THE BEST PHILADELPHIA SPORTS ARGUMENTS

THE 100 MOST CONTROVERSIAL, DEBATABLE QUESTIONS FOR DIE-HARD FANS

ERIC KARABELL

SOURCEBOOKS, INC.®
NAPERVILLE, ILLINOIS

Published by Sourcebooks, Inc.
P.O. Box 4410, Naperville, Illinois 60567-4410
(630) 961-3900
Fax: (630) 961-2168
www.sourcebooks.com

Library of Congress Cataloging-in-Publication Data

Karabell, Eric.
  The best Philadelphia sports arguments : the 100 most controversial, debatable questions for die-hard fans / Eric Karabell.
      p. cm.
  Includes index.
    1. Sports—Pennsylvania—Philadelphia—Miscellanea. I. Title.
  GV584.5.P46K37 2008
  796.0974811—dc22
                          2008015973

Printed and bound in the United States of America
          VP 10 9 8 7 6 5 4 3 2 1

For Emma, Zachary, Ryan, and Madeline:
Without argument, the best, most underrated
team I know.

CONTENTS

HOOPIN' IT UP

Who Makes—And Misses—The All-Time 76ers Dream Team?

THE BEST PHILADELPHIA SPORTS ARGUMENTS

INTRODUCTION

We love sports. We love Philadelphia. We are a fraternity. It's an odd fraternity, mind you, one that people who root for other cities' sports teams just don't get. We cheer, boo, love, hate, suffer, rejoice, argue, and debate. Oh, how we debate.

We are the Philadelphia sports fan, and we apologize to nobody. We don't have to. This book's for all of you, for all of us.

Go to a local watering hole in this tough town and the patrons aren't discussing religion. Or movies. Or politics. It's the Iggles and the Phils and the rest of our teams. Oh no, you don't discuss religion, unless it's how we pray for Donovan McNabb to get the Eagles back to the Super Bowl. In Philadelphia, sports are a religion. This book's for those who live and root in this tough town.

The politics we want to bounce off friends young and old aren't about the next election. It's about how some crooked ref stole a win from our team, how our front office people need to be educated or how the state of Pennsylvania is governed by a Philly fan, one of us. The honorable Ed Rendell says the right things when asked about Pittsburgh, but he's Philly through and through, maybe our biggest fan. This book's for Ed, too.

Just about every kid who grows up rooting for the Philly teams dreams of someday being an Eagle, Phillie, 76er, or Flyer. Unless your name is Vince Papale, though, focus of the inspirational Eagles flick *Invincible*, it's probably not going to happen. How many of us can say we ended up with a movie made about how we became a Philadelphia Eagle? Papale was representing the Philly fans, the ones who don't mind the well-earned reputation. This book's for Vince, too.

Our fans always believe in the Philly teams, through the good and the bad, and bleed our colors, from Eagles green to Flyers orange and black. We don't just root for our teams, and let everyone around us know it; we want to debate which local coach should be next to go, why a certain team is being run poorly, or where our next super-star, our next hero, should come from. This book's for the believers, the dreamers, too.

As you'll learn later in this book, the Philly sports fan is totally misrepresented. Nobody cares about their teams more than we do. We appreciate fine play, even from opponents, and demand effort from all, because we know the game. We also know why we go to the games. Not every word from our mouths will be a friendly one, but at least you're going to get feedback. We give a darn. We won't be fooled. This book's even for the fools, because there's a pot of gold waiting for us, whether we win or not. We're winners, just without the championship titles. This book's for the misrepresented, too.

If you grew up in Philly, you figured out early on who you're rooting for, and you don't change allegiances later in life. These are your teams forever. Sure, there must be some Dallas Cowboys fans that ended up in our midst, New York Mets loyalists who call our town home. Welcome. Just beware if you don your colors in our stadiums. This book's for the loyalists, near and far.

Some will say the Philly sports fan needs to be committed. Well, we certainly are committed, but not in the way you think. We don't need help, unless that help comes in the form of another pass-rushing defensive lineman, a young, healthy closer, a mobile defenseman who can score, more rebounding in the middle, you get the idea. This book's for the committed fan, too.

And this book is for me. I'm a Philadelphia sports fan, just like my family and friends, and we're part of the fraternity. I appreciate the support given to me on this project, which in this case means more arguing and debating, but in a totally good way. Hey, this is who we are! We've cheered, booed, loved, hated, suffered, rejoiced, argued, and debated. Oh, how we've debated. I debated with myself, even in writing this book, in deciding what we argue about and what the answers are. Only a hundred arguments? Why stop there?

THE BEST PHILADELPHIA SPORTS ARGUMENTS

Philly fans love a good debate, and trust me; we've had plenty to argue about over the years with our teams. Which team is our favorite? Which players have been our best? If we could pick one best-of team across the major sports, who would be on it? Our best, worst, most noteworthy, it's all one big debate, and it never ends. Statistics only tell part of a story, not all of it. There's always room for debate, and Philly fans can jaw with the best of them.

No matter what era of Philly sports you followed first, you never forget your roots. You're a fan. It's short for fanatic. Don't ever stop. This book's for you, especially.

Now it's time to start arguing. Keep the snowballs to yourselves.

BROTHERLY LOVE BASICS

ARE PHILADELPHIA SPORTS FANS THE BEST...OR WORST?

1 Say what you want about Philadelphia sports fans—and everyone pretty much has, by the way—but you can't deny the passion. The fans demand winning and, if forced, accept losing, but most importantly you've gotta put it all on the line, every time, or they'll let you hear it. Philly fans are truly misunderstood as sick, evil malcontents who booed Santa Claus and root for opponents to suffer misfortunes.

Yeah, so what? At least we're not apathetic. If you don't like it, you must root for Dallas or New York or Washington or Pittsburgh. This is Philly, a tough town where the athletes are doing more than swinging a bat and throwing a football. They represent Philadelphia when they're in battle, and if someone misses a block or doesn't skate as fast as they can, that's when trouble occurs. Because there is something worse than finishing second in Philadelphia, and it's finishing second while not giving extra effort.

Philly fans are smart and knowledgeable, and while that comes off as overly critical at times, to home and road teams alike, so be it. The stadiums aren't empty for big games, and neither are the parking lots before them. Eagles games are events, not just from one o'clock ET until the game ends, but for the entire day, the weekend, the season. When the Eagles made it to Super Bowl XXXIX, generations of fans came along for the ride to Jacksonville. It had been 24 seasons since the Eagles were in the biggest game. Not everyone could get tickets, of course, but Eagles fans stormed the Florida city and turned it green.

You want loyalty? Philly fans don't stop loving—or hating—their favorite teams in bad times, of which there are many. They demand the very best from the players. When the teams are good, there's no better time to be in the city and hop along for the ride. Kids wear the jerseys of their heroes proudly, and not only Donovan McNabb, Jimmy Rollins, and Andre Iguodala. How about Chad Lewis, Jim Thome, and Kyle Korver? Sure, the names change, because sports aren't like the 1970s anymore, but the passion doesn't end.

Philly fans get a bad rap nationally, but they don't care. In fact, the Philadelphia sports fan considers the notoriety an honor, a badge of overwhelming spirit to be passed on from generation to generation. There's no apathy here! If you're not from Philly you wouldn't get it, and you know what? It's your loss. That's what the Philly fan believes. They don't want your sympathy or forgiveness for the bad things that have happened over the years. Fair or unfair, consider Philly guilty for some wretched and raucous acts. There's no point in naming the bad events again, because you wouldn't understand our thinking. Hey, Michael Irvin walked again. J. D. Drew doesn't have scars from the batteries. And Santa Claus—look, that guy just plain deserved it.

Yeah, yeah, so we've booed our own, even the Hall of Famers. Well, maybe if Michael Jack Schmidt had talked to us once in a while, let us into his life, maybe we'd understand him better. Similarly, if you don't want to be here, Scotty Rolen and Curt Schilling, then get out. It's not just that Philadelphia fans demand more than 100 percent effort, you've gotta look like you're trying as hard as the fans would if they got that chance for one shining moment. Athletes get paid a lot of money to use their gift, and a tough town like Philly certainly recognizes that along with that gift comes a duty.

Philadelphia has enjoyed fantastic moments, unforgettable games, but for the most part the city has had to deal with bad teams more than good. That just makes us stronger, able to enjoy the good with a fervent zeal more than other towns. It's been 25 years since Philadelphia celebrated a winner, but in reality, we celebrate every day. Philly teams are rewarded with unbridled loyalty through thick and thin. That's a sports town.

Without even knowing the politics, Philly fans would elect any number of sports people mayor if they could. That's how much sports mean. Dick Vermeil has been gone for 25 years, but remains a beloved personality for what he accomplished as Eagles coach. Pete Rose might never make it to the Hall of Fame, for other reasons, but in Philadelphia, he got us over that proverbial hump. He caught the carom off Bob Boone's glove. He was a winner who never gave less than 100 percent. Bobby Clarke and Maurice Cheeks didn't get booed in Philadelphia when they were players, that's for sure. They were the little guys out there, the overachievers who made their teams better.

There's a rich history of sports in the City of Brotherly Love, and the fans have been through all of it. They care. More than you know. It's called passion. And it's what makes the Philly sports fan second to none.

WHO BELONGS ON THE MOUNT RUSHMORE OF PHILLY SPORTS?

2 Close your eyes. Pretend the Mount Rushmore you see in South Dakota is actually in South Philadelphia, right near the stadiums and the warehouses. Instead of four American presidents being honored with their faces carved into the side of a mountain, picture the greatest athletes Philly has seen being immortalized in this way. Maybe it's on the side of the Walt Whitman Bridge. Fans and admirers from all over could come to visit and debate who got left off, and whether the faces even look realistic in the first place. Really, if Honest Abe Lincoln could see his face now, modeled into a mountain of a state that didn't exist when he was alive, what would he say?

The purpose here, of course, is to properly distinguish the best athletes Philly has ever seen, regardless of the sport they played. These are the best of the best, the most important of the important. Local greats Steve Jeltz (Phillies), Shawn Bradley (76ers), and Bobby Hoying (Eagles) came oh so very close, but just missed the final cut. Sorry, boys.

Wilt Chamberlain has to be the first face carved. Born and raised in Philadelphia, he was a dominant figure at

Overbrook High and then with two different Philly professional basketball franchises. Chamberlain is arguably the
greatest hoops player of all time, and possibly the signature athlete as well. Who else had his size and grace and
could do so much to affect a game? Sure, Michael Jordan
won more championships and is better known today, but
the Big Dipper set records that even Jordan couldn't
approach. Really, is anyone ever again going to average
22.9 rebounds per game for a season, let alone a career?
What about 50.4 points for a season, or knocking down 100
in a game? Chamberlain's face goes on the mountain first
and foremost. Then he'd probably bring some of his lady
friends to see it.

Chuck Bednarik would love to see his face in stone. His
nickname is Concrete Charlie, after all. He'd fit right in.
Bednarik was a two-time All-American at Penn at center and
linebacker, and certainly didn't lose those skills upon joining
the Eagles. He was the last of the two-way players in the NFL,
a critical part of the 1960 team that won it all. Yeah, Bednarik
knocked the concrete out of pretty boy Frank Gifford, creating a lasting photographic memory for generations, but his
tackle of the Packers' Jim Taylor saved the championship
game. That's the photo Bednarik would be holding in his
hands on the mountain: the tackle that won a title.

Mike Schmidt and Steve Carlton each played such critical roles in the rise of the Phillies in the late 1970s that it
would seem difficult to choose just one. Well, we're

choosing one. It's Schmidt, the greatest third baseman in major league history. He was such a sensitive personality while in Philly, even during the really good years, that he'd probably shrug off how meaningful it is, being on the Philly Mount Rushmore. Maybe he'd choose his face to have sunglasses and a wig, like he did when he ran out to first base to break the tension with the fans late in his career. Carlton had a Hall of Fame career as well, and was one of the top left-handed starters ever, but Schmidt appeared only with the Phillies, and was on the field virtually every day, contributing at the plate and with Gold Glove play. Carlton, meanwhile, kind of sullied his rep by pitching (poorly) for the Giants, White Sox, Indians, and Twins until he was 43. Schmidt was productive until the day he wept farewell in San Diego.

Finally, in the corner of this Mount Rushmore would be a face with some missing teeth. Bobby Clarke carved his niche in Philly by refusing to lose and never letting his so-called handicap of having diabetes get the best of him. He might take his hockey stick and use it to whack the architect of this monument over the head if he didn't like his portrayal, but there's little question Clarke belongs on the mountain for all he did, and continues to do, for hockey in this town.

Basically, Clarke and the others noted here helped build the Philadelphia sports mountain, piece by memorable piece, to make it what it is today.

CAN THE PHILLY SPORTS YEAR 1980 EVER BE TOPPED?

3 Wow, 1980 was a great year to be a Philadelphia sports fan. All four major professional sports teams in the city went to their respective Finals during the 1980 season. It was an incredible year of accomplishment, even though only one of the teams won it all. Take a bow, Philly sports, that was a historic year!

One could argue that no city, with or without entries in all four major pro sports, can top what Philly did in 1980. It's never happened before or since in American sports history. Boston won a pair of titles in 2004 (Red Sox and Patriots), but the Bruins could only muster a division title, and the Celtics stunk. Other cities that fared well were Baltimore (1970) and Pittsburgh (1979), but neither has teams in four sports. Philly brought it that year in all four.

Also, one has to remember just how the Phillies, after making the playoffs three straight seasons in the late 1970s and winning a total of two postseason games once they got there, didn't have a great 1979 team. Halfway through the 1980 season it still wasn't a great team. Manager Dallas Green pushed the right buttons and forced that team into October, where it found a way to upend teams with better records and celebrate the franchise's first World Series title.

The Eagles were improving every year with the intense Dick Vermeil, and had a terrific 1980 regular season, going 12–4 and exorcising the demons of a decade-plus of abuse from the Dallas Cowboys. The January 1981 Super Bowl wasn't so super, as Ron Jaworski got picked off three times by the same linebacker, but Eagles fans were content with just getting there after rocking the Cowboys' world in below-freezing temps at the Vet. Little did Eagles fans know how long it would be until the next time a Super Bowl came calling.

The Flyers and 76ers didn't win it all either, but they came close. Something special occurred during each of their seasons. The Flyers didn't lose any games from October 16, 1979 to January 6, 1980, a North American sports record 35-game unbeaten streak. They breezed through three rounds of the playoffs, then lost to the upstart number five seed Islanders in the Cup Finals. Julius Erving's 76ers also got back to the Finals after a few unproductive playoff years, but fell to the Lakers in six games. One of the highlights of the regular season was man-child center Darryl Dawkins breaking backboards in separate games within a month: one in Kansas City, the other at the Spectrum. Another common thread between the Flyers and 76ers that year was the noteworthy way they were eliminated. The Flyers fell in overtime of the final game, and the loss was clouded a bit by linesman Leon Stickle missing an obvious offside call earlier in the game. The 76ers didn't expect to lose Game 6 knowing the Lakers would be without Hall of Fame center Kareem Abdul-Jabbar, but rookie point guard Magic Johnson filled in at center and scored 42 points.

The only way 1980 could be topped is if the Phillies, Eagles, Flyers, and 76ers each went to the final round of competition and more than one team ended up victorious, but at this point there's no hint that something like this is close to being realized. Regardless, just getting to the championship round is an accomplishment in itself, and Philly fans might have gotten a bit spoiled by the success. At this point, going on 25 years since any of the major professional teams won a title at all, with the fond memories of 1980 fading, Philly fans would be happy if any one of the four teams could be that successful again, and, of course, win the championship.

DID SANTA DESERVE TO GET BOOED?

4 First of all, for all children reading this chapter, Santa Claus is absolutely real. On Christmas Eve he glides through the night with his reindeer and toys, bringing presents to all the good little boys and girls. We need to make the important distinction here. The Santa Claus infamous for being booed by Philadelphia Eagles fans wasn't the real Santa. He was an imposter! Not real at all! What you're about to read, kiddies, has nothing to do with the real, honorable, jolly ol' St. Nick.

Hmmm, maybe that's why Philly fans booed this fake Santa as if he was Michael Irvin or Deion Sanders on that cold, snowy day 10 days before Christmas 1968. Of course, the real Santa couldn't make it, so why should Philadelphians settle for anything less?

Let's give some background here, if you don't mind. The Eagles stunk that season, losing their first 11 games, and had they continued on this winless path, the first draft pick the following year was theirs. Surely the Eagles would have used it on Heisman Trophy winner O. J. Simpson, and future Super Bowl riches would have been forthcoming. Then the Eagles even managed to screw that up, beating the woeful Lions and Saints. The final game of a miserable season was at home in Franklin Field against the Vikings, a decent team that won its division. Eagles fans wanted another loss, a new coach to replace hated Joe Kuharich, something to believe in.

Naturally, a mighty snowfall had filled the stadium the night before. The windchill factor was well below zero and the 54,000-plus fans who showed up for a meaningless, regular season finale were cold, angry, and sitting in half a foot of slush, since nobody had bothered to clean the stands at Franklin Field that day. It's a common misconception that this Santa incident is part of Veterans Stadium lore. People, the stadium didn't exist yet. Blame the Vet for other things, but not this.

Anyway, the Eagles had scheduled a halftime Christmas Pageant to brighten the mood, but it didn't quite go off as planned. First of all, a decent Santa Claus—not the real one, of course, but at least one who could play the part—never made it through the storm. He didn't show up. Second problem was that the Christmas float built by a local restaurant couldn't get on the field due to the snow and mud in its path. It might have been really nice, too, as it had a sleigh and fake reindeer, and the Eagles cheerleaders in elf costumes were going to accompany it.

Instead, desperate for a Santa, any Santa, the Eagles plucked a 20-year-old kid from the stands. It so happened he was from South Philly, dressed in a red suit and scraggly beard, not exactly the spitting image of the real thing.

The Eagles asked him to carry a bag of fake toys and walk across the field. Frank Olivo was his name, and he was 5'6", 170 pounds. The real Santa is a bit larger. Now what did they think would happen? He'd be cheered? Asked to play running back? Fans wanted blood, and since they couldn't get to incompetent (and soon to be canned) Coach Kuharich, Santa had to take one for the team. While a brass band played "Here Comes Santa Claus," Eagles fans mercilessly pelted Olivo with snowballs. He wasn't big and round and jolly, his beard was a joke, and the team he was representing wasn't going to deliver that O. J. toy fans wanted. He had to pay.

But that was it. It really was no big deal at the time. The Philly media barely mentioned the halftime incident, a footnote in a 24–17 loss. Olivo still lives in the Philadelphia region and remembers the incident as being funny. The Eagles got the third pick in the draft and messed it up, as Purdue's Leroy Keyes would score three touchdowns in his entire career. It was Howard Cosell who added insult to symbolic injury by showing the Santa incident as part of a highlights package on ABC's *Weekend Report*. If Cosell thought it was a big deal, then that's what it was.

Ever since then, Philadelphia sports fans have received a bad rap as mean, uncaring, vile people who booed and threw snowballs at a joyous figure, but the fact is, this fake Santa had it coming, knowing the circumstances. It could have happened in any beleaguered football city that day, with snow weapons and a cruddy team on display. It just happened to go down in Philly. Don't blame the fans. Maybe if the real Santa had showed up, history would have been a lot different and Philly fans would be known for class, sportsmanship, sobriety, and tact.

Well, maybe not.

IS PHILADELPHIA A FOOTBALL OR BASEBALL TOWN?

5 When the Philadelphia Phillies finally won the World Series in 1980, after nearly 100 years of mainly futility, the city celebrated appropriately. Baseball has been an integral part of the Philly sports scene since the 1880s, and the first half of the 20th century featured not one but two professional baseball teams.

That's great. But Philly remains unquestionably a football town. Imagine if the Eagles were to ever win a Super Bowl, and the celebration that would lead to. Baseball is the national pastime, but football in Philly is a passion, an obsession. It's discussed in bars, train stations, at the local barber, and on the radio year-round, whether the Eagles have a good team or not. The same can't be said about baseball, or any other sport, in the City of Brotherly Love.

When the Eagles are among the best teams in football, Philadelphians live and die with the team's results. One could argue this happens no matter the team's record, really. In the past decade the Eagles have had some very good teams, and went the distance in their conference, but only once made it to the Super Bowl. That year, the game was played in Jacksonville, and fans young and old wanted to be a part of the celebrations, whether they had tickets or not. The fans are devoted to the Eagles, through thick and thin. With baseball, Philadelphians love a winner, but let's just say Veterans Stadium was rarely packed, even in the World Series years, unless it was July and there was a promise of fireworks flying through the night air after the game. Eagles fans packed the Vet no matter what. Now that the Vet is gone this comparison is different. There aren't enough seats in the new, clean stadiums to prove the point.

Philly is a blue-collar town. Its inhabitants like to play the underdog role, in life and on the field of play, overcoming whatever gets in their way. You get hurt, rub some dirt on it, and get back out there. Be like Donovan McNabb and throw four touchdown passes on a broken leg. Chuck Bednarik didn't come out of games when he was hurt. Football mirrors what kind of city Philadelphia is. If Rocky Balboa wasn't a fighter, he'd be a linebacker, and he'd bust chops that way.

Baseball is a fine sport, of course, and Philadelphia deeply cares for the Phillies, but fans bleed for the Eagles. Each Sunday in the fall is a celebration; families and friends share in the jubilation when the team wins and the hurt when things don't go as well. In baseball—well, there are 162 of those games, always another one the next day. In football the joy and the pain lasts all week, and you live and die with your heroes.

Philadelphians get their identity from football, and likewise the players who suit up each Sunday in this town know that there's a price that comes with being an Eagle.

17

It can be a great price, or a tough one. If you're willing to leave your heart on the field, like the fans that root you on, give it a try.

WHICH FIVE TEAMS ARE PHILLY'S BIGGEST RIVALS?

6 Sports are better when there's a rival, a team or player to root against, something that can really draw the ire of the fans. All the great teams have those enemies the fans love to hate. In Philadelphia, there are plenty of enemies to root against, but some stick out more than others.

5. BOSTON CELTICS

Turn back the clock 25 years and the Celtics were truly evil to Philadelphians. The 76ers did win a championship without having to go through the Celtics to get there, but it seemed like every other playoff season they did. It started with Bill Russell and Wilt Chamberlain battling in the 1960s. Whether it was a miraculous John Havlicek stealing the ball or some other malady that cost the 76ers, the Celtics knocked the 76ers out of the playoffs in 1965, 1966, 1968, and 1969. Of course, a rivalry needs both sides to partake in the winning, and the 76ers did prevail easily in the championship season of 1967. After Russell and Wilt left, it was Larry Bird and Julius Erving taking center stage. For three straight seasons, and four out of six, they met in the conference finals, splitting the difference. Plus, who can forget Bird and Doc throwing punches. That's a rivalry, though it hasn't meant much for more than a decade.

4. NEW JERSEY DEVILS

Once upon a time the entire NHL was enemies with the Flyers. Dave Schultz would take on anyone and everyone on a night-to-night basis, Bobby Clarke would lodge his stick where the opponent's sun wouldn't shine, and the Flyers won a few Stanley Cups by pushing teams around. It took years for the Flyers to not be hated by most other teams. But which team was the Flyers' biggest rival? Division play wasn't big in the 1970s. The New York teams certainly weren't liked by Philadelphians, but the Flyers had moderate success against the Rangers, and when the Islanders won the first of four straight Cups against the Flyers, it was referee Leon Stickle who got blamed, not Isles coach Al Arbour or Bobby Nystrom. On the other side of Pennsylvania the Penguins were never really a rival until 2008, as the Flyers had won all three playoff series against them until then. The Flyers beat the Bruins in the postseason, but that's just it—they beat them. The answer is the New Jersey Devils. The Flyers can't do anything with them. The franchises have met in the playoffs four times, including when the Devils were the Colorado Rockies, and the teams have split. But the Devils won both times when it was the Eastern Conference Finals, as they advanced to the Stanley Cup Round. When the Flyers won, they merely went on to face another team in the East that would derail the championship hopes before the Finals. Remember Scott Stevens ending the Eric Lindros era in Philly? Maybe he did Flyers fans a favor, and nobody called the shoulder hit cheap, but since then the series has been one-sided, with the Devils winning 11 straight home games in the series at one point, and 14 of 16 at another point, including 2008.

3. NEW YORK METS

It wasn't always the Mets that Phillies fans disliked. In fact, these teams had little reason to hate each other, because when one franchise was flying high, the other one wasn't. The Mets entered the National League in 1962, and on the two occasions (only two!) the teams finished 1–2 in some order in the division, it wasn't a close race at all. That changed in 2007. The Mets had a seven-game lead in the NL East with 17 games to play, the kind of lead that had never been lost in major league history…and they lost it. The Phillies caught the Mets, in part by sweeping them in seven games in the final five weeks. The Phillies' Jimmy Rollins talked trash before the season, the Mets disregarded it, and then Rollins backed it up and those now-hated Mets didn't make the playoffs. It took four decades, but the Phils and Mets finally have a rivalry. The Pirates figured in there for a while—if there was any one visiting player Phillies fans

21

loved to boo in the 1970s, it was probably the Pirates' Dave Parker—but when the NL East was broken up and the Cubs and Pirates left for the NL Central, that effectively ended the rivalry. The Phillies and Braves have had their moments as well, but clearly the Mets are more a threat.

2. NEW YORK GIANTS

Let's make something clear before you read on: the Eagles' top rival is a football team, but not this one. But members of the Giants don't exactly join Eagles players for Sunday tea, either. Other than the legendary hit Chuck Bednarik leveled on deserving Frank Gifford in 1960, the Eagles and Giants didn't have much to hate about each other until the past few years. The 1978 Miracle of the Meadowlands was a critical play in Eagles lore, and embarrassing for the Giants, but it didn't add to the rivalry much. When the Giants beat the Eagles in the 1981 wild-card game in Philly, the year after the Eagles went to the Super Bowl, it was devastating, but didn't fuel the rivalry. The Eagles were slipping, and the Giants would win two Super Bowls in 1987 and 1991 before the Eagles got good again. There's some bad blood now, fueled in part by proximity and the way the Eagles got run over in two games in 2007, and it's a good rivalry because both teams are good, but the best is...

1. DALLAS COWBOYS

Eagles fans have always despised the Cowboys, or at least

the last two generations of Eagles fans. When Tom Landry was the Dallas coach, his teams would regularly feast on the poor Eagles, winning 21 of 23 games from 1967 into the Dick Vermeil era in the late 1970s. These games weren't close either. And there was so much for Eagles fans to dislike. They hated Landry's annoying fedora and Jimmy Johnson's perfect, fake hair. The quarterbacks always drew the ire of fans, from Roger Staubach to Danny White to Troy Aikman. Philly fans didn't enjoy the elegant Emmitt Smith. The Cowboys were America's Team in the 1970s, and the Eagles were just bad.

Buddy Ryan figured out early on that even if the Eagles have a bad season, it could be fixed by just beating the Cowboys. Ryan's teams swept Dallas from 1988–90, even while never winning a playoff game. Go to an Eagles game, no matter the opponent or year (since the 1980s), and you'll find plenty of fans wearing a T-shirt saying they root for the Eagles, and whoever plays Dallas.

Some of the Eagles' best moments in the Veterans Stadium era came against Dallas. So what are the highlights of this rivalry?

- The 1987 NFL players strike made things worse: when very few Eagles crossed the picket lines, many Cowboys did, and Ryan fumed about the Dallas replacement squad drubbing his team. After the strike when the teams met again, Eagles quarterback Randall

Cunningham was taking a knee to run out the final seconds of a 10-point win, but then threw a pass to the goal line to rub it in—on Buddy's orders, of course. The Eagles scored again in the final seconds of a 37–20 win.

- How about the time a bounty was supposedly placed on the head of Dallas kicker Luis Zendejas? The Eagles did knock him out of the 1989 Thanksgiving Day game, winning 27–0. A few weeks later coach Johnson needed a police escort from his own bench when snowballs flew from all over the Vet. Still, his hair didn't move.

- Michael Irvin's career ended in Philly to a chorus of cheers after a strong hit by defensive back Tim Hauck drove the wide receiver into the hard turf, rendering him briefly paralyzed. As Irvin lay motionless on the ground, Philly fans, unaware of the seriousness of the injury, rejoiced. The question is: had they known, would it have changed a thing? If this had been a San Diego Charger lying there, Eagles fans would not have had the same reaction.

And, of course, when the Eagles dumped Terrell Owens, he just happened to end up in a certain Texas town. The rivalry lives forever!

WHAT IS THE MOST MEMORABLE DATE IN PHILADELPHIA SPORTS HISTORY?

7 Some people just can't remember birthdays, whether it's their own or those of their children, pets, famous presidents, mailmen, you name it. For others, maybe it's a wedding anniversary that slips the mind, or getting the Flock of Seagulls haircut back in 1984. So many memorable days: how can you possibly remember them all?

When it comes to Philadelphia sports, is it merely championships that stand out? Quick, what's the number date the Flyers won it all in May 1974? How about the Eagles of December 1960? Do you remember where you were on those days? There are, however, numerous dates that do seem to stand out in Philadelphia sports history.

The first is October 21, 1980. The Phillies had been in existence for 98 seasons and never won a championship, but when Tug McGraw struck out Willie Wilson at 11:29 p.m. ET, it began a wild 24-hour period in the City of Brotherly Love. Sure, Philly is a football town, but the last time the Eagles won a championship, John F. Kennedy still hadn't been elected president. The Phillies did it a lot more recently, and the parade the next afternoon was attended by, in some estimates, three million people. Yes, schools were open that day, but, Phillies fans: how many of you didn't show up?

Not all memorable dates in Philly sports history, of course, are associated with good things. There are games that stand out, like Black Friday for the 1977 Phillies, or the October Saturday night in Toronto when Joe Carter took Mitch Williams deep. Then there are those dates worse than the mere losing of games. The death of goaltender Pelle Lindbergh on a Sunday morning in November 1985, during the Flyers season, was felt all season and beyond. Eagles defensive lineman Jerome Brown passed away, also in an auto accident, in June 1992, and had his number 99 retired by the team. And Phillies outfielder-turned-announcer Richie Ashburn died from a heart attack in September 1997, the night he called a game against the Mets. McGraw's death in January 2004 also hit Philadelphia fans hard.

But it's unlikely those exact dates are so ingrained in the minds of Philadelphians that they can recall them. Not like March 2, 1962. That's the night Wilt Chamberlain, then with the Philadelphia Warriors, scored 100 points in one basketball game. That has never been accomplished since; it's never even come close. The second-best points total in a game is 81, by Kobe Bryant in January 2006, and no other player has ever topped 73.

There are a few interesting things about why this date is so memorable, though. For one, the game wasn't played in Philadelphia, but in Chocolatetown, USA, also known as Hershey, PA. Second, the franchise for which Wilt was playing left Philly a few years later for the West Coast, and now stands as the Golden State Warriors. Chamberlain returned to Philly to win a championship, but the actual 76ers franchise mark for scoring in a game is nowhere near 100. It's Chamberlain, of course, but the mark is 68 points.

There wasn't a full house when Chamberlain broke the century mark in the 169–147 win over the New York Knickerbockers. In fact, the listed attendance for the game at the half-empty Hershey Sports Arena was 4,124. Amazing that so few people were witness to sports history. Chamberlain said he was approached by thousands of people who claim to have been there. Show us your ticket stub! (My dad has one. He *was* there.)

Chamberlain's signature individual game stands as not only a memorable one for Philadelphia sports fans, but for all the NBA, and every year on March 2 sports fans are reminded of the significance of the date. It's a record not likely to ever be approached. The fact that it happened 90 miles away from Philly with no TV cameras or reporters only adds to the intrigue.

WAS THE VET REALLY THAT BAD?

8 Okay, the Vet was kind of a dump. There, we said it right off the bat. Most of the stories you've heard about the place were true. Yes, the stadium needed the cats so they could devour the rats. The field was rock hard and cold and like playing in the street, except it was green and not supposed to be a street. (Well, it was mostly green.) The stands were too far away, especially for baseball, with a dour atmosphere like being at a funeral. And sure, there was a notable stench each time you visited, in the stadium and often in the product the home team would put on the field.

Now South Philly has a pair of beautiful stadiums that people actually want to go visit. Lincoln Financial Field and Citizens Bank Park are nice—maybe *too* nice. Should we take our shoes off first? You don't want to spill a drink under the seat. There are no hideous rodents in the corners. And men don't use the sinks for, um, things other than washing their hands. The Vet was a dump, but it was Philly's dump, and it had its advantages. It had the home field advantage.

Of course, when Veterans Stadium opened in 1971, it really was a state-of-the-art place, a nice place to visit, as shocking as it seems. Multipurpose stadiums were all the rage back then, and the city of Philadelphia could stick both the Eagles and Phillies, and whatever else it wanted, into one place. Other cities, like Pittsburgh and Cincinnati, also introduced cookie-cutter stadiums. It didn't take long for people to realize—regular people and the athletes—that the Vet was not such a nice place. There wasn't much love put into building it, as corners were cut and it was rushed out the door. Its construction was hampered by a labor strike, financial problems, numerous design delays, and later, an indictment by the grand jury.

A few years later—more like a decade later—it became clear the Vet was a bit dangerous. Careers were lost at the Vet, nobody more famously than poor Chicago Bears wide receiver Wendell Davis, who blew out both knees thanks to the turf. But was that really the Vet's fault? If the turf had been pristine and soft, would it have made the Vet that much more appealing? You still couldn't see downtown from the stadium. You couldn't see much of anything!

Fathers didn't want to bring their children anywhere near the dangerous 700 Level, for fear of bodily or auditory harm. The Philly fans—loud, rough, honest, rowdy, you name it—made the Vet their home. Fans would throw snowballs from the raucous upper deck at opposing players and coaches like Jimmy Johnson and one of those fans was attorney Ed Rendell, who would eventually become Philadelphia's mayor and Pennsylvania's governor. A

Common Pleas court judge was eventually given a makeshift courtroom to levy fines and jail time in the Vet basement. Not to Rendell, of course.

If you ask whether the Vet became an outdated, dank dump, the answer is yes. Repairs and upgrades were seemingly never made to the stadium after the 1980s. Heck, it was hard to tell if it was ever cleaned at all. But was the old dog as bad as people made it out to be? Veterans Stadium was home to some fantastic memories over the years, with the Phillies winning it all on that field in 1980, then driving through the stadium in celebration a few days later. Wilbert Montgomery might have had a longer career playing home games on softer turf, but he didn't care on that 42-yard jaunt against evil Dallas that sent the Eagles to the Super Bowl. The Vet might have been bad, really bad in the end, but it still was home. It was *our* home.

And when it got knocked to the ground on March 21, 2004, along with it went a lot of memories.

FLY LIKE
THOSE EAGLES

WHAT WERE THE EAGLES' FIVE MOST MEMORABLE GAMES?

9 Fifty-six to zip. That was the score of the very first Philadelphia Eagles football game, way, way back on October 15, 1933. You might have missed it, as cable TV hadn't quite made it to every town. The Eagles lost the game to the New York Giants, and endured some tough times in terms of wins and losses those early years. In fact, in the entire decade of the 1930s, the Eagles won just 18 games, losing 55, and three were ties. The Eagles would eventually score a touchdown, in game number 3 at Green Bay, as Roger Kirkman found Swede Hanson for a 35-yard touchdown pass. It's not quite as famous a duo as Montana to Rice or Manning to Harrison, but it worked that day. Philly was just happy to have a team after its first NFL entrant, the Frankford Yellow Jackets, folded during the 1931 season.

Then things got better. The Eagles won a few championships, stunk again for a decade, won another title, stunk for nearly two decades and, well, you get the story. Those who have been Eagles fans for only a few seasons since 2000 have seen success, division titles, even an official Super Bowl run. Their parents and grandparents saw championships.

The Eagles have played many memorable games in their history, and not just games that decided league titles. Basically, if a game earned its own title, it's big; but let's also not forget the other ones that mattered the most.

5. CHAMPIONSHIP WINS IN 1948, 1949, 1960

All three of these games were, of course, memorable because they're the only championships the Eagles have won, but now we're nearly 50 years after that last title, so...how good is your memory? For those who wouldn't be born for decades, the Eagles shut out the Chicago Cardinals 7–0 on Dec. 19, 1948, in a blinding blizzard to win their first title, followed up the next year with a 14–0 win in the Los Angeles rain on Dec. 18 to beat the Rams, and 11 years later, the day after Christmas, held on to beat the Green Bay Packers 17–13. All three games were memorable, but we're going to focus on more recent events, while giving these games their due as well.

4. ON THE FOURTH TRY, FINALLY

Eagles 27, Falcons 10—January 23, 2005

It's not easy to get to four straight conference title games. The Buffalo Bills managed to do this, and won all four times, though each season from 1990–93 ended with a Super Bowl loss. The Bills don't get much credit for this, but they should. The Eagles, no less impressively, went to four straight NFC title games from 2001–04, but it wasn't until the final year that Donovan McNabb and pals got the team over the proverbial hump and into the big game. In the first conference title game, Kurt Warner's powerful Rams beat the Eagles 29–24 in St. Louis on the way to a title, which Eagles fans couldn't really complain about. The future looked bright; everyone figured there would be another chance. Well, there was. The next season the Eagles closed down the Vet and hosted the Tampa Bay Buccaneers on January 19, 2003. How could a team from Florida win in cold Philly? Playing in games with the temperature below 40 degrees, the Bucs were 1–22...make that 2–22, as we still see Joe Jurevicius running for a 71-yard touchdown. The next season in the bright and shiny Lincoln Financial Field, a wild-card team from Carolina beat the Eagles 14–3. Would the Eagles ever make it to the Super Bowl again? On January 23, 2005, yet another warm-weather team entered Philly, and this time the Eagles tamed Michael Vick and his Falcons 27–10. The Eagles led only 14–10 at halftime, but on a bitterly cold day Atlanta wouldn't score again. Tight end Chad Lewis scored two touchdowns, the last of his season as he injured his left foot on a scoring play. Dorsey Levens registered the final touchdown, and David Akers kicked two field goals. The game itself might not stand out for its individual heroics, but ultimately it provided the Eagles the opportunity to play in the Super Bowl, which of course didn't go as well.

3. PASS THE BODY BAGS

Eagles 28, Redskins 14—November 12, 1990 •

Buddy Ryan wasn't the best coach the Eagles ever had, that's for certain, but he did have a way of motivating his players. Leading up to a key Monday night clash against the Redskins at the Vet on Nov. 12, 1988, Coach Buddy didn't mince words when he gave a preview of the game between rivals, noting there would be a beating so severe "they'll have to be carted off in body bags." Philly fans, of course, loved that kind of talk, and they loved that Ryan could back it up, even though he'd never win a playoff game. League officials weren't as pleased, but it did make for must-see television. The Eagles followed through and dished out pain all night, sending at least six Redskins out of the game with injuries, including quarterbacks Stan Humphries and Jeff Rutledge. Future Eagle running back Brian Mitchell had to finish up at quarterback in the 28–14 Redskins loss, otherwise known as the Body Bag Game. The Philly defense directly supplied three of the four touchdowns.

2. OH SAY, CAN YOU SEE?

Bears 20, Eagles 12—December 31, 1988

Well, it could be all you remember from this one is the fog that pervaded over Chicago's Soldier Field on New Year's Eve 1988. While the temperature was 29 degrees and skies were sunny for the opening gun, by halftime nobody could see a thing. I was there, a college kid in the west end zone, and I couldn't see the people in my own row. The pea-soup fog from Lake Michigan covered the field, making viewing impossible for players, fans, and frustrated announcers like Terry Bradshaw. The Eagles blew this game, by the way. Randall Cunningham threw for 407 yards, but couldn't get the team into the end zone. Twice the Eagles had touchdowns called back due to penalties. The Eagles settled for three Luis Zendejas field goals in the first half, and trailed 17–9 at intermission, even though they had outplayed the Bears. That's when the dense fog rolled in. That was it. There would be no come-back, even though the Eagles were a second-half team and might have been able to deliver one.

1. NEW ORLEANS, HERE WE COME

Eagles 20, Cowboys 7—January 11, 1981

One could make the case that the Eagles left everything on the Veterans Stadium field that gray January day when they exorcised past demons and topped the Dallas Cowboys. Dallas had won all but four of the previous 27 games in the series, and was clearly the bully, America's Team. The Eagles pulled out all the stops, even choosing to wear their white road jerseys, thus forcing the Cowboys to don supposedly unlucky blue ones. Wilbert Montgomery's 42-yard touchdown jaunt on the Eagles' second offensive play got things started in the 20–7 victory played with a sub-zero windchill, but the fans didn't care; there was plenty to feel warm about. Heavily favored over the wild-card Oakland Raiders in the Super Bowl two weeks later, the Eagles came out flat and lost 27–10. However, so dramatic and emotional had the Dallas game been, it seemed fans and players were just happy the team had made it that far, actually referring to the game as the team's Super Bowl. Plus, the Phillies had won the World Series just a few months prior, and the Flyers and 76ers were championship caliber. Who knew titles would be so hard to come by the next...well, forever.

WHAT WERE THE FIVE GREATEST PLAYS IN EAGLES HISTORY?

10

5. FOURTH AND 26

Freddie Mitchell never did live up to expectations in his career, which ended prematurely at age 26 after four seasons and only 90 catches. However, the first-round draft pick did make one play that, in a way, justified his disappointing tenure. On January 11, 2004, while the 12–4 Eagles were on their way to losing a home divisional playoff game to Brett Favre's Packers, Donovan McNabb and friends faced a desperation fourth-and-26 from the Eagles 26-yard line. What did Andy Reid say before the play? "Get a first down," Reid said. He's not a great coach for nothing. Mitchell listened. With Green Bay playing a soft zone, Mitchell made the biggest play of his career when he leaped for a McNabb fastball near the middle of the field and held on after a strong Marques Anderson hit. The play went for 28 yards. How often does a team convert a play like that? One out of 100 times? Seven plays later, kicker David Akers sent the game to overtime, then won it in overtime 20–17. After the game, Mitchell thanked his hands. A week later, the

Carolina Panthers came to Philly and the Eagles' prayers went unanswered.

4. STAY AWAY FROM BANKS

Randall Cunningham played for four teams in his NFL career, breaking quarterback rushing marks, having regular season success and showing his skills as one of the more exciting players of his time. His playoff record, however, left much to be desired. As an Eagle, Cunningham was victorious in one playoff game he started, a 1992 wild-card game at New Orleans. Other than that, Eagles fans are left to remember the big plays. Cunningham's signature play came on *Monday Night Football* on Oct. 10, 1998, against the Giants. Early in what would become a 24–13 win, on a third-and-goal from the four-yard line, Cunningham rolled to the right as if he was going to try and run for a score, and Giants linebacker Carl Banks hit Cunningham above the knees. Quarterbacks go down from hits like that. Cunningham, however, didn't go down. He twisted his body in the air, balanced himself with his left hand on the turf, regained his composure, and found tight end Jimmie Giles open in the end zone for a touchdown.

3. MIRACLE OF THE MEADOWLANDS

Has anyone seen a quarterback and running back bumble an exchange like this since that memorable November 17,

1978, game in the swamps of New Jersey? The Giants led the Eagles 17–12 in the final minute, with the Eagles out of timeouts and the game seemingly over. For some unknown reason, Giants quarterback Joe Pisarcik, who would join the Eagles as a backup two seasons later, attempted to hand off to Larry Csonka, but the running back wasn't expecting it, and the ball popped loose. Eagles cornerback Herm Edwards, normally not even on the field for defensive situations like these, scooped up the fumble and gleefully ran 26 yards for the winning score, a pivotal 19–17 win that helped send the Eagles to their first playoff berth in 18 seasons. There would be more. What there wouldn't be were more plays like that. Quarterbacks always drop to one knee now, forever scared of what might happen.

2. GIFFORD GETS CRUNCHED

The picture of an excited, animated Chuck Bednarik pumping his right fist can still be found today, and many an Eagles fan probably hangs one on their wall. On November 20, 1960, at Yankee Stadium, the Eagles and Giants were playing a key Eastern Conference game, with first place at stake. The Eagles led 17–10 late in the game, and the Giants were driving, until star halfback Frank Gifford, a former league MVP, caught a pass over the middle. He probably doesn't recall what happened next. Bednarik knocked him out with a legal but violent hit that cost Gifford the next 18 months of his career. That's right,

Gifford missed the rest of the season and all of 1961 recovering from the concussion. The ball popped out, of course, Eagles linebacker Chuck Weber fell on it, and the win was secured. Bednarik claims he wasn't exulting in the motionless Gifford's pain, just that the Eagles had won. Likewise, a Bednarik hit was the signature moment as the Eagles won the 1960 championship, with Green Bay's Jim Taylor getting stopped inside the 10-yard line in the final minute. Bednarik flattened Taylor and didn't let him up, as time ran out on Philly's last football championship. At least Taylor wasn't injured.

1. RUN TO THE SUPER BOWL

While Bednarik's hits were critical to that 1960 title, the lasting image for a more recent generation is from Wilbert Montgomery taking the Eagles to their first Super Bowl on one magnificent play. The Eagles were terrible most of the years after 1960, until Dick Vermeil came along and built a Super Bowl contender. The 1980 Eagles were ready to take that final step to the big game, having made the playoffs after the 1978 and 1979 seasons. In 1980 the team started 11–1, won the NFC East, and beat the Vikings to earn a home game with the rival Cowboys to send one team to the Super Bowl. The Eagles were favored but hadn't had much luck against America's Team, and they were a beat-up squad, nobody more so than Montgomery himself. Dallas had to punt on its first possession, giving the Eagles great field position. On the team's second play, quarterback Ron Jaworski handed off to Montgomery, and the star running back juked left, turned right, and dashed like a missile through a hole provided by center Guy Morriss, guard Woody Peoples, and tackle Jerry Sisemore. Montgomery was gone, rambling 42 yards for the first score in a 20–7 win that sent the Eagles to New Orleans for Super Bowl XV. Sure, the Eagles didn't win the championship, but anyone who watched that run will never forget Wilbert Montgomery.

WHO WERE THE EAGLES' FIVE MOST IMPORTANT DRAFT PICKS?

11 Fans love to point out those sleeper draft picks made good. However, the value of a draft pick isn't always measured just by what round he gets picked in. While the Eagles have acquired some of their top players through the draft, others were picked up in trades, some even for draft picks. Bill Bergey was a defensive stalwart who cost a pair of first-rounders and a second-rounder in a deal with the Bengals, but could anyone say that wasn't worth it? Bergey even announced his presence right away in the locker room by pointing out he *was* the team's draft. Of course, not all those draft pick deals worked out. See Boryla, Mike. He cost the team a few picks, including the first one in 1976. The Eagles also once dealt for Bill Cowher. He went on to better things as a coach.

So we're mixing and matching with the most important picks in Eagles history. There are no Tom Bradys here, as the Eagles haven't won multiple Super Bowls, or any for that matter. Some of the Eagles' best picks over the years came in the first round; some came later on when they were just hoping to catch lightning in a bottle. But their most important selections—those come in all shapes and sizes.

5. REGGIE WHITE (DE, 1984 USFL SUPPLEMENTAL DRAFT), TAKEN FOURTH OVERALL

Few remember how the Eagles got this guy, and it was technically through a draft—the supplemental draft of 1984 for USFL players to get to the NFL. White had played two years with the Memphis Showboats of the defunct league, and the Eagles wisely snapped him up with the number 4 pick of the historic draft. White would end up arguably the most dominating defensive lineman in NFL history, with more sacks than games played, but his importance for the Eagles wasn't just on the field. He gave the team an intimidator and someone for opponents to fear, and the Buddy Ryan defenses more credibility. In case you were wondering, the first three picks in that USFL draft were Steve Young (Buccaneers), Mike Rozier (Oilers), and Gary Zimmerman (Giants). The other Eagles picks were Darryl Goodlow and Thomas Carter. (Who?)

4. DONOVAN MCNABB (QB, SYRACUSE), DRAFTED SECOND OVERALL IN 1999

The Eagles hadn't held a draft pick as high as number 2 overall in 35 years, so this was a big one. They couldn't mess it up, and rookie coach Andy Reid wasn't sharing his thoughts with anyone on who the pick would be. Reid's tone would be a harbinger for his coaching regime. As noted elsewhere in the book, there were a number of quarterbacks available, plus the reigning college player of the year, Ricky Williams. Philly fans wanted Williams, the Heisman-winning running back. Reid disagreed. He took McNabb, and he's turned out to be the team's winningest quarterback, and one of the league's best, while also boasting the finest stats. How important was this pick, once Reid had decided to go with a signal caller? Ask the Bengals, who chose Akili Smith with the next pick, got six touchdowns from him in four years and have had one winning season in the 2000s.

3. BRIAN WESTBROOK (RB, VILLANOVA), DRAFTED 91ST OVERALL IN 2002

When Philadelphians think of college football, their attention generally turns to Penn State, where Joe Paterno has ruled for about 100 years, and where plenty of top-level prospects have had successful careers. The Eagles have picked their share of Nittany Lions along the way as well, most notably Kenny Jackson with the number 4 overall pick in 1984. The Eagles have taken a few Penn players, including the first guy on this list, and Temple alums show up once in a while. But what about Villanova, a program that went under for a time in the 1980s until being resurrected in Div. I-AA? Other than Howie Long, how many NFL players from Villanova can you name? That all changed in the third round of the 2002 draft, when Andy Reid chose Westbrook, the only player in college history to amass

45

more than 1,000 yards rushing and receiving in a season. In Philly the Westbrook pick was viewed as an afterthought, a nice gesture for a local kid, but then he returned a punt for a score in a 2003 game against the Giants, and by the next season was one of the most versatile running backs in the league. With two more good seasons he'll be the franchise's leading rusher.

2. WILBERT MONTGOMERY (RB, ABILENE CHRISTIAN), DRAFTED 154TH OVERALL IN 1977

He made the run that started the 1981 championship game rolling for the Eagles, rambled for 194 yards on a battered body to lead them to their first Super Bowl, and when his eight years in Philly were over, no running back had gained more yards. Even now, no running back has. And this is a guy the Eagles stole in the sixth round of the 1977 draft, with a draft pick acquired from the Bears for a guard named Mark Nordquist. The Eagles drafted Nordquist in 1968 in the fifth round, got 96 games out of him, and then drafted their all-time leading rusher, a quiet, unassuming gentleman of a player who never got into any trouble. After years of non-productive running backs in Philly, Montgomery was important because Dick Vermeil had managed to fill a great need without using early draft picks or making a trade. He didn't have the requisite early draft picks anyway: the prior era had traded away all the picks in the first four rounds. Didn't matter: the Eagles' all-time leading rusher and receiver (Harold Carmichael) were each selected in the sixth round or later. Maybe those Rich Kotite Eagles teams should have just skipped the early rounds!

1. CHUCK BEDNARIK (C-LB, PENNSYLVANIA), DRAFTED FIRST OVERALL IN 1949

While Montgomery's pick was critical, the bottom line is that the Eagles never won a championship with him. Meanwhile, Concrete Charlie was plucked out of Penn as the first overall pick in 1949, and helped define the franchise for the next 14 seasons, winning two championships and being voted All-Pro 10 times. You might be wondering, how did the Eagles win the NFL title in 1948 yet still get the first pick the next season? The NFL decided to make the first pick back in 1947 a bonus pick and used a lottery to decide the team to get it. The champion Bears got that pick in 1947 and the Eagles would follow suit two years later. Bednarik became the Eagles' most important draft pick, but he might have been a Detroit Lion had the Eagles not won a random lottery!

12 There is no shortage of bad draft picks credited to the Eagles franchise, but there's obviously more pressure to perform on the first guy taken.

The very first draft pick in league history went to the Eagles, way, way back in 1936, and University of Chicago two-way legend Jay Berwanger was chosen. He was the first Heisman trophy winner, so how could Philly fans fault the pick? Well, turns out ol' Jay didn't want to play professional football. The Eagles dealt his rights to the Chicago Bears, and he never played there either, choosing to become a sportswriter, a coach, even a manufacturer of plastic car parts. Hey, at least he didn't pull a J. D. Drew and play elsewhere, right?

In the Andy Reid era the team has generally chosen well when selecting in round one. Donovan McNabb was a fine choice; Corey Simon had his moments on the defensive line; and Lito Sheppard became a Pro Bowler. The worst first-rounder for Reid would probably be Freddie Mitchell, the number 25 pick out of UCLA in 2001. Mitchell was never a consistent target for McNabb and, other than one memorable play in the postseason, didn't make his mark on the field. His FredEx nickname and the way he praised his hands were proof he thought he was a star, even though those 90 receptions and five touchdowns in four years say otherwise. Still, that was a late-first rounder. The Eagles have done worse. Like with these guys.

5. LEROY KEYES (RB, PURDUE), DRAFTED THIRD OVERALL IN 1969

In fairness to Keyes, Philly fans initially gave him grief not because of who he was, but because of who he wasn't. In 1968 the Eagles had a miserable season. They lost their first 11 games, and seemed right on track to get hotshot USC running back O. J. Simpson. Then the Eagles shut out the Lions on Thanksgiving Day. Ten days later, the Eagles beat the fellow lowly Saints. Losing the finale to Minnesota, better known as the day Santa Claus got booed and pelted by snowballs, wasn't good enough; the Eagles had blown their chance at Simpson and had to pick third. Nobody remembers that Keyes seemed like a decent pick at the time, as he had finished second to Simpson in the Heisman Trophy voting. All they remember is that he wasn't Simpson, and his pro stats would show it. While O. J. went on to break records (and do some interesting things off the field later in life), Keyes carried the ball a grand total of 125 times, at three yards a pop, scoring three touchdowns, in five underwhelming seasons.

4. JON HARRIS (DE, VIRGINIA), DRAFTED 25TH OVERALL IN 1997

Now we get to some of the interesting linemen chosen by Rich Kotite, Ray Rhodes, and even Buddy Ryan. Harris was a favorite of Rhodes, but he really reached in making him a first-rounder, even at pick 25. Harris, who wasn't even a regular starter at Virginia, and was projected as a third- or fourth-round pick, was stunned when he was selected that early. So was everyone else. Two seasons and only two sacks later, Harris was dealt to the Packers for John Michaels.

3. ANTONE DAVIS (OT, TENNESSEE), DRAFTED EIGHTH OVERALL IN 1991 BERNARD WILLIAMS (OT, GEORGIA), DRAFTED 14TH OVERALL IN 1994

These not-so-fine offensive tackles are grouped together for their closeness in year drafted and for being taken way too high. Davis was a ridiculous choice by Kotite, who traded the team's first choice in 1992 to move up in the 1991 draft to get him. An All-America from Tennessee, Davis started as a rookie and played five years in Philly but never reached his potential. Williams came from Georgia, another SEC school, and also had unrealized talent. He started as a rookie, then failed a few drug tests—well, 15 of them—and needed years to knock his marijuana habit. He was banned from the league, but did play in the XFL, so he's always got that going for him.

2. MIKE MAMULA (DE, BOSTON COLLEGE), DRAFTED 7TH OVERALL IN 1995

To some, Mamula wasn't so bad a draft-day bust since he did have five seasons as a regular player in Philly. However, Ray Rhodes traded up from the number 12 pick to get him, when he could have drafted him much later. Who went in that number 12 spot? Just Warren Sapp, that's who. Well, Mamula was a constant source of derision from fans and the tough media. Too small to be a dominant defensive end, not quick enough to get to the quarterback, the Boston College product put on a show at the NFL pre-draft combine in 1995 with his bench pressing and 40-yard draft times. Most NFL experts saw through the façade. The Eagles didn't. He had fooled Rhodes into trading up to get him, and unless Mamula became a star, he would have a rough time in Philly. Since then scouts have been more careful about overestimating players at pre-draft camps, also known as Mamula Syndrome. Mamula finished his career with 31 ½ sacks and a lifetime of hatred from Eagles fans.

1. KEVIN ALLEN (OT, INDIANA), DRAFTED NINTH OVERALL IN 1985

Buddy Ryan made this pick, thinking he had his left tackle for the next decade. Other NFL teams projected this guy as a third-rounder at best. Even they were wrong, apparently. Early on, even Ryan could tell Allen looked like a bust.

Then the word bust took on different meaning. Allen tested positive for cocaine in training camp his sophomore year, went to jail for sexual assault, and never played again. Yep, that was a first-round pick who played one season. And of course, who can forget this all-timer from Ryan: that Allen was a good player to have around "if you want someone to stand around and kill the grass." At least Ryan never lost his sense of humor.

SHOULD THE EAGLES HAVE DRAFTED RICKY WILLIAMS?

13 The Ray Rhodes 1998 Eagles were an unmitigated 3–13 disaster, and changes had to be made. It wasn't just a position or two; this whole team needed an overhaul. Eagles fans were mad, or at least madder than normal. So a guy nobody knew named Andy Reid was summoned from Green Bay for his first head coaching stint and the rebuilding process was underway. But who would be selected with that number 2 overall pick?

The fans obviously and desperately wanted University of Texas running back Ricky Williams, the Heisman trophy winner who broke or tied 20 NCAA records, including the ones for career yards and touchdowns. The guy was going to be great. It would have made sense to pick Williams, despite the fact that the Eagles also desperately needed a quarterback, because while Duce Staley was coming off a productive 1,000-yard season, few saw him as a long-term answer. Plus, this draft was loaded at quarterback with Tim Couch, Donovan McNabb, Akili Smith, Daunte Culpepper, and Cade McNown, among others, and the Eagles could have found a way to get someone, right? All these guys would end up going in the top 12.

But only Couch went higher than McNabb, at number 1. When the Eagles made their pick, one of the most notorious things to happen at a live draft occurred. Thanks to a Philly radio promotion, at least 30 of the fans in attendance in New York's Madison Square Garden were angry, liquored-up Eagles fans who had been bused to the Big Apple to root for Williams to get picked. Everyone wanted Williams. Even Philadelphia mayor Ed Rendell made it clear he wanted the running back. The fans weren't so much angry with McNabb, but while their intent wasn't to ruin the biggest day of his life, they did by creating an embarrassing scene. They booed. They booed loudly. The cameras ate it up, as did those who wanted more fodder about the psyche of the Philadelphia fan. It didn't reflect well on Philly and it certainly got the McNabb era off on the wrong foot, but that didn't matter. Philly's used to that.

The question was, of course, should the Eagles have chosen Williams? In hindsight, the McNabb pick looks very smart. While Williams did have some good seasons, he's been in and out of football, having made it quite clear he'd prefer to smoke pot than play the game. He bolted from the Dolphins on the eve of the 2004 season, putting them in a bind they haven't gotten out of, and it's certainly looking like his career is on the verge of extinction.

Meanwhile, McNabb has been one of the best quarterbacks in the league since becoming a full-time starter in 2000, leading the Eagles to four conference title games and a Super Bowl. He's won more than 60 percent of his starts, been to Pro Bowls, and his jersey is worn by kids and adults all over Philly. But back in the spring of 1999, who knew it would work out this way?

Even without hindsight, the Eagles made the right move. In fact, we should laud the Eagles for picking the quarterback they did. Couch, Smith, and McNown were busts. Imagine what Philly fans would have done to poor McNown, for example. The Eagles needed to end the Bobby Hoying era, after he managed to throw nine interceptions and fumble six times without throwing a single touchdown in 1998. The pick had to be a quarterback. Despite the booing, it was the right one.

DID DONOVAN MCNABB PUKE AWAY SUPER BOWL CHANCES?

14 Of course, whether the drafting of Donovan was smart or not, it doesn't mean he's above criticism on the field, even in a Super Bowl. The Eagles team that finally got over that NFC Championship Game hump would fall a field goal short in Super Bowl XXXIX, losing to Tom Brady's Patriots 24–21. Brady was impeccable in a big game, as was normally the story, and the Patriots defense forced four turnovers. The game was tied 7–7 at the half, and 14–14 heading into the fourth quarter, the first time in Super Bowl history that had happened. Brady got his team 10 points in the fourth, and we skip to the part where the Eagles took over at their own 21-yard line with 5:40 left in the game, needing two scoring drives, one a touchdown, to send the game into overtime.

Here's where Philly fans got infuriated. While Reid and McNabb were never known for their clock management, this was a bit ridiculous. The Eagles acted like time was not a factor, eschewing a no-huddle offense and looking like they thought there were 20 minutes left to play. Little by little, the team moved down the field, the clock ran, and when McNabb hit Greg Lewis with a 30-yard touchdown pass, the two-minute warning had already passed. Why did the Eagles take so long? The onside kick attempt failed, and while the Pats did punt, the Eagles were pinned inside their own 5-yard line with under a minute to go, and McNabb threw his third interception of the day to seal the loss.

However, a few days after the game the news came out that McNabb had been sick in the huddle on the final drive, which gave insight to why the Eagles didn't seem to attack with much immediacy. Center Hank Fraley noted McNabb was "mumbling, and Freddie [Mitchell] yelled out the play we were trying to bring in. He was puking at the same time, trying to hold it in." Other offensive linemen confirmed the gory details of how the Chunky Soup spokesman had, well, lost his Chunky Soup at the most inopportune time. Mitchell, never at a loss for self-serving words, said afterward that he had called the play.

The Eagles have qualified for two Super Bowls in 42 years of the big game, and in the first one quarterback Ron Jaworski threw an early pick, ended up with three, and the Raiders had a blowout win. In the second one, the quarterback had three more picks and supposedly threw something else on the field as well.

Or did he? While it's difficult to know exactly what did happen on that Jacksonville field in the fourth quarter, the postscript on this tale is that whether McNabb did or didn't vomit, is it relevant? The quarterback says he was fine, but what is he going to say? If he did get ill, he'll be forever

57

known as someone who failed in the clutch and couldn't handle the pressure. Of course, McNabb haters can make that claim anyway. We've seen him vomit on the field since then, in far less meaningful games. Players do this from time to time, but it's rare a loss can be blamed on—well, you know.

No matter how much of McNabb himself became part of the Jacksonville field, he didn't lead his team to victory. Neither did Andy Reid, who had to know what was going on, but couldn't make things better. Even if the final scoring drive had gone quicker, which was no guarantee with a team on the other side that has nearly a full hand of Super Bowl rings, there's no telling if McNabb could have driven the Eagles to a game-tying field goal. We're left to wonder about what might have been earlier in the game, when the Eagles had chances, not about what was left on the field.

WAS THE TERRELL OWENS ERA WORTH IT?

15 Terrell Owens didn't seem to make many friends in his Philadelphia tenure, which started out well and ended rather poorly after 21 games. But was it worth it to bring T. O. to Philly in the first place?

Next question.

Okay, so we still can't get the words of Owens's agent Drew Rosenhaus out of our collective heads. As for the T. O. era, first let's examine the facts. The 2003 Eagles had lost in the NFC title game for the third straight season and had scored a grand total of one touchdown in the two home title games. Donovan McNabb was in the prime of his career, the running game was deep and productive, and there were no outstanding weapons at wide receiver at McNabb's disposal. In 2002 Todd Pinkston and James Thrash led the team in receptions and touchdown catches, though neither was exactly feared. The following season nobody on the team caught as many as 50 passes, with Thrash and running backs Brian Westbrook and Duce Staley leading the way. Freddie Mitchell, drafted three years prior, wasn't looking like the answer. McNabb needed help.

Enter Owens, arguably the most productive wide receiver in the league and a future Hall of Famer. Owens had been to four straight Pro Bowls as a member of the 49ers and was still in his prime heading into his 30s. Owens wanted out of San Francisco, but as Eagles fans would find out, there was even controversy in his exit. Owens and the 49ers disputed whether the player was a free agent or not, with the team claiming Owens's prior agent David Joseph had missed the deadline to void the final years of his contract. The 49ers tried to trade Owens to Baltimore. Owens thought he was a free agent. In the end, after negotiations with the Eagles, 49ers, and Ravens, the Eagles dealt a conditional fifth-round draft pick and defensive end Brandon Whiting to acquire Owens, and rewarded him with a seven-year contract worth $49 million, including a $10-million signing bonus.

Owens was brash, outspoken, and a major pain in the butt to coaches and teammates in Philly, but nobody could dispute his talent. He hauled in 14 touchdowns in 14 games that first season before breaking his leg and spraining his ankle in Week 15 against Dallas. The 13–1 Eagles didn't know if Owens would return for the playoffs. As he tried to heal, the Eagles lost their last two games, each meaningless with the NFC's top seed sewn up. In the playoffs, the Eagles beat the Vikings and Falcons with relative ease sans Owens, and got to Super Bowl XXXIX anyway.

The two weeks between the title game win over Atlanta and the big game in Jacksonville against the Patriots seemed to be all about T. O. Would he or wouldn't he play?

Doctors said he wouldn't be ready, Owens didn't listen. In a way it took the pressure off the other Eagles, with so much of the media focusing on Owens. In the end Owens did play, and he played spectacularly, catching nine passes for 122 yards in the Eagles 24–21 loss. Owens was labeled heroic for playing, but even he couldn't get the team a Super Bowl title.

Things didn't go quite as well in the 2005 season. Owens hired new agent Rosenhaus, and demanded a new contract, one that would make him one of the top-paid wide receivers in football. He said he needed to feed his family. Who are we to doubt that? The Eagles stuck with their policy of not renegotiating contracts. Owens was thrown out of practice in August for arguing with Reid, and a media circus ensued, with him doing situps in the driveway of his New Jersey home, then having Rosenhaus memorably and repeatedly answer "next question" at an impromptu press conference at Owens's house when he didn't like the questions. Owens and McNabb continued trading barbs, Owens didn't want to talk to any of his teammates and coaches, and it was getting clear Owens wasn't fitting into the Eagles team concept. According to Owens, the team showed a lack of class by not properly acknowledging his 100th career touchdown catch. Before the Week 9 game the Eagles suspended Owens for conduct detrimental to the team, but basically they just didn't want him around any longer. An arbitrator said the team was within its rights, and that was it. Owens never played for the Eagles again, and was cut the following March.

So, was it worth it? Naysayers point out Owens didn't help the Eagles win any playoff games, as he was injured for the NFC playoffs, and Philly lost the Super Bowl. McNabb's Eagles had finally gotten over the hump and won an NFC title game, but Owens didn't have anything to do with it. Then he pretty much torpedoed the 2005 season and was gone, hated by much of Philly. So—could this have been worth it?

It was worth it because the Owens era showed Eagles fans that they were trying anything to build a winner, and for one season, even though Owens missed January, it worked. Owens was that feared wide receiver McNabb never had, and hasn't had since. He helped give the team a chance in the Super Bowl, and even when things went horribly awry the summer of 2005, the fact that Reid and management refused to budge did endear them to fans. It was the right thing to do, hiring Owens, then firing Owens. And it was worth it.

SHOULD THE SECOND HALF OF THE FOG BOWL HAVE BEEN PLAYED?

16 Even though the Eagles had to go on the road to play the Bears in this infamous divisional playoff game on New Year's Eve 1988, they were as good as the Bears, if not better. But foggy Soldier Field got in the way. Or did it?

The fog that day was a freak of nature, for the long history of Soldier Field had never seen a weather situation like this. At home the Bears have dealt with rain and snow and ungodly temperatures, but thick, billowing fog that resembled smoke from a nearby fire covering the stadium? Not so much. The Eagles were their own worst enemies in the first half, not converting in the red zone, having two touchdowns called back by penalties, settling for field goals, and trailing 17–9. When the fog moved in off Lake Michigan from the south, it became nearly impossible to see. Visibility was slim for players and coaches, not to mention fans and announcers.

Football isn't like any other sport. It gets played in all types of weather, except dangerous lightning. Fog isn't dangerous. At least, it isn't when you're off the road, and nobody was driving near a cliff in this fog. In fact, nobody was driving much at all. Eagles coach Buddy Ryan was asked after the game if he thought the second half should have been delayed, to let the fog clear, and he said, "That's baseball, where you delay for rain and all that. This is football."

And that's why Ryan makes our argument for us. The fog affected both teams. It's true the Eagles were far more dependent on the passing game than the Bears were, but Randall Cunningham, the Eagles' leading rusher, had a career full of making unexpected big plays. He threw for 407 yards on this day, but never did get his team into the end zone. The fog was an excuse for the Eagles, not the reason they lost. They had chances. After the game, Eagles management and some players whined the game should have been stopped until the fog lifted, but they wouldn't have done that if the Eagles had won.

Ironically, the fog lifted about a half hour after the game ended, but too late to give the Eagles more chances, chances there's no guarantee they would have done anything with anyway.

WHY IS DICK VERMEIL SO BELOVED?

 The Eagles stunk in the 1960s and early 1970s, as coaches Joe Kuharich, Ed Khayat, and Mike McCormack managed one winning season between them from 1964 through 1975. Change was needed, and when owner Leonard Tose and general manager Jim Murray tried to coax UCLA coach Dick Vermeil to come aboard and coach at the NFL level, there were plenty of skeptics, including leery Philly fans. A college coach, in Philly? He'd get eaten alive! Vermeil had won the Rose Bowl, but he was only 37. Could he even handle a town like Philly?

Vermeil put his stamp on things early on, with a renewed work ethic and intense practices. He turned over the roster, and by season two the scrappy Eagles were showing signs of building something. The 1977 team was competitive, and won its final two games, beating the Jets and Giants at home to finish 5–9. Ron Jaworski had finished his first year as quarterback, Wilbert Montgomery was poised to take over the running back chores, the defense was as good as it had been in years, and 1978 actually held promise.

The next two years saw the Eagles in the playoffs, and in 1980 the Eagles rolled through the regular season, winning 11 of the first 12 games, beating the Vikings and

Cowboys in January, and going on to Super Bowl XV. Vermeil and his upstart team lost to the Raiders, but just getting to the big game was historic.

After that, the Eagles made one more playoff appearance, losing at home in a wild-card game to the Giants after the 1981 season before the strike season of 1982. That strike year changed everything. It was Vermeil's toughest, and not only for the 3–6 record. The players weren't responding to him anymore, the nights of sleeping on the office couch were taking its toll, and the losses were too tough to deal with. Vermeil's best attributes—his energy, drive, and will to win—were now his downfall. He was burned out, and he said so, in a tearful goodbye shortly after the season.

Vermeil became a successful announcer for ABC, but you knew he'd someday come back to coach. He was young. He just didn't look done when he resigned. Vermeil almost came back to Philly in 1995, but either his contract demands were too much or it just wasn't the right time. Eventually, Vermeil would win a Super Bowl with the Rams and then move across Missouri to lead the Chiefs, but Philly fans never stopped loving him. In fact, Vermeil was more popular than the coaches who followed him, even in retirement. The Eagles have had bad seasons since Vermeil stopped coaching in 1982, but for a guy with a career 57–51 record, including playoffs, to be so revered long after leaving the job is a bit odd. Why the love?

Is it because of the way he built this franchise up after years of poor play? Is it because he left in a moment of weakness, showing a tough, never-give-up city that grown men can cry? He became a sympathetic figure, and it seems that feeling never went away.

Neither did he. Vermeil became a spokesman for Independence Blue Cross insurance, and 20 years after leaving the Eagles his face remains seen in local TV ads and on billboards along highways. Vermeil never left Philly, really, even when he took other coaching jobs, still making his home in the suburbs.

Maybe it all comes down to this: The franchise's biggest play (Wilbert Montgomery strafing Dallas), and biggest game, in that glorious 1980 Super Bowl season, came with the ebullient Vermeil on the sidelines, and those moments will never be forgotten.

TAKING OFFENSE: WHO'S ON THE ALL-TIME EAGLES OFFENSIVE DREAM TEAM?

It all starts with the quarterback. Without him, it's tough to have a winning football team. The Eagles have had some terrific signal callers, some of whom were just passing by on their way to making history, others who stuck around awhile. And there have been some terrible ones as well: Ask Eagles fans who had to endure watching Bobby Hoying, Pat Ryan, or Mike Boryla at quarterback, and they'll tell you how much they longed for someone else.

Of course, the case can be made that the quarterback, while he gets a lot of the attention, is only as good as the players who block for him and the weapons he has at his disposal. There are 18 Eagles players or personnel enshrined in the Pro Football Hall of Fame, and only a few are quarterbacks. The offensive line is represented, as well as a few players who did the dirty work at end, which was the precursor to the current tight end position.

Eagles fans appreciate their Hall of Famers and the others whose outstanding work got them placed on the Eagles Honor Roll, but awards still don't guarantee a spot amongst our greatest Eagles of all time. Let's go position by position on the offensive side of the ball to pick the very best.

18 QUARTERBACK: DONOVAN MCNABB (1999–PRESENT)

What about: Ron Jaworski? The Polish Rifle deserves a lot more credit for what he accomplished. This was the league's preeminent ironman at the position until a guy named Brett Favre came along, and that counts for a lot. He also got the Eagles to a Super Bowl, and nobody has thrown for more passing yards in team history, though McNabb should pass him in 2008. Jaws, currently a well-respected commentator and analyst for ESPN and *Monday Night Football* who still resides in the Philly suburbs, set club passing records in completions, touchdowns, and yards, and he was the key to turning things around on the field for new coach Dick Vermeil. The underwhelming Boryla was the quarterback before Jaws, necessitating the trade before the 1977 season from the Rams for tight end Charles Young. Jaws started right away and began building an impressive resume. Even today, he remains a popular figure in town, like his coach Dick Vermeil.

What about: Randall Cunningham? No Philly quarter-back was flashier than Cunningham, who in his 11 seasons, once he replaced Jaws, piled on impressive, historic rushing totals. But that wasn't all. He also delivered jaw-dropping moments and multiple playoff appearances, and he certainly had a fine regular-season record. The four-time Pro Bowl pick could even lay down a fine punt inside the 20 if you needed it. However, when it mattered most—

in the fog of Chicago in his first playoff game, or relieving Rodney Peete in a divisional playoff loss to Dallas to finish his Eagles career in 1995—Cunningham was more flash and dash than results. We'll never forget the elusive Carl Banks play on *Monday Night Football*, one of the top Eagles plays mentioned in Argument 10, or the 95-yard bomb he threw to Fred Barnett in Week 13 of 1990, after eluding numerous Bills in the end zone, but The Ultimate Weapon, as he was dubbed by *Sports Illustrated*, still won only one playoff game.

What about: Norm Van Brocklin? For those who go a bit further back, Van Brocklin was the league MVP in 1960, when the franchise last won it all, and the only man to beat the great Vince Lombardi in the playoffs. Van Brocklin played the final three years of his Hall of Fame career in Philly, but only one of these years was exceptional. And like The Dutchman, Sonny Jurgensen had his moments in Philly, but wasn't an Eagle for very long and did much of his Hall of Fame work elsewhere.

Yeah, but: The best is McNabb. He has combined terrific statistics with winning, and has been a critical leader in arguably the franchise's top era. While his Eagles career began somewhat ignominiously by being booed at the NFL draft by liquored-up Eagles fans, how can anyone say the McNabb era hasn't been a success? The team has never won a Super Bowl, but McNabb got the team to four consecutive NFC Championship Games, and once to the biggest game of all. Entering the 2007 season, no active quarterback with as many starts had a better winning percentage than his .663 mark, and only a handful had managed to pass for 20,000 passing yards while running for 2,500 more. The McNabb era might not last much longer, but it's certainly been a positive one, especially when compared to those other signal callers from the same class like Tim Couch, Akili Smith, and Cade McNown. Yes, Philly fans, McNabb has been a lightning rod for controversy and probably misunderstood, but it could have been much worse. And no, A. J. Feeley wouldn't have done better.

19 RUNNING BACK: STEVE VAN BUREN (1944–51)

What about: Wilbert Montgomery? This guy made a lot of big plays as an Eagle, with the most memorable one getting the team past Dallas and into Super Bowl XV. His best statistical season wasn't that 1980 campaign, but the years before and after, when he finished in the top 5 in rushing yards. When he retired, no Eagle had more rushing yards, attempts, or more rushing yards in a season. The Abilene Christian product returned kicks his rookie year but became one of the franchise leaders soon after, and remains beloved in Philly.

What about: Brian Westbrook? Like Montgomery, Westbrook was an undersized speedster from a small school who wasn't expected to be as great as he was, but he continues to amaze. Westbrook led the NFL in yards from scrimmage in 2007 and topped Montgomery's franchise mark while remaining one of the top receiving options at his position. Westbrook's punt return touchdown as a rookie in 2003 sparked the team to a win over the Giants and 10 wins in the final 11 games. Every year since, he has continued to pile on the rushing and receiving yards like few others in the league.

What about: Duce Staley and Ricky Watters? They each had their moments in Eagles green, gaining 1,000 yards in multiple seasons, but neither fully endeared themselves to fans. Staley had numerous injuries that held him back and more than one contract dispute with the club. He finished his career as an afterthought in Pittsburgh, but did retire as an Eagle, getting a halftime ceremony and everything. Watters was labeled a selfish player early on, which he was, but few can argue with his productivity. A Pro Bowl selection twice in three seasons in Philly, Watters is a motivational speaker and author of the book *For Who For What: A Warrior's Journey.* No, we did not make up the title of the book.

Yeah, but: It's gotta be Steve Van Buren. Young Philly fans never saw him play, but Van Buren put up terrific stats in an era when stats weren't what people noticed. Back then, it was about the championships, and the bruising 200-pounder from LSU scored the lone touchdown in the 1948 7–0 title game blizzard win over the Chicago Cardinals at

Shibe Park. A season later he pounded his way to 196 yards in a 14–0 whitewash of the Los Angeles Rams. Van Buren was a four-time league rushing champ who wasn't merely famous by Philly standards, but was inducted into the Pro Football Hall of Fame in 1965 and 30 years later named to the league's 75th anniversary team. Van Buren could have run in any era and succeeded. When a knee injury curtailed his career, he left the NFL as its leader in rushing yards and rushing touchdowns. Put simply, he's probably the greatest Eagle of all time.

20 WIDE RECEIVER: TOMMY MCDONALD (1957–63)

What about: Harold Carmichael? Eagles fans of the current generation grew up watching the 6'8" Carmichael patrolling the field, standing out like a giraffe over smaller defensive backs. Ever the professional, Carmichael and Ron Jaworski teamed up for big seasons in the late 1970s, both setting standards for durability. Carmichael caught a pass in 127 consecutive games, and remains the franchise leader in consecutive games played (162) and most touchdowns scored. You can still see him down at the Linc as the team's director of player programs, but don't bring up the fact he finished his career with rival Dallas. Let's remember the good times.

What about: Pete Pihos? The versatile Pihos played his entire career in Philly, going to six Pro Bowls in nine seasons and, while he's best known for his work at wide receiver, also went to a Pro Bowl as a defensive end. Pihos wasn't the fastest receiver the Eagles have seen, but he made up for it with physical play and terrific hands. He once remarked that he never dropped a pass he could reach. He had his best statistical seasons at the end of his career, leading the league in receptions three straight years, then retiring in his prime.

What about: Mike Quick? Who can forget the 99-yard touchdown catch the aptly named Quick hauled in from Jaworski to win an overtime game at the Vet against Atlanta in 1985? Quick was one of the top receivers in football in his prime—which, sadly, was short due to knee injuries— but he went to five straight Pro Bowls and averaged double digits in touchdowns in that span. Like Carmichael, Quick was always a fan favorite and remains so as the team's announcer with Merrill Reese on radio broadcasts.

What about: Harold Jackson and Irving Fryar? Both were explosive receivers who topped 1,000 receiving yards a pair of times in Philly. Coming off a league-leading 62 catches for 1,048 yards, Jackson was traded to the Rams for Roman Gabriel after the 1972 season and went on to play for another decade. Fryar was near the end of his career when he starred for the Eagles from 1996–98, twice making the Pro Bowl with more than 80 receptions. Fryar caught five passes in the 14–0 shutout loss in San Francisco after the 1996 season and finished his career down

Interstate-95 with the Redskins. And don't forget Fred Barnett. He made a Pro Bowl and twice topped 1,000 yards, but because it all came in the Rich Kotite era, few remember.

Yeah, but: McDonald stood only 5'9" and 176 pounds, becoming the smallest player enshrined in the Pro Football Hall of Fame, and he starred in the 1960 championship season, scoring a league-best 13 touchdowns. Hey, you win a title in Philly, they tend to call you the best, and it's the fearlessness that helped McDonald stand apart. Known for his toughness and energy, McDonald took many a hard hit but kept getting up, playing through whatever the big linebackers of the day could dish out. He played halfback at Oklahoma, but was given a chance at wide receiver due to others being hurt and stayed at the position. The six-time Pro Bowl player caught 66 touchdown passes in his seven seasons in Philly, and his 84 touchdowns ranked him second in the league when he retired. McDonald finished his career with a bunch of other teams, but still makes his home in the Philly suburbs. He knew where his heart remained, in the city that drafted him.

21 TIGHT END: PETE RETZLAFF (1956–66)

What about: Keith Jackson? Based on his phenomenal rookie season, Jackson seemed on his way to being one of the best tight ends in the league for years. Jackson caught 81 passes for 869 yards a few months after being the team's first-round pick, but never had a season like it again. Could Jackson have left his best on Soldier Field that foggy New Year's Eve when he dropped a key touchdown pass? While he would go on to make two more Pro Bowls as an Eagle and two more with the Dolphins and Packers, Jackson didn't win a playoff game in Philly. He does have a Super Bowl ring, along with Andy Reid, from the 1996 season in Green Bay.

What about: Charles Young? He was an All-America at Southern Cal and the sixth overall pick in 1973, and an instant hit in the NFL. What is it with first-round tight ends having great rookie seasons in Philly, then bolting for Super Bowls elsewhere? Like Jackson, Young did some fine work in Philly, but for some horrible pre-Vermeil teams. Young's best season came in 1973 with 854 yards and six touchdowns, but he's best known in Philly for being the guy dealt to the Rams to acquire Ron Jaworski. Hey, that deal worked out just fine for the Eagles. Young won his championship with the 49ers.

Yeah, but: While Jackson and Young were more modern tight ends seemingly groomed to play the position, Retzlaff was basically dumped by the Detroit Lions, the team that drafted him in the 22nd round in 1953. The Eagles acquired him off waivers for only $100! Retzlaff was a fullback who never caught a pass in college or the NFL until the Eagles picked him up. After a few seasons, he was installed mainly as the tight end. Nice move. Retzlaff tied for the league lead in catches in 1958, led the Eagles in receptions each season from 1963 to 1966, and made five Pro Bowls, retiring as the Eagles all-time leader in receptions and yards. Retzlaff might also be remembered for his work off the field, as he was the team's player union representative and later served as the general manager for four years. On second thought, seeing those Eagles teams he helped manage, let's remember Retzlaff *on* the field.

22 CENTER: CHUCK BEDNARIK (1949–62)

What about: Vic Lindskog? He started at center on the title teams of 1948 and 1949, and while he was rewarded with only one Pro Bowl selection, in 1951, he was considered one of the top centers in the league at the time. (Pro Bowl voting doesn't always correspond to what's actually happening on the field.) Lindskog also played linebacker early in his career, bringing a boxer's mentality to the field, since he had trained in Los Angeles and considered a career as a heavyweight. Lucky for the Eagles he chose football, as he would help mentor Bednarik.

What about: Guy Morriss? Pretty underrated, Morriss snapped the ball to Jaworski on the 1980 team and for years before and after as well. He's fourth all time in games played for the team, having brought a strong work ethic and dependability, and he missed only one game in his 11 seasons. He finished his career with the Patriots and later went on to coach at Kentucky and Baylor.

What about: Jim Ringo? Better known as a Green Bay Packer, Ringo finished his career with four solid seasons in Philly, on his way to an eventual Hall of Fame selection. Using quickness and technique, he wasn't a particularly large man for the center position.

Yeah, but: Much better known for his big hits at linebacker, Bednarik was also the team's center, the last of the league's 60-minute players who never left the field. (You'll be seeing Concrete Charlie mentioned later as well.) While at Penn he was the first offensive lineman to win the Maxwell Award and his third-place finish for the Heisman was, at the time, the best for an interior offensive lineman. Bednarik seamlessly moved to the NFL and continued his fine work as center with the Eagles.

23 GUARD: BUCKO KILROY (1943–55)

What about: Jermane Mayberry? He was the Eagles first-round pick in 1996, and while it took him awhile to reach expectations, he was the franchise's first full-time guard to go to the Pro Bowl, in 2002. Mayberry was also very active off the field while in Philly, having helped fund the Eagles Eye Mobile, which gives free eye examinations to underprivileged youth in the Philly area.

What about: Jim Skaggs? He had an underappreciated 10-year career as an Eagle, missing most of his first two years after coming from the University of Washington, but then settling in as right guard in the late 1970s. He had a chance to play with the Raiders in the then-new AFL, but chose Philly.

Yeah, but: Kilroy was a rough, intense Philly guy who played in 134 games, going to three Pro Bowls, and he might have done his best work as a two-way tackle. But Philly has been loaded at tackle over the years and Kilroy also enjoyed Pro Bowl appearances at guard. Kilroy had a nasty mean streak, something he and teammates never denied, but he did take offense to a 1955 *Life* magazine article that labeled him an ornery player, as well as dirty. The headline read "Savagery on Sunday," and Kilroy was labeled "the orneriest of ornery critters." He sued for libel and won damages. Kilroy was also a player-coach of the Eagles, and later had a distinguished career running teams, including the Patriots in the 1980s. Born in the Port Richmond section of Philadelphia, Kilroy attended North Catholic high school and Temple University, and was once described by a Chicago newspaper writer as a "knuckle duster in knee pants who gives our fellows that boyish grin while knocking their teeth loose in a pileup." Sounds Philly to us.

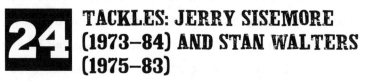

24 TACKLES: JERRY SISEMORE (1973–84) AND STAN WALTERS (1975–83)

What about: Al Wistert? Likely would be the pick of old-timers who saw him, and as one of seven Eagles to have their number retired, he would be a fine choice as the team's top tackle. He even won a few championships, having captained the 1948 and 1949 teams. He's gotten support for the Hall of Fame, though he's never been enshrined. Wistert was one of three brothers who were named All-American tackles at Michigan, and he played his entire nine-year career with the Eagles.

What about: Jon Runyan and William Thomas? Big ol' Jon Runyan, as he's often affectionately referred to by John Madden, and William Thomas have actually played together longer as a tandem than Sisemore and Walters. Runyan was Andy Reid's first major free agent acquisition, and totally worth it, as the 6'7", 330-pounder hasn't missed a game since 1996. You try suiting up for work 176 consecutive times—oh, and with Michael Strahan trying to run you over. Thomas was a first-round pick in 1998 and has been protecting Donovan McNabb's blind side ever since. (He used to be called Tra Thomas, not William.)

What about: Bob Brown? A tremendous talent, Brown shined for five excellent seasons in Philly, after the team used the number 2 overall pick in 1964 to draft him from Nebraska. At 6'4" and 300 pounds he had the size and mean streak to dominate and did, earning three Pro Bowl nods and making a name for himself as a drive blocker. It took awhile, but Brown ended up in the Hall of Fame. So how isn't he number 1 here? Brown forced a trade out of Philly before the 1969 season, ostensibly so he could play for a winner, so can we really fault him? Um, yeah, he should have stayed an Eagle!

Yeah, but: Sisemore and Walters anchored the Vermeil teams of the late 1970s and early 1980s, and because each played in so many games as a tandem (95 games) and were key to the 1980 Super Bowl run, they get the nod. Sisemore was the third overall pick in the 1973 draft and made two Pro Bowls, while Walters was acquired via trade with the Bengals and played in 122 consecutive games, also making a pair of Pro Bowls. Sisemore did move over to guard later in his career, but was no less effective there. Basically, Vermeil and Jaws never had to worry about the tackles while they were in town, as Sisemore and Walters had everything under control.

DEFENSE NEVER RESTS: WHO'S ON THE ALL-TIME EAGLES DEFENSIVE DREAM TEAM?

Take a guess when the Eagles had their best defensive seasons: it shouldn't be too tough. Four times the Eagles have led the NFL in fewest points allowed. In 1949, the Eagles were champs, and the defense remained solid the following season. The 1980 squad went to its first Super Bowl and the following year—well, at least the Eagles made the playoffs. The Eagles have had some pretty bad defensive units as well, notably in the early 1970s and, oddly enough, in 2005 under Andy Reid.

You might be wondering, what about the terrific 1991 team that had loads of Pro Bowl selections on defense and allowed the fewest yards in the league? Yeah, we'll give that one its due also. It was a great defense, arguably the best one an Eagles team has put together. Most people think so-called defensive genius Buddy Ryan was the architect of the defense, but the head coach at the time was Rich Kotite. Try to find *his* name and the word *genius* in the same sentence.

Anyway, the Eagles have been fortunate to send many top-notch defensive players to the field, so let's check out the best at each position.

25 DEFENSIVE END: REGGIE WHITE (1985–92)

What about: Carl Hairston and Clyde Simmons? They were fine players who deserve credit, but they're just not going to beat one of the top Eagles of all time. Simmons is actually number 2 on the team's sack list with 76.5, with his 1992 campaign standing out for his league-leading 19 sacks. Hairston was also a sack master before the statistic technically existed, but anyone who watched him knew he was the key to the 1980 team's defensive line. Hairston recorded 100 or more sacks in five straight seasons.

Yeah, but: C'mon, did you think anyone else got serious consideration here? White was beloved in his Philly seasons and beyond, when fans would watch Packers games and root for White to get the Super Bowl trophy he so wanted. White revolutionized the defensive end position with his speed and power, registering more sacks than games played and being selected for the Pro Bowl seven straight times. In the strike year of 1987 he totaled 21 sacks in only 12 games. His 124 sacks with the Eagles aren't just a club record; they are 47.5 more than

Simmons, who is second in club history. Still, White wasn't defined only by his on-field performance, as he was a very opinionated man and an ordained minister as well, known for his deep faith.

26 DEFENSIVE TACKLE: JEROME BROWN (1987–91)

What about: Charlie Johnson? He went to Pro Bowls in his final three seasons with the Eagles and played in the Super Bowl after the 1980 season. He expressed dissatisfaction with coach Dick Vermeil's intense ways in the summer of 1982 and asked for a trade. He finished his career with the Vikings. Johnson was a fine player, a difference maker on the line, but not the best the Eagles have had.

What about: Vic Sears? He played 13 seasons and 131 games with the Eagles, starting at tackle on both sides of the ball for a very long time, including the 1948 and 1949 title teams. He was named to the league's all-decade team of the 1940s. Sears was tough and durable, a professional rarely cited for dangerous play, unlike some of his teammates of the era. Old-time Eagles fans might choose Sears as the best, but he'd be a close second here.

What about: Jess Richardson? One of the key linemen on the 1960 team, Richardson grew up in Philly, and after going to college at Alabama, the Eagles made him an eighth-round draft pick in 1953. Richardson missed one game in nine seasons, and while he didn't make his money getting to the quarterback, he was one of the team's top run stuffers. Richardson grew up an Eagles fan and lived his dream of winning a title. If sacks were counted back then, it's unlikely Richardson would have piled them on, but he was a solid player.

Yeah, but: Jerome Brown left this world too soon, after five seasons with the Eagles. He died in a car accident in Florida after the 1991 season, but had clearly left his mark with his play. His final season was likely his best, as he made his second Pro Bowl and helped anchor the line of that terrific defense, stopping the run and registering nine sacks. Brown had his number retired and remained an inspiration to teammates and fans after his death. Some would argue that choosing Brown here is based more on sentiment than statistics, but his final season was a terrific one, and Brown was among the best linemen in the league at the time.

27 MIDDLE LINEBACKER: BILL BERGEY (1974–80)

What about: Jeremiah Trotter? He was a third-round pick in the 1998 draft, and in his second season tallied 174 tackles to lead the team. He went to Pro Bowls after the 2000 and 2001 seasons, yet decided he was worth more than the Eagles wanted to pay and bolted for the Redskins. Big mistake. After two seasons, Trotter was desperate to return to Philly, and the Eagles gave him the opportunity. Trotter wasn't just a popular player upon his return; he was a key reason the Eagles became strong in run defense. Trotter went back to two more Pro Bowls before becoming a training camp casualty before the 2007 season.

Yeah, but: Although he was acquired from the Bengals for a pair of first-round draft picks and a second-rounder, nobody ever questioned whether the Bergey deal was worth it. With his trademark beard and passion for the game, Bergey was the team's best defensive player for years, often looking like he was tackling opponents all by himself. On the field Bergey had the size, speed, and confidence needed to control the game, which he often did as he piled on the tackles: nearly 1,200 of them in seven seasons. Off the field everyone wanted a piece of Bergey, and he once joked that he had signed enough autographs for every Philadelphian, three times over. Even when his 1979 season ended in New Orleans with his knee torn on the AstroTurf, Eagles fans expected Bergey to continue playing. He came back for the 1980 Super Bowl season, then retired. He remains a popular figure in town, and can be heard on radio and TV broadcasts.

28 OUTSIDE LINEBACKER: CHUCK BEDNARIK (1949–62)

What about: Seth Joyner? He was a track and football star in college, showing his speed on Buddy Ryan's signature defenses. Originally cut by Ryan in his first preseason, Joyner was brought back and eventually earned a starting role by Thanksgiving of 1986. Joyner was wildly confident and outspoken, not caring which opponents, teammates, or front office personnel he angered along the way. His best season was 1991, when *Sports Illustrated* named him the league's player of the year.

What about: Maxie Baughan? Baughan was merely a rookie in 1960, but still started every game for the champs at right outside linebacker. He made the Pro Bowl in five of his six seasons in Philly after a decorated career at Georgia Tech. Baughan eventually got tired of the losing in the mid-1960s and was traded to the Los Angeles Rams.

What about: Alex Wojciechowicz? The Fordham product ended up in the Hall of Fame and played only five seasons with the Eagles after a trade from Detroit, but he performed like the seasoned pro he was. Wojciechowicz played outside linebacker on the 1948–49 championship teams and was known as a ferocious hitter and tackler.

What about: Frank LeMaster? He played next to Bill Bergey during the Dick Vermeil years and was another aggressive athlete key to the Eagles success. His only Pro Bowl appearance came in 1982, but this former basketball player at Kentucky always brought a working class mentality to the field and was admired for it. LeMaster could play outside or inside at linebacker. He led the Eagles in tackles in 1981, and scored three touchdowns in his career.

Yeah, but: And here we see that name again, as Concrete Charlie wins the nod at two different positions, one on each side of the ball. Bednarik dominated at outside linebacker, and not only on the hit that changed Frank Gifford's life. In the 1960 title game he stopped Jim Taylor to save that win, and the great Jim Brown called him the best linebacker he ever saw—and he should know. After being leveled by Bednarik, Gifford missed the rest of that 1960 season and all of the next year before coming back to play. Bednarik also knocked Packers top gun Paul Hornung out of the title game. There hasn't been a two-way player since Bednarik called it quits, and there never will be. The Hall of Fame inducted him in 1967, and even today Bednarik looks like he could step on the field and deck someone.

29 SAFETY: BRIAN DAWKINS (1996–PRESENT)

What about: Wes Hopkins? A ferocious hitter who played both safety positions for the Eagles from 1983–1993, Hopkins registered 30 interceptions and many broken bones. Hopkins made the 1986 Pro Bowl and recovered 16 fumbles in his career.

What about: Randy Logan? He never missed a game in his 11 seasons with the Eagles, playing in 159 consecutive games, three games short of Harold Carmichael's team record. A hard hitter who was quiet off the field, Logan is arguably the best strong safety the club has had.

What about: Andre Waters? An undrafted free agent in 1984 from Cheyney University, Waters was a fierce tackler who often crossed the line, but Philly fans loved him for it. Waters led the team in tackles four times and had his best season in 1991, when the Eagles led the league in run and pass defense. Waters made headlines in 2006 when he shot himself to death, causing the league to examine whether cumulative concussions led to depression in retired players.

What about: Bill Bradley? He picked off 34 passes in his eight seasons with the Eagles, and was known as one of the best in the league in reading quarterbacks and using instincts to get to the ball first. He was the first player to win back-to-back interception titles, and his accomplishments in 1971, with 11 picks for 248 yards, remain a standard to shoot for today. Bradley went to three Pro Bowls.

Yeah, but: An Eagle since being drafted in the second round in 1996, Dawkins is a six-time Pro Bowl selection and one of the hardest hitters in the game. He's already played in a franchise-record 15 playoff games, the free safety's next interception will tie him for the franchise lead, and no Eagle has been involved in more wins. Is he nearing the end? Absolutely, and who knows, he might have to join other Eagle greats in the Andy Reid era who have left town to finish their careers—but Dawkins is the spiritual leader of the defense and should return.

30 CORNERBACK: TOM BROOKSHIER (1953, 1956–61)

What about: Eric Allen? A fan favorite for his

seven seasons in Philly, five of which ended in Pro Bowl berths, it wasn't just that Allen made interceptions, tying the franchise record with 34: what he did with them was exceptional. He returned four picks for scores in 1993, including two in a memorable day-after-Christmas win over the Saints, and another was a 94-yard run against the Jets. Allen doesn't have any true negatives, and he went on to star with the Saints and Raiders, but he gets beaten out by someone who became a fixture in Philly.

What about: Roynell Young? He was a first-round pick in 1980 out of Alcorn State, and started immediately for the team that went to the Super Bowl. Young was Pro Bowl his sophomore season, but played in only two playoff games after that, including the legendary Fog Bowl, which was his last NFL game.

What about: Herman Edwards? You either know him from that miracle fumble recovery and touchdown to steal the 1978 victory against the Giants, or for his work as head coach of the Jets and Chiefs, but this was a pretty good cornerback in his day. Edwards totaled 13 interceptions in his first two seasons, despite being undrafted out of Cal-Berkeley.

What about: Troy Vincent? He made four consecutive Pro Bowls as an Eagle, a terrific free agent signing from the Dolphins who played with Brian Dawkins and Bobby Taylor for eight seasons in the secondary. A native of Trenton, Vincent would become the president of the NFL

Players Association. Vincent had 28 interceptions in 118 games with the Eagles, and made his mark but, like Eric Allen, loses out to someone who only wanted to play in this town and won a championship.

Yeah, but: Philly loves players who overachieve, and that seemed to be the case with Brookshier, a 10th round draft pick who spent two years in the Air Force after his rookie season but returned to have a memorable career on and off the field. A tough, hard-hitting cornerback, Brookshier brought an attitude and swagger to the defense. Eight of his 20 career interceptions came that first season. While his playing career ended with a compound fracture of his leg in 1961, his notoriety didn't, as he became a fixture on local radio and TV, then moved on to CBS Sports, where he and Pat Summerall became one of the better-known broadcasting duos made up of former players. The Eagles have been blessed with terrific cornerbacks, but Brookshier played a major role in the 1960 title-winning season as well.

31 KICKER: DAVID AKERS (1999–PRESENT)

What about: Bobby Walston? Also an accomplished wide receiver, Walston held the club record for points until Akers broke it in December 2007, as Walston was the team's primary kicker for much of his tenure of 12 seasons as an Eagle. Walston is also in the team's top 10 for catches, yards, and touchdowns, and he ranked second in the league in touchdown receptions in 1954.

What about: Sam Baker? He took over the kicking duties two seasons after Walston retired, and made two more Pro Bowls, giving him a career total of four. Baker was also the team's punter in this span. When Baker retired at the age of 40 after the 1969 season, he held the league mark for scoring in 110 consecutive games.

Yeah, but: Akers began his Philly career in a dubious way, as a journeyman lefty on a tryout signed for kickoffs, but early on it was apparent he was a better field goal option than incumbent Norm Johnson. Akers became the regular kicker, and holds the franchise mark for field goals and points, while also becoming one of the most accurate kickers in league history. Akers hasn't had his best seasons since tearing a hamstring in 2005, and he's begun to hear it from the fans, but few kickers have been as reliable in the decade.

32 PUNTER: JOE MUHA (1946–50)

What about: Jeff Feagles? His name rhymes with the team he played for from 1990–94, but Feagles wasn't acquired as a stunt, nor was he even close to done when he left Philly. Feagles is still kicking, 17 seasons after becoming an Eagle, and is the league's record-holder for consecutive games played, punts, and most punts downed inside the 20-yard line. He finally made his first Super Bowl, in 2008, and won it!

What about: Sean Landeta? Like Feagles, Landeta has seemingly been around forever, and he kicked for the team from 1999–2002, as well as a return engagement for five games at the age of 43 in 2005. Landeta punted 107 times for that terrible 1999 team, the first year of the Reid and McNabb era, but also averaged nearly 43 yards per punt in his tenure.

Yeah, but: Feagles and Landeta did fine work in their tenure as Eagles, but Joe Muha won championships. He was a fullback and linebacker on the title teams of 1948 and 1949, and played a key role as punter, averaging 42.9 yards in that role for his career, and an incredible 47.2 yards per kick in 1948. When Randall Cunningham boomed a 91-yard punt in 1989, the franchise record he broke was Muha's 82-yarder in 1948.

PHILLIES
PHODDER

WHAT WERE THE PHILLIES' FIVE MOST MEMORABLE PLAYOFF WINS?

33 When you play in nearly 19,000 games, some of them are going to be very memorable. Then again, that's just the regular season. In 125 years the Phillies have been involved in only 60 playoff games, and quite a few of the memorable ones saw the Fightin' Phils walk away on the losing end. In fact, the Phillies have won 22 playoff games in their history—not even one playoff win for every five years of existence—but there was a World Series championship in there, after all. And don't forget the 1915 World Series, which the Phillies lost to the Red Sox 4 games to 1, the postseason series in the late 1970s, and the one win in the 1983 World Series against Baltimore. That said, here are the five most memorable playoff wins in team history.

5. 1993 NL CHAMPIONSHIP SERIES, GAME 5—OCTOBER 11, 1993

The series was tied at two games apiece, and some thought even that was quite a trick for the Phillies, as they were facing the juggernaut Braves, a 104-win team. The Phils took Game 1, when Kim Batiste got the winning hit in extra innings in his only postseason at-bat, but lost the next two games by scores of 14–3 and 9–4. Danny Jackson outdueled John Smoltz to win Game 4 by a score of 2–1, and Game 5 pitted Curt Schilling against Steve Avery. Schilling was masterful, scattering four hits and no runs through eight innings, and the Phils had a 3–0 lead. Schilling started the ninth allowing a walk and Batiste committed an error, and manager Jim Fregosi brought in Mitch Williams. With Schilling covering his head with a towel, hardly instilling confidence in the team's closer, the lead soon evaporated on a single, a sacrifice fly, and two more singles. Now Williams faced runners on the corners with one out, and Mark Lemke at the plate. Tension was high as the Phils saw Schilling's great outing about to turn into a loss, and Williams desperately tried to avoid letting the team fall into a 3-games-to-2 hole. Lemke fanned, and Bill Pecota flied out to Lenny Dykstra, sending the game to extra innings. With one out and the count full, Dykstra homered to deep right center field off Mark Wohlers, giving the Phils a 4–3 lead. Larry Andersen retired the Braves in order in the bottom half of the inning, and the Phillies came home ready to clinch. In Game 6 Tommy Greene rebounded from his awful Game 2 start with seven strong innings, while Dave Hollins homered off Greg Maddux to help send the Phils to the World Series.

4. 1993 WORLD SERIES, GAME 5—OCTOBER 21, 1993

The Phillies were still deflated from the way Game 4 of the Toronto World Series had ended, as leads of 7–3, 12–7, and 14–9 evaporated in a miserable top-of-the-eighth inning. The Blue Jays scored six runs and held on for a 15–14 win at the Vet. Mitch Williams was on the mound in that eighth inning, allowing two of Larry Andersen's runs and three more of his own to blow the game. One had the feeling with ace Curt Schilling on the mound in Game 5 that he wouldn't leave the game in the hands of any relief pitcher. Schilling is one of the best postseason pitchers in history, establishing himself in this 1993 postseason by beating Juan Guzman 2–0 and sending the World Series back to Toronto, where Williams and Joe Carter would meet for history. Schilling allowed five singles and threw 147 pitches. What would have happened had Schilling not retired the side 1-2-3 in the ninth inning? Would Williams have come in? Would Schilling have let him? Let your imagination wander.

3. 1983 NL CHAMPIONSHIP SERIES, GAME 4—OCTOBER 8, 1983

The upstart Wheeze Kids, as the old Phillies were known that year, didn't fare well against the Dodgers during the regular season. In fact, the Phillies won exactly one game in 12 attempts. That's it. So it wasn't a surprise that the

Dodgers entered the playoff series with a decided mental edge. Steve Carlton and Mike Schmidt took care of Game 1, as Schmitty swatted a first-inning home run, and Carlton, with help from Al Holland, outdueled Jerry Reuss for a 1–0 win. The Dodgers tied the series the next day, but Charles Hudson went the distance in Game 3 and Gary Matthews homered for a 7–2 win. For Game 4 it was Carlton vs. Reuss again, but Matthews set the tone in the very first inning with a three-run home run, and the Phillies cruised the rest of the way, qualifying for the World Series against the Orioles. Matthews had a huge series, hitting three home runs and driving in eight in the four games, and was named series MVP. The Phils carried their momentum to Baltimore and took Game 1 on homers by Joe Morgan and Garry Maddox. They wouldn't win again, but Matthews's heroics in vanquishing the Dodgers carried the entire off-season.

2. 1980 NL CHAMPIONSHIP SERIES, GAME 5—OCTOBER 12, 1980

Arguably the greatest postseason series in major league history, the Phillies and Astros played five close, tense games, with the final four going to extra innings. Rookie pitcher Marty Bystrom hooked up with Hall of Famer Nolan Ryan, 11 years his senior, in the finale in Houston on a Sunday afternoon. Things didn't look so good for the Phils when the Astros got to Larry Christensen and Ron Reed for three runs in the seventh. But then Ryan, the leading strike-out pitcher of all time, allowed three straight singles in the eighth, and walked Pete Rose, making the score 5–3 and bringing in Joe Sambito to pitch. Keith Moreland pinch hit for Bake McBride and grounded out to score a run. After Schmidt struck out, Del Unser singled in the tying run and eventual series MVP Manny Trillo tripled in two runs. The Phils led 7–5! Tug McGraw quickly gave the lead right back, and neither team scored in the ninth. In the top of the tenth inning Unser stroked a one-out double, and two batters later Maddox doubled him in. Dick Ruthven, the team's number 2 starter during the season, had retired the Astros in the ninth inning, and did the same in the 10th, with Maddox catching an Enos Cabell lazy fly out to end the game. For the first time in 30 years, the Phillies were heading to the World Series!

1. 1980 WORLD SERIES, GAME 6—OCTOBER 21, 1980

The Phillies took the first two games of the series at home, then lost the next two in Kansas City. In the critical Game 5, the Phillies trailed the Royals 3–2 in the ninth inning, with ace closer Dan Quisenberry on the mound, when pinch-hitter Unser followed a Schmidt single with a clutch RBI double down the right field line, tying the game. Two groundouts later, Trillo lined a shot off Quisenberry for an RBI hit. McGraw loaded the bases in the ninth, but held on for the 4–3 win, and the Phillies had their chance to clinch in Game 6 at home. In the series winner, Schmidt singled in a pair of runs in the third, and by the time Carlton left after seven innings, the Phils led 4–1. McGraw made things interesting yet again, escaping a bases-loaded situation in the eighth, then loading the bases in the ninth. The Royals had the bags full with one out and Frank White at the plate, and the second baseman hit a pop up near the Phillies dugout, which catcher Bob Boone let bounce out of his glove. However, before it hit the ground, Pete Rose famously reached out and caught it for the second out. McGraw then struck out Willie Wilson to end it, at 11:29 p.m. ET, and give the Phils their lone World Series title.

WHAT WERE THE PHILLIES' FIVE MOST MEMORABLE REGULAR SEASON WINS?

34 Okay, we've checked out the playoff wins, nearly a quarter of the victories in team postseason history. The regular season is a different story, but there have been plenty of memorable wins there as well. In order to be truly memorable, the game needed to really mean something. So that removes the night Von Hayes clubbed a pair of home runs in the first inning of a 26–7 home win over the Mets, as well as the night—er, morning—Mitch Williams delivered the game-winning hit off then-rookie Trevor Hoffman's Padres, ending a rain-delayed doubleheader at 4:40 a.m. ET. Who can forget Bob Dernier hitting an extra-inning, inside-the-park homer, a three-run, twelfth inning shot to give the Phils a 3–2 win, or when Punch-and-Judy hitter Steve Jeltz, who finished his career with five home runs, somehow managed to come off the bench against the Pirates in June 1989 and hit a pair of home runs, one from each side of the plate in a startling come-from-behind 15–11 win. That had never been done in Phillies history, and for Jeltz to do it was amazing. Pirates announcer Jim Rooker announced after the Bucs' 10-run first inning, "If we lose this game, I'll walk home." That was to Pittsburgh, folks. He didn't walk home, but did raise money for charity.

Here are the most memorable Phillies regular season games that were worth walking home for.

5. SCHMITTY SWATS FOUR HOMERS—APRIL 17, 1976

Boy, did Mike Schmidt enjoy hitting at Wrigley Field! Schmidt had a record-breaking April 1976, as he hit 11 home runs in the season's first month. In the fifth game of the season, the wind was blowin' out and the Phils fell behind 12–1 as Steve Carlton got lit up for seven runs. Then Schmidt really got going. He hit homers in the fifth and seventh innings off Rick Reuschel, and hit a three-run shot in the eighth to close the score to 13–12. The Phils took the lead in the ninth, but Tug McGraw blew the lead, and then it was 15–15 in the tenth inning when Schmidt came up after a Dick Allen walk. And there it goes! Schmidt knocked in eight runs in the game, and became the 10th player in history to swat four home runs in one game, an exciting, wind-blown 18–16 win for the Phillies.

4. ANOTHER WILD ONE AT WRIGLEY, 23–22—MAY 17, 1979

One had the feeling this wouldn't be an ordinary game when neither of the starting pitchers—the Phils' Randy

Lerch and the Cubs' Dennis Lamp—escaped the first inning! In fact, Lerch homered in the Phils' seven-run first inning, then allowed five runs on one out in the bottom half, and was removed from the game. The Phillies added eight runs in the third inning—yep, the wind was blowing out again at Wrigley Field—and led 15–6. Then the Cubs came back. Bill Buckner hit a grand slam off Tug McGraw in the fifth inning, and Dave Kingman clocked his third home run of the game in the sixth, cutting the Phillies lead to 21–19. No, this was not football. The game was tied at 22 into extra innings, and with two outs in the tenth, future Hall of Fame closer Bruce Sutter on the mound, Schmidt hit his second home run of the game, and Rawly Eastwick closed the door on the 23–22 win.

3. A PERFECT FATHER'S DAY AT SHEA— JUNE 21, 1964

Not only was it a perfect day for Phillies ace Jim Bunning, but the Phils and Mets played a doubleheader on a Sunday afternoon in which the home team got a total of three hits! Bunning's game was the first one of the day, and he didn't allow a single base runner, throwing 79 of 90 pitches for strikes and fanning 10 in the 6–0 win. A father of seven, Bunning made history on Father's Day, becoming the first National Leaguer in 84 years to throw a perfect game, and later that night he appeared on the Ed Sullivan Show. The Phillies won the second game 8–2 and a lot more games until the final two weeks of the season, when it all fell apart. But we're not talking about that here.

2. DIVISION TITLE IN CANADA—OCTOBER 4, 1980

The upstart Phillies, led by fiery manager Dallas Green, went to Montreal for the final series of the regular season with an 89–70 record. The Expos had the same mark. This weekend would decide the NL East division title. The Phillies took the Friday night game 2–1, as Schmidt hit a sacrifice fly in the first inning and homered in the sixth. Tug McGraw saved Dick Ruthven's 17th win, striking out five of the six batters he faced. The next day was Saturday, and the Expos took a 4–3 lead into the ninth inning, aiming to make the season's final game matter. With two outs and Bake McBride on second base, Bob Boone singled to center field, tying the score. In the eleventh inning, Pete Rose singled and McBride popped out, bringing Schmidt to the plate. He already had the franchise record for home runs in a season, and the season mark for homers by a third baseman, so what's one more? With Stan Bahnsen pitching, Schmidt launched one way over the left field fence for his 48th home run of the season. McGraw, who pitched two perfect innings the night before, threw three innings on Saturday, allowing one base runner as the Phillies clinched the NL East in style.

1. FINALLY, A PENNANT—OCTOBER 1, 1950

Everyone remembers the 1964 Phillies blowing a big September lead and ceding the pennant to the Cardinals, but the 1950 Whiz Kids nearly gave them the blueprint, losing most of a seven-game lead with 11 games left to play. The Brooklyn Dodgers made a furious comeback to set the stage for the final day of the season at Ebbets Field. If the Dodgers won, it would mean a three-game playoff to decide who would meet the Yankees in the World Series. In a 1–1 game in the bottom of the ninth, Phillies center fielder Richie Ashburn made a throw that would define his career, pegging Cal Abrams at the plate to send the game into extra innings, where Dick Sisler won it with a three-run opposite field home run. The Phillies made their first World Series in 35 years, though the Yankees would sweep them. Sisler's home run made him a celebrity, as he was honored along with Joe DiMaggio in Ernest Hemingway's novel *The Old Man and the Sea*. It's also arguably the most famous home run in franchise history, at least in a game the Phillies won.

35 You know all about Hall of Famers Mike Schmidt and Steve Carlton and the roles they played in the lone World Series championship in 125 years of Phillies baseball. Schmidt bashed 48 home runs—29 more than any teammate—earning the league MVP award, hit the clutch homer to finally knock off the Montreal Expos in the division clincher, and continued to hit in the World Series. Carlton won 24 games and the Cy Young that season, striking out nearly 200 batters more than any teammate, and winning three of his four post-season starts.

But they couldn't have done it alone. Who else played the most critical roles that season?

5. DICK RUTHVEN

The clear-cut number 2 starter on the staff won 17 games during the regular season, saving the bullpen along the way and joining Carlton as the only other pitcher to reach as many as 152 innings. Ruthven relied on defense and guile and wasn't afraid to pitch inside. In the championship series against the Astros, he started and pitched well in Game 2, and his performance in Game 5 was critical as he came on in relief, after closers Tug McGraw and Ron Reed had been used, to pitch two perfect innings and earn the win. In the World Series, Ruthven started Game 3 in Kansas City, going nine innings of what became a ten-inning loss. The innings were critical to a tired staff.

4. BOTTOM OF THE ORDER

Larry Bowa and Bob Boone batted eighth and ninth in the World Series—remember, the entire series used the designated hitter—and combined to hit 16-for-41, for a .390 batting average. They each scored and knocked in six runs as well, with extra credit for both scoring runs in the clinching Game 6. In contrast, top-of-the-order guys Pete Rose, Lonnie Smith, and Bake McBride weren't nearly as productive, though McBride did homer in Game 1. Against the Astros the duo batted .270. Further, Nos. 5 and 6 hitters Manny Trillo and Garry Maddox excelled against the Astros, batting a combined .341 with seven RBIs. Trillo was named the series MVP, and Maddox doubled in the Series-clinching run in the tenth inning of the final game.

3. THOSE OTHER RELIEVERS

While most people think there was only one relief pitcher on the staff, right-handers Dickie Noles, Ron Reed, and Warren Brusstar were solid during the regular season, winning 10 games and saving 15, with Reed filling in as closer when McGraw was injured. This group came up big in the postseason. Noles and Brusstar combined to throw 5.1 innings in the Astros series, allowing two hits and one run, and Brusstar won Game 4 in extra innings. In the World Series, the trio allowed one run in nine innings, with Reed saving Game 2. Noles was particularly helpful in relieving ineffective Larry Christensen in the first inning of Game 4, saving the rest of the staff by throwing 4.2 innings of one-run ball. Plus, his memorable knockdown pitch against George Brett showed the Phillies weren't going to be intimidated.

2. DALLAS GREEN

The fiery, intense, tell-it-like-it-is Green began managing the Phillies during the 1979 season, taking over for Danny Ozark. He got the Phillies to the playoffs three straight seasons, but was deemed too nice a guy for rich ballplayers, and was unable to motivate them to greater heights. Green could. He didn't care if the players hated him or not, and they probably did, but he also coaxed their best on the field, demanding raised performance. Green's legendary tirade in Pittsburgh in August, between games of a doubleheader while the team was struggling, had great impact. He nearly fought Ron Reed. He cursed out everyone. And everyone started to play better, winning 9 of 11, didn't they? Green was pushing the right buttons to get the most from the team, and seemed to make all the

109

right moves. The Phillies won 26 of 39 games and a crucial final weekend series in Montreal to get to the playoffs. Then Green led them through an intense series against the Astros, in which the team lost two of the first three games, and trailed 5–2 in the eighth inning against Nolan Ryan in Game 5. What other Phillies manager could have led this team to the World Series?

1. TUG MCGRAW

Ultimately the Phillies wouldn't have been able to win the World Series without the lovable McGraw who, though he was pretty much on fumes by the time the postseason arrived, pitched in nearly every game in October, wriggling out of trouble in a number of them. During the regular season, McGraw saved 20 games and sported a 1.46 ERA, with a 0.52 ERA, 5–1 record, and 13 saves in 52.1 innings down the stretch. Just as important was his never-quit attitude that pumped his teammates up. In the 11 postseason games the Phillies played in, Tugger pitched in nine of them, going 1–2 with four saves. Carlton and Ruthven were the only Phillies to throw more innings in the playoffs. McGraw allowed only one run in 7.2 innings in the World Series and fanned Willie Wilson to end it, setting off the great celebration. Thanks Tugger; the Phillies couldn't have done it without you.

WHAT WERE THE PHILLIES' FIVE BEST TRADES?

36 For a franchise as old as the Phillies, there had to have been some great trades, *right?* Um, right? Well, the Phillies have also lost more games in history than any other franchise, so not all players wanted to come to Philadelphia. Until the 1970s, the Phillies weren't known for a whole lot of great deals as their owners were, for the most part, too cheap to acquire top talent, or were not interested in racial integration, being the final NL team to actually integrate. The Phillies aimed to build through the farm system, which didn't work much. But as the 20th century came to an end, the Phillies became wiser when it came to taking chances on players. For this argument, the top trades were ones in which the Phillies acquired one of the top players of his era or someone who directly influenced a (near) championship run.

5. DODE PASKERT TO THE CUBS FOR CY WILLIAMS—DECEMBER 26, 1917

You might have missed this one when you were growing up, but Williams was one of the top sluggers of the era, before Babe Ruth. The Cubs oddly gave him away for Paskert, just a serviceable right-handed hitting outfielder who had hit as high as .265 once in the previous six seasons. Williams, a lefty-hitting outfielder, had speed and power and a solid glove, and was among the league home run leaders in 1915 and 1916. He slumped the next year and fell into disfavor with the Cubs, who moved the 29-year-old for a 36-year-old Paskert. Williams would star in Philly for a decade, winning three home run titles, including 41 in 1923. He became the NL's career home run leader until Rogers Hornsby broke the mark in 1929.

4. JUAN SAMUEL TO THE METS FOR LENNY DYKSTRA, ROGER MCDOWELL, AND A PLAYER TO BE NAMED (TOM EDENS)—JUNE 18, 1989

Samuel was one of the most exciting players in Phillies history, but he seemed allergic to taking walks and ultimately was not a very good leadoff hitter. Plus, he had already begun his decline, while Dykstra was ready to assume a full-time role after sharing center field with Mookie Wilson for years. Dykstra played in Philly for seven-plus seasons and made it through a full season healthy only twice, but 1990 and 1993 were really good years, so good that this trade is a no-brainer in hindsight. In 1990 Nails batted .325 with 33 steals and 106 runs, and sported a .418 on-base percentage. In 1993 he scored an amazing 143 runs and finished second in the league's MVP voting as the Phillies went to the World Series. McDowell closed for the 1990 Phillies, but was dealt to the Dodgers the next season for Mike Hartley, who in turn was dealt a year later to the Twins for David West, a key bullpen part of the 1993 team. Samuel just continued his decline with the Mets, Dodgers, and a number of other teams. Edens pitched in only three games with the Phillies and retired the following season.

3. KEVIN STOCKER TO TAMPA BAY FOR BOBBY ABREU—NOVEMBER 18, 1997

Stocker was a decent shortstop for the most part, but not really much of a hitter. He was called up in mid-1993 and batted .324, helping the Phillies to the playoffs and World Series, but he proved to be a below-average player for four years after that. Why the expansion Devil Rays wanted him as their starter is anyone's guess. Of course, this trade really isn't Tampa's fault. The Houston Astros owned the rights to Abreu, but hadn't used him much and decided they would be committed to Richard Hidalgo in right field instead. Tampa chose Abreu in the expansion draft so they could get Stocker from Philly, and the deal was made. While Stocker batted .208 as the Tampa regular, the Phillies got through the next three years with Desi Relaford and Alex Arias at short until Jimmy Rollins came along, and Abreu blossomed into an immediate star. By the time he

113

was traded to the Yankees nine seasons later, only Chuck Klein had a higher OPS in franchise history, and Abreu had a pair of 30/30 seasons to his name.

2. JASON GRIMSLEY TO HOUSTON FOR CURT SCHILLING—APRIL 2, 1992

Grimsley had showed a bit of promise in parts of his first three seasons with the Phillies but he was wild, walking 103 hitters against 90 strikeouts in 136.2 innings. That's a lot of walks. The Astros showed interest and didn't mind parting with Schilling, who had been there for just a year after coming over from Baltimore along with Steve Finley and Pete Harnisch for Glenn Davis. We'd assume that went down as one of the best trades the Astros ever made. This one didn't. Schilling pitched in relief in 1991, but the Phillies made him a starter during the 1992 season and he became one of the league's best, finishing fourth with a 2.35 ERA his first year in Philly. By the time Schilling talked his way outta town he had won the sixth-most games in more than 100 years of Phillies baseball and had begun to prove his worth as a big-game playoff pitcher. Meanwhile, Grimsley managed to hang on as a major leaguer for 15 undistinguished seasons, with a 42–58 record and 4.77 ERA. He'll be better remembered in history for his drug suspension and being named in the Mitchell Report.

1. RICK WISE TO ST. LOUIS FOR STEVE CARLTON—FEBRUARY 25, 1972

Those were all nice trades for the Phillies, but c'mon, Steve Carlton for Rick Wise seems like highway robbery. Yes, Wise was a good pitcher, having won 17 games in 1971 with a 2.88 ERA, plus throwing a no-hitter at Cincinnati that season while hitting two home runs in the same game. Wise was a good pitcher who would finish his 18-year career with a 188–181 record. But Carlton won 329 games in his career! The Cards were willing to move the future Hall of Famer because he was a bit eccentric and often embroiled in contract squabbles. The Cards got 32 wins out of Wise in two seasons before dealing him to Boston. The Phillies got 27 wins from Carlton in 1972 alone and a franchise record 241 over the next 15 seasons. Carlton is one of the top left-handed starting pitchers in major league history.

WHAT WERE THE PHILLIES' FIVE WORST TRADES?

37

Not that the Phillies didn't make any stinker deals for their first 90 years, but for a trade to really be classified as bad the team had to part with someone who could have really helped the team be a contender. There are many reasons a team would make a poor trade, and a few of those are represented below. Maybe a player had to be moved because he had worn out his welcome, or because he was a young player few thought would become a star. The Phils have dealt future Hall of Famers away, and still lived to tell the tale. Here are the worst deals they've made.

5. CURT SCHILLING TO ARIZONA FOR TRAVIS LEE, OMAR DAAL, NELSON FIGUEROA, AND VICENTE PADILLA—JULY 26, 2000

4. SCOTT ROLEN, DOUG NICKLE, AND CASH TO ST. LOUIS FOR PLACIDO POLANCO, MIKE TIMLIN, AND BUD SMITH—JULY 29, 2002

We group them together because they are pretty similar. On a pair of otherwise delightful July days two years apart, the

Phillies dealt their best pitcher since Steve Carlton and best third baseman since Mike Schmidt for...well, not much, and mainly because the stars didn't want to be in Philly anymore. Hey, deal them if you must, but this is all you could get? Let us count the disappointments, shall we? Lee was a slick-fielding first baseman with moderate power, but he hit barely .250 in Philly and the fans hated him from day one. Padilla won 14 games twice in Philly, but then couldn't stay healthy—or according to teammates and reporters, sober—and ended up in Texas. In the Rolen deal Polanco became a good player at second base until Chase Utley came along and made him expendable, but the trials and tribulations of Bud Smith kinda summed these deals up. As a 21-year-old Cards rookie, Smith tossed a no-hitter and finished fourth in the Rookie of the Year voting. Then things went downhill. In 2002 he developed shoulder problems, struggled with a 6.94 ERA with the Cardinals, and got demoted to the minors. The Phillies thought they could fix him, and dealt for him. However, he'd already torn his labrum and would never pitch for the team. Oh well; at least Schilling and Rolen didn't end up winning World Series for other teams...oh. Never mind.

3. JULIO FRANCO, MANNY TRILLO, JAY BALLER, JERRY WILLARD, AND GEORGE VUKOVICH TO CLEVELAND FOR VON HAYES— DECEMBER 9, 1982

In fairness to Hayes, he wasn't a bad player. He was never a great player, however, and that's what was expected of someone on the solitary end of a 5-for-1 trade. Hayes never lived the deal down, especially when Franco emerged. But to be fair, let's not overrate what the Indians got in the deal. Franco was a 23-year-old shortstop prospect who didn't have power and couldn't field. In fact, in his first three seasons of full-time work he averaged 33 errors per year, and only once in his career, which was still going as he approached 50 (!), did he hit more than 15 home runs. The other guys weren't special. Trillo was a wonderful fielder and the MVP of the 1980 championship series against the Astros, but wasn't much of a hitter overall and never a full-time player again after this trade. Baller, Willard, and Vukovich didn't have distinguished careers. So really, while Hayes angered everyone in Philly, the fact is the cost to get him wasn't all that high. Hayes did have his moments in nine years in Philly. In 1986 he led the NL in runs, doubles, and extra base hits, and in a June 1985 game against the Mets at the Vet, Hayes smacked a pair of home runs in the first inning, including a grand slam, in a 26–7 win. Ol' 5-for-1 belongs on this list, but it's not close to the worst deal the Phillies have ever made.

2. FERGUSON JENKINS, JOHN HERRNSTEIN, AND ADOLFO PHILLIPS TO THE CUBS FOR LARRY JACKSON AND BOB BUHL—APRIL 21, 1966

I suppose one can see why the Phillies made this deal. Jackson was 35 at the time, but the four-time All-Star was one of the winningest pitchers of his era and, with the help of three solid years in Philly, he'd finish with 194 career wins. Jackson was established, and Gene Mauch's staff needed more depth after Jim Bunning and Chris Short. While Jackson became the team's number 3 starter, Buhl was the number 4, though at 37 he was just about done. He would struggle in 1966 and pitch only three times in 1967 before retiring. Jenkins was 23 at the time and had appeared in only eight games with the Phillies. Who knew he'd turn out to be a 284-game winner who would win 20 games each of the next six seasons with the Cubs? Man, can you imagine him and Steve Carlton anchoring the rotation for a decade? Jenkins won a Cy Young and in 1991 became the first Canadian inducted into the Baseball Hall of Fame. Not that the Phillies could have used a pitcher like that or anything. It wouldn't be the last time the Phillies parted with an unknown youngster and got fleeced by the Cubs.

1. LARRY BOWA AND RYNE SANDBERG TO THE CUBS FOR IVAN DEJESUS—JANUARY 27, 1982

Dallas Green giveth, and he taketh away. He managed the Phillies to the World Series title in 1980, but a year later he was general manager and executive vice president of the Cubs, having been lured by a bigger deal. Little by little he brought Phillies coaches and acquired Phillies players, but this deal was the topper. DeJesus was an average shortstop, but certainly younger than Bowa, a Philly

119

favorite who had turned 36 and wasn't in the team's plans. DeJesus was 29 and not brimming with promise, either. Had this been a 1-for-1 deal, nobody would have thought much of it. Green, however, insisted on getting the prospect Sandberg, then 22. Phillies scouts didn't think much of Sandberg. Manny Trillo and Mike Schmidt were established at second base and third base, and everyone agreed Sandberg wasn't a shortstop. What boggles the mind, however, is why Phillies brass couldn't see his future at the plate. Sandberg raked in the minor leagues. Oh well. Sandberg became one of the best power hitting second basemen in history, hitting 282 home runs, making seven All-Star teams, and winning the 1984 MVP. He also stole 344 bases, batted .285, and won nine straight Gold Gloves starting in 1983. Maybe the Phillies wouldn't have won the World Series if not for Green, but one wonders how many Fall Classics the team missed by simply throwing some kid named Sandberg into a deal.

WAS JOE CARTER'S HOME RUN ALL MITCH WILLIAMS'S FAULT?

38 Mitch Williams never threw another pitch for the Phillies after serving up the Joe Carter home run that won the 1993 World Series for the Blue Jays. Fans revolted against the controversial closer even before Game 6 of the Series, peppering him with death threats because he was erratic. Okay, so maybe he wasn't the best closer the team had ever had, but can the loss be wholly attributed to him?

The short answer is no: Williams had help along the way, or make that not enough help. While it seemed like every time he went to the mound it would become a roller coaster ride, the fact is the team would not have been there without him, and he's the only one blamed because he threw the final pitch. There were other Phillies who played a role in the Series loss to the Blue Jays.

First of all, Phillies manager Jim Fregosi failed to realize Williams was out of gas well before Game 6. In Game 4, which went down in history as the highest-scoring game in World Series play, the Phillies scored six runs in the first two innings, and held a 12–7 lead after five. Williams, who would admit later his arm was pretty much toast in

September, was brought in anyway to protect the lead in the eighth inning. When the inning began, the Phils led 14–9. By the time Williams came in, the score was 14–10 and 40-year-old Larry Andersen had left two men on base. Williams would register a walk and a strikeout, but then Rickey Henderson hit a two-run single and Devon White smacked a two-run triple to give the Blue Jays a 15–14 lead, and win.

Where were the other Philly relievers? Andersen had a 12.27 ERA in the Series, but he came back in 1994 for another year. Fans didn't hate him. Lefty David West, so good during the regular season, pitched in three games in the Series, retiring three hitters and allowing five hits, a walk, and three runs. West allowed two runs in the sixth inning of Game 6! The rest of the Phillies bullpen should take some criticism, as well as the Phillies brass for relying on them.

The Blue Jays had a very good team, led by Roberto Alomar, Paul Molitor, and Carter, but the Phillies had their chances, leaving eight men on base in the 15–14 game, five in the sixth and seventh innings. The Phillies should have won Game 4, which in turn wouldn't have made Game 6 the do-or-die game it became.

In Game 6, the Phillies scored five times in the seventh inning to take a 8–6 lead, and again Fregosi insisted on using Williams to try to save the game. However, his earlier moves can be questioned. Starter Terry Mulholland gave up three Toronto runs in the first inning but settled down after that, and was removed in the sixth despite not being pinch hit for. The game was in Toronto, with the designated hitter rule in play. Mulholland, an All-Star and one of the team's aces, had thrown only 70 pitches, and could have remained in the game. Roger Mason replaced him and mowed the Blue Jays down, retiring seven of eight hitters, allowing no runs. West and Andersen finished up the eighth inning with no damage, giving Williams an 8–6 lead to work with.

Should Williams have been brought out for the final inning, with everyone in the park knowing he was tired? Was it at all under consideration to just leave Andersen in the game? The Blue Jays were bringing to the plate a number of right-handed hitters, including Henderson, Molitor, and Carter, and all fared better against lefties, which the Wild Thing was. Why not Bobby Thigpen? He wasn't used much during the season, but he did and still does hold the major league record for saves in a season, with 57 for the 1990 White Sox. He and Mason were the team's lone thriving relief pitchers in the World Series. Thigpen didn't allow a run in 2.2 innings of work. What about available starting pitchers? Danny Jackson would have started Game 7, but Tommy Greene had to be available to pitch. Why hold out hope for Game 7 pitchers if you can't get to a Game 7? Had Mulholland been allowed to go to a pitch count near 100, Mason could have closed the game, or ground ball specialist Andersen could have.

Regardless, it was clear Williams was a ticking time bomb. The Phillies didn't help matters by leaving nine men on base.

Williams threw the pitch that lost the World Series; that point can't be denied. But should he have been in there to throw that pitch? The Phillies didn't have a good bullpen to start with, which certainly isn't Williams's fault, and those who were pitching well weren't available or weren't used to close games in the Series. The death threats couldn't have helped. Watching Curt Schilling ridiculously hide his face with a towel, whether he started the game or not, couldn't have helped Williams's confidence, either. All-time stolen base champ Henderson walked to lead off the ninth, and Williams was so worried about him running he used a slide-step delivery, the first time he had ever done so. Isn't the ninth inning of Game 6 of the World Series a peculiar time to be experimenting with a new delivery? Who authorized that? Ultimately, the Blue Jays were probably just a better team, and deserved to win.

The Wild Thing lost it, so blame him the most; but he had help.

The best part of the story, if there is one, is that Williams took it all in stride and ironically returned to Philadelphia years later, where he opened a bowling alley, managed and pitched for the Independent League's Atlantic City Surf, and has been seen and heard on local TV and radio discussing Philly sports.

WHY DID THE PHILLIES DRAFT J. D. DREW?

39

J. D. Drew certainly looked like he was going to be one of the best hitters in the game when the Phillies selected him with the second overall pick in the 1997 amateur draft. With a sweet lefty swing, power, and speed, Drew broke many records at Florida State and was the first player in college baseball history to have a 30/30 season. Drew was money in the bank, so to speak, and the woebegone Phillies were coming off a 67-win season in 1996, and won only one more game the next year. Drew would have fit in nicely.

The problem was, the Phillies didn't have enough money in the bank, or if they did they didn't intend to spend it. Drew didn't want to play for the "pittance" the Phillies were offering, and he and his notorious agent Scott Boras made that quite clear before the draft. It wasn't so much that Drew didn't want to play in Philadelphia; he was making it clear he was a financial mercenary and wanted a contract worth at least $10 million, more in line with the heist Travis Lee had won a year earlier. (The Phils would end up with him years later, as you'll remember.) There were loopholes in the rules about signing draft picks, so while most teams only wanted to spend standard amounts in line with past seasons, agent Boras found a way to circumvent the system, sending his players to the Independent Northern League while they negotiated contracts. If the player and team couldn't agree to a deal, the player would go back into the next draft so another team could select him.

Drew and the Phillies weren't even close in the negotiations. In fact, it's unclear if there ever were any serious ones. The Phillies offered around $2 million. Drew wanted at least $10 million. Obviously, no deal was worked out. Drew played in the Northern League and kept his draft status, and the following year was the number 5 pick by the St. Louis Cardinals. Soon after, Major League Baseball adjusted the draft loophole to include Independent Leagues, so this situation wouldn't happen again and a team like the Phillies would retain the player's rights, forcing an eventual agreement, or the player wouldn't play.

Drew is having a star-crossed career, with a few good seasons and others fraught with injuries, but his career .890 OPS with the Cardinals, Braves, Dodgers, and Red Sox entering 2008 would rank him in the top five for the Phillies franchise over the last 30 years.

The Phillies knew Drew would be difficult, if not impossible, to sign, so why did they draft him anyway? Drew was so talented; the Phillies figured they'd work something out and have a cornerstone player on the team for years.

The Phillies clearly underestimated the situation, as Boras and Drew made it clear the Phillies shouldn't select him if they weren't willing to pay up and there was another team willing to do so, which there was. They flat-out asked the Phillies to not draft the player. Of course, this monumental miscalculation implies that Drew became a superstar, which he didn't. He made one All-Star team, in 2008, and has generally been disliked at each of his career stops. But it doesn't change the fact that the Phillies knew the difficult road ahead, and traveled it anyway.

However, drafting Drew sent a message that the Phillies, and other baseball teams, wouldn't stand for this nonsense. That clearly didn't work out, though it did result in an MLB rule change, albeit too late for the Phillies. It also sent a message that the Phillies were stepping to the plate, as it were, in an effort to get the best players, which Drew was believed to be. Maybe it would result in more tickets sold, free agents wanting to play in Philly, stuff like that. Well, maybe not.

It's very possible that even had the Phillies not taken Drew, they would have blown the pick on someone else. Consider the Phillies had used their first pick in 1994 on pitcher Carlton Loewer, who won 10 career games with a 6.12 ERA, and in 1995 their first pick was outfielder Reggie Taylor, who played 14 games with the club and hit .231 in his short career. The Phillies took Drew and passed on, among others, Troy Glaus, Vernon Wells, Michael Cuddyer, Jon Garland, and Lance Berkman, all of whom went later in the first round. Chances are the Phillies would not have selected one of them anyway.

Maybe the Phillies wanted to instill crowd confidence and unity by taking Drew, knowing the fans would join together to boo him and send other animated insults his way. Who knows, maybe the Phillies made a deal with battery manufacturers, as the AA battery—or was it the 9-volt?—became the guided missile of choice for angry fans whenever Drew visited Philly as a visitor in future seasons. Okay, this is a stretch, but Phillies fans have joined together in their hatred of Drew, the player who didn't really refuse to play in Philly, but refused to accept the money given to him.

Ultimately, the Phillies were thinking like a fantasy baseball owner, trying to get the best player without considering consequences. In real life, other factors come into play, and the Phillies misread the signs.

WAS CURT FLOOD JUST TRYING TO AVOID PHILADELPHIA?

40 The 1969 Phillies won 63 games, finishing fifth in the newly created NL East division, with only the expansion Montreal Expos behind them. Meanwhile, the St. Louis Cardinals won 87 games that year, and had been to the World Series three times in six seasons, winning twice. It was a no-brainer that a player would prefer to be with a winner than with the Phillies.

Curt Flood wanted to play for a winner, but was that what bothered him most about the October 7, 1969, trade that sent him to the Phillies? Or was it the fact that he didn't agree with the famous W. C. Fields statement, "On the whole I'd rather be living in Philadelphia"? Regardless, Flood was traded to the Phillies, but refused to report and never played for them. What was his ultimate reasoning?

History reflects poorly on the Phillies, the losingest franchise in major league history, so it's understandable why Flood didn't want to leave a standout Cardinals team to start anew, but Flood's real problem with the trade was that he wanted to choose where he played. The trade itself was fair and full of big names: the Phillies sent powerful but enigmatic first baseman Dick Allen, steady second baseman Cookie Rojas, and pitcher Jerry Johnson to St. Louis for Flood, a standout defensive center fielder, catcher Tim McCarver, outfielder Byron Browne, and pitcher Joe Hoerner. Flood would have been the starting center fielder and a speedy, top-of-the-lineup presence for the Phillies.

While Flood didn't want to play for the Phillies, calling them a bad team in a bad ballpark (Connie Mack Stadium) in what he believed to be a bad and racist baseball town, Phillies fans should realize there was something far more important at stake. This really wasn't about Philly's inferiority complex. Had Flood been dealt to New York, he wouldn't have wanted to go...well, who really knows?

Flood challenged baseball's reserve clause, believing it unfair for teams to wield so much power over the players that they could control their contracts for an indefinite amount of time. He wanted to be declared a free agent and play where he chose, at the time a preposterous notion. Fueled by the Civil Rights Movement and the bigger picture, Flood courageously gave up his $100,000 contract, writing a letter to commissioner Bowie Kuhn announcing his intent to become available for all teams, noting he wasn't a piece of property to be bought and sold, and that his rights as an American citizen were being violated. He was angry and defiant, but others also believed antitrust laws had been violated. Flood was the one who took a stand. He had conviction.

Flood's case would be heard and end up in the hands of the Supreme Court. He'd lose the decision, sit out the 1970 season, and finish his career a shadow of the player he had been with the 1971 Washington Senators, but Flood had made his point, even falling on his sword to do it. Six years later the reserve clause would be tested again by pitchers Andy Messersmith and Dave McNally, and shortly after free agency became the norm in professional sports. Flood is credited with fighting the system and opening doors for thousands of professional athletes.

In this case, the Phillies were just window dressing one of the most famous lawsuits in sports history, one that had historical influence.

IS THE PHILLIES LOSING 10,000 GAMES SUCH A BAD THING?

41

On July 15, 2007, a Sunday evening at Citizens Bank Park, the Phillies lost 10–2 to the St. Louis Cardinals. No big deal, right? In a normal baseball season, each team will suffer plenty of losses, with the best teams losing only 60 or so. Well, this loss was different, as it was the 10,000th loss in franchise history, and the first time any professional sports team had reached that magic number. It was significant, and to most, embarrassing and emblematic of 125 years of mostly bad baseball. But to others, this was quite an achievement.

The Phillies are known for a lot of things in their history, and winning would not be one of them, but longevity—doesn't that count for something? And most of this losing happened at least a generation ago, so Philly fans can be forgiven for not blaming this on Pat Burrell and Brett Myers.

The original Philadelphia Quakers, soon to be Phillies, lost their first game on May 1, 1883, and 81 of 98 contests that first season. From 1918 to 1947, the Phillies had one winning season. The 1950 team made the World Series, but didn't win a game once it got there; the 1961 team lost a record 23 straight games; and the 1964 team infamously suffered one of the biggest collapses in sports history. This franchise has suffered through bad management, bad players, bad stadiums, and bad luck. The Phillies can't say they didn't deserve to lose 10,000 games.

But therein lies the positive. The Phillies were good enough to be around for 125 years to lose that many games. They are the oldest continuous one-name, one-city franchise in all of professional sports. In fact, only a few franchises have been around longer than the Phillies, even as attendance was as futile as the team's records for most of the 20th century. Doesn't this speak to the love between a team and its town, that through all the losing the team would remain and keep its loyal, devoted supporters?

When the Phillies lost game number 10,000, fans embraced the attention and notoriety rather than shunning it. Anyway, those fans in attendance haven't had to deal with most of the 10,000 losses. The Phillies have had 72 losing records in 125 years, but no 100-loss seasons since 1961. In fact, 13 of the team's 100-loss seasons came in the first 63 years, only one since. How's that for improvement?

The Phillies aren't the Cubs, a franchise of lovable losers that hasn't won a World Series in 100 years. They aren't the Red Sox, who suffered a number of crushing losses in post-season play after winning it all in 1918. The Phillies haven't been cursed. They've just lost a lot of games. Big deal. They've also played a lot of games.

Think of all the good things that have happened to the Phillies. Wasn't 1980 a great season, with a World Series title?

Four other times the Phillies have appeared in the Fall Classic. Mike Schmidt, Steve Carlton, and quite a few other Hall of Famers starred for the team. Four other franchises, including the Padres and Rangers, have a worse winning percentage than the Phillies. And in the season in which they lost the 10,000th, a furious great September comeback against a hated rival resulted in a division title and playoff berth.

Plus, entering 2008, they had won 8,853 times!

WHO MAKES—AND MISSES—THE ALL-TIME PHILLIES DREAM TEAM?

Numerous Hall of Fame players have been with the Phillies at one time or another in their history, but not too many of the great players hung around long enough to make the kind of impact one would associate with a dream team. The Phillies made it to the World Series only two times in the first 90 years of the franchise, and historic players were kind of at a premium. That's why you'll see that most of the top Phillies played with the team in the past 20 years, or were on the 1950 team that made it to the World Series.

42 CATCHER: BOB BOONE (1972–1981)

What about: Darren Daulton? One could argue the key to the 1993 NL championship team wasn't Lenny Dykstra at all. Sure, Daulton had a monster season, one he never matched again, but Daulton was also the guts of the team and handled the pitching staff. Knee injuries seemed to always set Daulton back, but in 1992 and 1993 he had what appeared to dwarf any other offensive seasons for a Phillies catchers in franchise history, knocking in more than 100 runs each year and being a spiritual leader. Of course, that last comment would become more ironic years later, when Dutch would share his unconventional thoughts about time travel, physics, and conspiracies, even writing a book about his theories. On the field Daulton didn't have terrific career numbers, with a .245 batting average and only two seasons with more than 15 home runs, but his two-year prime was terrific, and helped get the Phillies to a World Series. If only he would have had Mitch throw a fastball on that 2–2 pitch to Joe Carter...

What about: Andy Seminick? The 1950 Whiz Kids featured Seminick behind the plate and, like Daulton, his best year coincided with a World Series trip. In 1950 Seminick hit 24 home runs and knocked in 68 runs, identical power to the year before, but he hit .288, 45 points higher than the preceding season and his career mark. Also like Daulton, Seminick dealt with injuries much of his career, with an ankle injury holding him back in the 1950 World Series against the Yankees and arm woes later in his career. Seminick was a good catcher, probably the Phillies' finest until the 1970s.

What about: Mike Lieberthal? Nobody caught more games in Phillies history than Lieberthal; and really, the guy did have some good seasons. In 1999 he smacked 31 homers and knocked in 96 runs, making the first of two All-Star teams, and when he left after the 2006 season for the Dodgers he had hit .275 over 13 seasons with 150 home runs, a franchise record 149 as a catcher. Not bad at all. Not the best in club history, but Lieberthal was pretty underrated.

Yeah, but: Don't even look at Boone's offense, because it wasn't the most important part of his game. The Phillies teams he came up on had others to hit for power, like Schmitty and the Bull, and Boone's main job was to handle the pitching staff, which he did as well as anyone in baseball. Boone won two Gold Gloves with the Phillies, seven overall, and he made three All-Star teams while in Philly. Meanwhile, while his role as a hitter was secondary and Boone was merely average at best, remember that not too many catchers in the 1970s were great hitters. Boone struggled at the plate in the 1980 regular season, but when it mattered most he came up big, with a .412 batting average in the World Series and four RBIs.

43 FIRST BASE: PETE ROSE (1979–83)

What about: Fred Luderus and Don Hurst? For pre-1970 fans, we've got Luderus and Hurst to throw at you, but neither makes the cut. The fact that they're mentioned here speaks more to the franchise being a bit thin at the position over the 125 years. Luderus logged 1,298 games at first base from 1910–20 and was one of the better power hitters of the decade, twice finishing second in the National League in home runs, and two other times ranking second in doubles. Hurst, who played six-plus seasons as a Phillie from 1928–1934, held the club record for career home runs at the position with 111 until Ryan Howard came along and broke it in about two years. Dolph Camilli would have broken Hurst's mark had he been in Philly more than three-plus seasons, but he smacked 92 home runs in that time.

What about: John Kruk? He had a nice run with the Phillies after being acquired from the San Diego Padres, and was generally the team's number 3 hitter for the 1993 World Series run. The portly Kruk, who some say weighed more than 300 pounds at one point in 1993, walked 111 times that season and batted .316, making the All-Star game for the third time in as many seasons with the Phillies. Kruk will certainly be remembered for dodging a Randy Johnson fastball near his head in a 1993 All-Star at-bat, then feigning a heart attack while drawing laughs. Kruk was never the best-looking or best-dressed

Phillie, giving fans an everyman vibe as someone who might be holding a beer and playing for your local softball team. His autobiography is wisely titled *I Ain't an Athlete, Lady*, and maybe he wasn't, but he was a pretty good baseball player.

What about: Ryan Howard? Too soon to reward him with the top spot? Well, it won't be much longer. As of this writing, Howard had played only two full seasons in the majors, though he had already won the Rookie of the Year award in 2005, the MVP award the next season with a club record 58 home runs, and in 2007 "slumped" to 47 home runs and 136 RBIs. Howard has the most home runs by a first baseman in franchise history, and at the rate he's going, he'll catch Mike Schmidt's overall club record by the time he's 35.

Yeah, but: Okay, this has not really been a great position through 125 years of Phillies baseball. Consider that only four players have more games at first base than Rose in team history, and none of them were particularly great hitters. Look, Rose helped the Phillies get their only World Series championship, and ultimately that made his then-record free agent signing totally worth it. Rose wasn't just a member of that team; he was a productive leadoff hitter who did what he had to to get on base. He also played a mean first base, learning the position and thriving. Rose hit .331 in his first campaign in Philly and .325 in 1981, so his 1980 batting average of .282 wasn't great for Rose, but he played in every game and scored 95 runs. He was 38 by the time he joined the Phillies but still hit .291 over five seasons, and in the five playoff series while in Philly he batted .326.

44 SECOND BASE: JUAN SAMUEL (1983–1989)

What about: Tony Taylor? Taylor played the most games at second base in Phillies history, more than a thousand over two tenures with the club. Acquired from the Cubs in 1960 for Don Cardwell and Ed Bouchee, Taylor wasn't a great hitter, compiling a .261 batting average and never once reaching double digits in home runs, but if you looked over at second base at just about any point in the 1960s, he was probably there. That's gotta be worth something. Taylor was there for the great collapse of 1964 and was still playing at age 40 in 1976 when the brief Dave Cash era was underway and the Phillies were getting good again. Only one season did Taylor play in the postseason, while with the 1972 Tigers. He deserved better in Philly.

What about: Manny Trillo? He played only four seasons with the Phillies but won three Gold Gloves as one of the best defensive second basemen in team history. In 1982 Trillo set a since-broken major league record with 479 straight errorless chances in the field, going 89 games without a miscue. Ironically, the streak ended when he booted a Bill Buckner ground ball. Maybe Buckner should have been taking notes. Trillo also could hit a bit, winning the 1980 National League Championship MVP award with a .381 batting average and four RBIs against the Astros, but he made his name with the glove. How did Trillo leave Philly? Oh, he was one of the five players in the Von Hayes deal. You do recall that one, don't you?

What about: Chase Utley? Like first base with Ryan Howard, the case can be made that Utley is already the club's best second baseman in history, but we're going to give him a second-place nod. Utley has played three full seasons and parts of two more, earning two All-Star berths and twice being in the top 10 for MVP voting. Utley enters 2008 with three straight 100-RBI seasons, and already holds the franchise record for home runs at the position, with 91 of his 97 career dingers coming at second base. Juan Samuel hit 90 homers as a second baseman for the Phillies. Utley smacked a grand slam for his first major league hit, in his major league start on April 24, 2003, and while he had to wait patiently for the Placido Polanco era in Philly to end, it did, and Utley has been terrific.

Yeah, but: Samuel had faults, to be sure. He wasn't a particularly good fielder. Lacking instincts, he made 33 errors his first full season and two years later committed 25. Few, if any, middle infielders struck out at the rate he did, and Samuel seldom walked, leading to low on-base percentages, especially for a guy who normally led off. But man, was this guy exciting to watch, or what? There was one season between the Trillo and Samuel eras, and then in 1984 Samuel made the All-Star team and finished second in Rookie of the Year voting, hitting 15 home runs and 19 triples, and scoring 105 runs, while stealing a modern club record 72 bases. Samuel would never run as much, but he developed more power, culminating in the 1987 season in which he hit 28 home runs and batted in 100, while scoring 113 times, adding 15 triples, 35 steals, and batting .272. He had become the first player in history to register double digits in doubles, triples, home runs, and stolen bases in his first four big league seasons. Things got tougher for Samuel after that as he was dealt to the Mets in 1989 for Lenny Dykstra and Roger McDowell, then was sent to the Dodgers, and, after a few below-average seasons, became a well-traveled journeyman. For five-plus seasons in Philly, however, he was one of the most exciting players fans had seen.

45 SHORTSTOP: JIMMY ROLLINS (2000–PRESENT)

What about: Larry Bowa? An intense and fiery leader while playing and coaching, Bowa will always have a special place in the hearts of Phillies fans who watched him in the 1970s. Bowa made his mark as a fielder, winning two Gold Gloves but probably deserving more. Bowa set league marks for fielding average in a career and single season, and retired with the NL record for games played at shortstop, with 2,222. More than 1,600 of those games came with the Phils, whom Bowa signed with as an undrafted free agent. At the plate Bowa wasn't much of a hitter. Only once in his career did he hit .300 for a season, he never scored 100 runs, despite hitting second in the order for much of the time, and he hit only .254 in the playoffs. Then again, in the 1980 World Series Bowa batted .375. Even after being a part of one of the worst trades in Phillies history—going to the Cubs with then no-name prospect Ryne Sandberg for Ivan DeJesus—Bowa came back to manage the Phillies. He didn't get the team to the playoffs, but nobody in Philly could say he didn't try.

What about: Granny Hamner? He was one of the leaders of the 1950 Whiz Kids, finishing sixth in the MVP voting that season. Maybe people liked him for his name, but Granville Wilbur Hamner was a solid player for the Phils for 15 seasons, with his top offensive season coming in 1953 with 21 home runs and 92 RBIs. Hamner also played second base, becoming the first player to start All-Star games at two different positions. He made his major league debut at age 17 and became a regular when he was 21.

Yeah, but: Rollins has been one of the most popular Phillies since being brought up to the majors in September 2000 and hitting .321 in 14 games. He makes it as the best at his position in a way that Howard and Utley don't, for example, because he's played longer and doesn't have quite the same competition at his position. It's not just his play on the field, however; he brings a confidence to the

143

team, which was certainly on display when he guaranteed the NL East title to the Phils before the 2007 season. It seemed kind of out-there to make a statement like that, but Rollins backed up the words by having an MVP campaign and helping the Phillies catch the Mets for the division title, literally. Rollins hit 30 homers, knocked in 94 runs, and stole 41 bases, and was the first player in history to tally 30 homers, 30 doubles, 30 steals, and 20 triples in one season. Rollins wasn't bad before that, though. At some point he'll catch Bowa for most games played at shortstop as a Phillie, but he's already got the club mark for home runs at the position, easily.

46 THIRD BASE: MIKE SCHMIDT (1972–89)

What about: Willie Jones? So how did Willie Jones get the nickname Puddin' Head, anyway? Did he really have puddin' in or on his head? Of course not. Before we get to who this player was—the only one in this section who had a good relationship with the Phillies fans by the way—Jones got his nickname from the popular 1930s song "Wooden Head, Puddin' Head Jones." No, it's not on my iPod either. On the field he was a clutch player known for big home runs and he was one of the top fielding third basemen of the era and a member of the 1950 Whiz Kids. Jones played nearly 1,500 games at third base for the Phillies, a figure topped only by Schmidt.

What about: Scott Rolen? Some will argue Rolen was and is a better fielder than Schmidt, as he entered the 2008 season with seven Gold Gloves to his credit. At the plate, Rolen never hit 40 home runs or came close to winning an MVP in Philly, but he did win the Rookie of the Year award in 1997 and hit 25 or more home runs in his final four full seasons before being such a pain in the butt the team shipped him to St. Louis for far less than he was worth. The Philly fans never seemed to like Rolen, but he never really liked them either. To play in Philly you need thick skin, and that wasn't Rolen at all. It wasn't only that he wasn't Schmidt, who also had a special relationship with the fans, but it was more that Rolen wasn't having fun. He seemed miserable all the time, acting like playing in Philly was such a horrible thing. It's not, if you know how to handle it.

What about: Dick Allen? There's no question Richie could hit a baseball, but there were so many other things that helped define who he was, and not all of them were good. Allen won the NL Rookie of the Year award in 1964, a season that is of course remembered in Philly for another reason (the biggest collapse ever), and he had to overcome racial prejudice in Philly to do so. That wasn't always so easy for him. He was, after all, the franchise's first black star, and he didn't handle it well. Allen didn't want to practice, follow any rules, listen to coaches, get along with teammates, or skip a party. He fought with popular teammate Frank Thomas, who got released because of it, and

Philly fans blamed Allen and didn't forgive him until his second tour of duty with the club. His erratic behavior eventually got him sent out of Philadelphia, where he didn't stop hitting, winning the AL MVP with the White Sox in 1972. While Allen probably wasn't treated fairly by Phillies fans early on, he was a rebel and they sensed weakness. A horrible fielding third baseman (67 errors his first two seasons) who eventually moved over to first base, Allen will be remembered by some as one who hit mammoth home runs deep into the night, and hit over .300 while on the Phillies.

Yeah, but: Michael Jack Schmidt is the greatest third baseman of all time, with 548 career home runs, three MVP awards, 10 Gold Gloves and, of course, one World Series ring. Let's move on.

47 LEFT FIELD: DEL ENNIS (1946–56)

What about: Sherry Magee? He's third on the Phillies list in games for an outfielder, having played for 11 seasons from 1904 to 1914, and considering the time he played in, when home runs weren't plentiful, Magee was productive, leading the NL in RBIs while in Philly three times. Magee had a big 1910, leading the loop in batting average, on-base percentage, slugging percentage, runs scored, total bases, and RBIs.

What about: Ed Delahanty? He batted better than .400 three times with the Phillies, and his career mark of .346

ranks the Hall of Famer fifth all-time. Of course, nearly all of this happened before 1900, so it's tough to ask people on the street what they thought of Big Ed, as he was called. One of five brothers to play in the major leagues, Delahanty smacked four home runs in a game in 1896, all of them inside-the-parkers, and three times led the NL in RBIs. Delahanty died while still a major leaguer in 1903, when his body was swept over Niagara Falls as he either jumped or was pushed off the International Falls Bridge.

What about: Pat Burrell? Many have wanted Pat the Bat out of town for years, but the truth is he's been rather productive, entering the 2008 season with 218 home runs over eight seasons. While Greg Luzinski had bigger seasons, his and Burrell's overall numbers are pretty similar, and neither were—ahem—known for their speed or defense. Burrell often draws the ire of Phillies fans, but the six-year, $50-million contract he signed in 2003 pretty much made him untradeable. Maybe that was a good thing, as Burrell played a key role in the 2007 division title with a big second half, putting him back in good graces, at least temporarily.

What about: Greg Luzinski? It's a tough call between Ennis and the Bull, but Ennis was the better all-around ball player. Luzinski had massive power, and his Bull Blasts into the left field seats at the Vet were legendary. While Mike Schmidt was winning the MVP awards and home run titles, Luzinski was productive as well, as he often protected

Schmidt in the batting order and had three Phillies seasons with at least 30 home runs and 100 RBIs. He was also selected to four straight All-Star games. Bull finished his career with the White Sox and he came back to Philly to open Bull's Barbeque at Citizen's Bank Park, where he visits with fans and talks about the good ol' days. Try the pulled pork; it's very tasty.

Yeah, but: At the time he left Philly in 1957, Ennis was the franchise's all-time leading home run hitter, a three-time All-Star who knocked in 100 or more runs on six occasions, and just missed two other times. Ennis was born in Philadelphia, was signed right out of Olney High School in 1942, and, after serving in the South Pacific for the Navy in World War II, joined his hometown club and had a big rookie season. His best year, like many of the Whiz Kids, was that wonderful 1950 season, when he hit career bests with 31 home runs and 126 RBIs. Ennis dealt with the fickle Phillies fans, who loved and hated him, by ignoring the abuse and being a consistent run producer for more than a decade. Upon retiring, his career accomplishments proved he should have been more loved than not.

48 CENTER FIELD: RICHIE ASHBURN (1948–59)

What about: Garry Maddox? It was once said that two thirds of the earth is covered by water, the rest by Maddox. This was one of the great defensive center fielders ever, as Maddox won eight straight Gold Gloves upon reaching the Phillies, who got him from San Francisco for Willie Montanez. Maddox finished fifth in MVP voting in 1976, when he batted .330, and he played a key role on the 1980 title team, knocking in 73 runs during the regular season, and doubling in the series-winning run in Game 5 at Houston to win the pennant.

What about: Cy Williams? Stolen from the Cubs after a down 1917 campaign, Williams played for the Phillies from 1918 until his retirement in 1930, winning three of his four NL home run titles. In 1923 he swatted 41 home runs, the same number as Babe Ruth. While Ruth got all the attention for his accomplishments, Williams was the first NL player to reach 200 home runs, and he remains in the Phillies' top 10 for games, extra base hits, hits, RBIs, and slugging percentage, and he's sixth in home runs.

What about: Lenny Dykstra? The best individual season for a Phillies center fielder is likely the Dykstra campaign in 1993, when the Dude scored 143 runs and led the team to the World Series. He hit 19 home runs during the regular season; in his seven other seasons with the club he hit a total of 32. Dykstra was second in MVP voting in 1993, but much of his time in Philly was spent on the disabled list. Overall Dykstra played in Philly from 1989 through 1996, but in only two of those seasons was he healthy enough to play in more than 90 games. But ah, those two years, for the guy they referred to as Nails, were very, very good.

Yeah, but: Ashburn is one of the most popular Phillies ever, and this is before he and Harry Kalas became a beloved announcing team. Ashburn started in center field for the Phillies from the time he came up in 1948 through the 1959 season, a durable, likeable leadoff man who thrived on getting on base and helping to keep runners off the bases. At the plate Ashburn was one of the top singles hitters in history, leading the league four times and finishing in the top three each of his first 13 seasons. He also led the league in walks four times and won two batting titles. While he didn't win as many Gold Gloves as Maddox, he played a lot longer in Philly and was a premier leadoff man. In the field Ashburn routinely led the league in fielding percentage and helped save the 1950 pennant by throwing out Dodgers' runner Cal Abrams at the plate in the bottom of the ninth inning of the final regular season game, which the Phillies won in the tenth. After repeatedly being denied admission into the Baseball Hall of Fame by the writers, Ashburn was elected by the Veteran's Committee in 1995, and was inducted along with Mike Schmidt, giving the ceremony a Philly twist, especially when a congregation of Phillies fans were on hand to cheer.

49 RIGHT FIELD: CHUCK KLEIN (1928–33, 1936–44)

What about: Bobby Abreu? It had to look odd when the Phillies "dumped" Abreu on the Yankees at the trade deadline in 2006 after so many years of service, but that's what happened, and it was really a financial issue more than anything else. What's also odd is that, even with the help of hindsight, this isn't thought of as one of the Phillies' worst trades. Abreu had terrific seasons in Philly, being a perennial .300 hitter with 20-plus home runs and 100 or so RBIs, and twice joining the 30/30 club for homers and steals. He remained productive to the day he was dealt, but his contract had become expensive and the Phillies wanted someone younger and more energetic in right field, and a better leader. Abreu was neither a big home run hitter nor a great fielder, but he won baseball's midseason home run derby in 2005, then won the Gold Glove at the end of the season. In truth, Abreu wasn't a natural power hitter, and he went into a big home run slump after winning the contest, and was often painted as lazy in right field, though he did have a strong arm. All told, only Mike Schmidt drew more walks in a Phillies uniform, only Chuck Klein had a higher OPS, and only Schmidt and Ed Delahanty hit more doubles.

What about: Gavvy Cravath? Okay, this isn't a household name in Philly these days, but it was back in 1915 when he broke the major league home record and helped lead the team to the World Series. Cravath was the Babe Ruth of his era, winning six home run titles in seven years and hitting 24 of them in 1915, which was the most home runs in the century and most ever by a Phillie. Of course, Ruth was just about to become a whole lot better.

What about: Johnny Callison? A fan fave who manned right field for the Phillies the entire decade of the 1960s, Callison reached the 30–100 mark for home runs and RBIs twice. Arguably the Phillies signature hitter of the era, Callison went to three All-Star games, and famously won the 1964 game at New York's Shea Stadium with a walk-off three-run home run. Callison also suffered with Phillies fans for the collapse later that season, though he didn't play badly while the team was losing 10 straight and the pennant. In one game Callison hit three home runs, though naturally the Phillies lost that game to Milwaukee. Callison entered 2008 ranked ninth on the club's all-time home run list.

Yeah, but: Klein finished his career with a .935 OPS, best in franchise history. In his first tour of duty with the club, before being sent to the Cubs in a controversial 1933 trade, Klein put up startling statistics, winning four NL home run titles in a five-year span, leading the league in RBIs twice, earning an MVP award, and finishing second twice. Klein won the Triple Crown in 1933 as well and had 44 outfield assists in 1930. This was a Hall of Fame player who didn't play on very good Phillies teams, but looking at the franchise record book, his name is strewn throughout.

50 LEFT-HANDED STARTER: STEVE CARLTON (1972–86)

What about: Chris Short? Despite the name, he was actually quite tall, a 6'4" southpaw who won 17 or more games four times in five years from 1964–68, and twice topped 200 strikeouts. Short ranks fourth on the franchise's innings, wins, and shutouts lists, and third in starts and strikeouts.

What about: Curt Simmons? He made his mark on the 1950 Whiz Kids, winning 17 games and establishing himself as one of the league's top lefties, though he was called to serve in the Korean War in September that year, missing the World Series and the entire 1951 season. Simmons returned in 1952 and was one of the team's top starters until being released in 1960. He ranks fifth on the Phillies' list for innings and wins.

Yeah, but: Carlton won 241 of his 329 career games with the Phillies, and all four of his Cy Young awards, giving himself a place as one of the top lefty starters in major league history. Phillies fans affectionately called him Lefty, though their affection for him—like that for Mike Schmidt—was only present when things were going really well. The Phillies acquired the 1971 20-game winner from the Cardinals for Rick Wise, a shrewd move, and in his first season in Philly Carlton had one of the greatest individual pitching seasons ever, certainly in comparison to how bad his team was. Carlton won 27 games, completed 30, fanned 310 hitters, and had a 1.97 ERA, all for a team that won 59 games. Carlton won 46 percent of all Phillies games that year. Of course, things went a bit astray the next year, when Carlton lost 20 games and had his stringent training techniques questioned; as a result, he decided he would no longer talk to the media, which continued for years. The Phillies built an offense from within around Carlton, and he was the ace for all the division titles and World Series triumph, winning his second of four Cy Young awards in 1980 with a 24–9 record. It was a shame seeing him try to latch on with other teams after the Phillies let him go, and nobody really hears from him anymore, but in his prime Lefty was the best.

51 RIGHT-HANDED STARTER: ROBIN ROBERTS (1948–61)

What about: Grover Cleveland Alexander? Also known as Pete, he was the Phillies' first great pitcher, dominating the National League from 1911–17, winning 190 games in that short span with a sparkling 2.18 ERA. Alexander led the Phillies to the World Series in 1915, which they lost to the Red Sox, and was controversially sent to the Cubs in a December 1917 trade, because the team needed money and feared Alexander would be called to World War I, which he was. Alexander was also a notorious drinker, though it didn't seem to hold him back on the mound, as he won pitching's Triple Crown four times, twice with the Phillies. He ranks in the Phillies' top 5 in wins, ERA, innings, strikeouts, and starts, and owns by far the best winning percentage in club history.

What about: Jim Bunning? The well-known senator from Kentucky had a career before politics, as in the 1960s he was one of the top pitchers in the game, winning 19 games each of his first three seasons and 17 in the fourth. Bunning ranks eighth in team history in starts and sixth in strikeouts, and, other than being overused in the 1964 September collapse, is probably best known as a player for throwing a perfect game at Shea Stadium on June 21, 1964. No NL pitcher had thrown a perfect game in 84 years.

What about: Curt Schilling? He never knew how to stop talking, and talking way too honestly, while with the Phillies or any team after, but the man who is fourth on the franchise's career strikeout list delivered some great moments in his eight-plus years with the club. Schilling emerged as a staff ace in 1992, not long after the Phillies stole him from the Astros for Jason Grimsley, and he went 16–7 for the 1993 World Series-bound team. Schilling won the NLCS MVP award for his two starts against the Braves, and though he did not pitch well in Game 1 against the Blue Jays, with the Phils down 3 games to 1 he tossed a five-hit shutout in Game 5. It wasn't uncommon to see Schilling with a towel over his head on the bench that season, symbolic of him not wanting to watch closer Mitch Williams try to protect his leads, and ultimately that called into question Schilling's value as a teammate. Eventually the Phillies got tired of Schilling's complaints about the team not doing enough to win, and they kind of showed he was right in dealing him off to Arizona for four players, one of them underachiever Travis Lee.

Yeah, but: Roberts won 234 games and fanned 1,871 hitters with the Phillies, each second-most in club history, and he ranks first in games, complete games, and innings. Roberts was selected to seven straight All-Star games beginning in 1950, and the Hall of Famer was known for durability and throwing strikes. He started three games in the final five days of the memorable pennant-winning 1950 season, going 10 innings in the exciting clincher at Brooklyn. After that season he was often a victim of lack of run support; otherwise he probably would have won 300 games. As it was, despite topping 20 wins for six straight seasons, he fell 14 short. He'd leave the Phils and pitch for the Orioles, Astros, and Cubs, as the Phillies released him after a 1–10 season in 1961. Roberts started opening day every season from 1950 through 1961, a record for one pitcher with one team. He's still fondly remembered today in Philadelphia.

CLOSER: TUG MCGRAW (1975–84)

What about: Ron Reed? At first an NBA player with the Detroit Pistons, Reed started his baseball career with the Braves in 1966, playing both sports for a year. Reed was a starting pitcher in Atlanta and St. Louis, but when the Phillies acquired the intimidating, 6'6" right-hander for Mike Anderson in December 1975, he became a full-time reliever, an innings eater who also accumulated 90 saves. Reed's best years in Philly came in his first three, when his ERA was below 3 each year and he saved an average of 15 games per year, but he also played a key role in the 1980 World Series team, the main right-handed closer compliment to McGraw.

What about: We'll combine the Phillies top-3 all-time save leaders into one section, because none of the three really had great careers with the club, their lofty save totals more a byproduct of the era. Jose Mesa, Steve Bedrosian, and Mitch Williams were each fine relief pitchers in their day, incidentally. Mesa garnered a record 112 saves for the team, 87 of them in 2001–02, though he wasn't an All-Star or considered a great pitcher at the time. Bedrosian did win the Cy Young award in his second of three-plus seasons with the team, as he had 40 saves and a 2.83 ERA. Williams threw the fateful pitch that lost the 1993 World Series for the Phillies, but many fans gloss over the fact the team wouldn't have made it that far without his 43 saves that year. In 1991 Williams went 12–5 with a 2.34 ERA and 30 saves, his best statistical year for the club. Of course, as Joe Carter was rounding the bases in Toronto, it was clear Mitch would have to resume his career elsewhere. He was dealt to Houston in December 1993.

Yeah, but: The Tugger ranks fourth in club history for saves, but that's only because closers weren't used the same way in the 1980s. Few pitchers accumulated more than 30 saves in a season back then. McGraw was on the mound for the franchise's biggest save, when he fanned Willie Wilson to end the 1980 World Series. In fact, McGraw was on the mound quite a bit in the memorable 1980 postseason, hurling in all five games of the Astros series, saving two of them, and appearing in four of the six games against the Royals, getting a win, a loss, and two more saves. McGraw was more than statistics for Phillies fans. He represented the team's and city's heart, but was also very fun-loving. The word screwball could be used to describe his personality, and his best pitch. The colorful McGraw's best season came in 1980, when he was fifth in the Cy Young voting with 20 saves and a 1.46 ERA. When McGraw retired after the 1984 season, he ranked eighth in major league history with 180 saves. McGraw remained a cult hero in Philly after leaving the game, and his death from a brain tumor in 2003 was felt by all Phillies fans.

HOOPIN' IT UP

WHAT WERE THE 76ERS' FIVE MOST MEMORABLE WINS?

53 One of the amazing things about Philadelphia 76ers history is that there aren't a lot of truly memorable wins. In fact, the losses are much more memorable. This is a franchise known for telling fans "We Owe You One" after the 1977 Finals loss to Portland, and reminding everyone of it for years until finally winning it all in 1983. We all remember a rookie named Magic Johnson going wild for 42 points and 15 rebounds in place of Kareem Abdul-Jabbar to clinch the 1980 Finals for the Lakers. John Havlicek stole the ball 15 years earlier to seal a 110–109 win for the Celtics. A year after winning the 1983 championship, the 76ers somehow managed to lose in the first round of the playoffs to the upstart Nets at home in Game 5. It seemed the 76ers were making memories for other franchises.

Well, we did come up with five games to think about, however, five games the good guys won. (And if you're looking for Wilt Chamberlain's 100-point game in Hershey, Pa., it's not here, because he did it while playing for the Philadelphia Warriors, a franchise that makes its home in San Francisco. We do, however, count this game for Philly's most memorable sports date, from Argument 7.)

5. THE FIRST TITLE

The 1966–67 76ers were arguably the best team in NBA history (see next argument), so it was no surprise when Wilt's crew drubbed the hated Celtics 140–116 in Game 5 of the East Finals to advance, then beat the San Francisco Warriors in six games. The final game of the series was a 125–122 win in San Francisco at the Cow Palace, a hard-fought game in which the 76ers came from behind in the final quarter. Chamberlain hauled in 23 rebounds in the clincher and recorded all six of his blocks in the fourth quarter, while sixth man Billy Cunningham scored 13 points late. The champion 76ers finally flew home as NBA champions.

4. WILD WILLIE

Not all memorable games happen to Hall of Famers. How about Willie Burton? Remember him? You probably don't, but when he had his best night he ended up with the record for most points in a game at the Spectrum, which is hard to believe. On December 13, 1994, Burton poured in 53 points in a 105–90 win over the Miami Heat, breaking Michael Jordan's arena record of 52 points. He hit 24 of 28 free throws. Burton just had one of those nights when you can't miss. He played only 53 games of a journeyman's career in Philly, ironic in that it matched the points of his best game. Burton had joined the 76ers only a month earlier, after being released by guess which team. Yep, it was the Miami Heat. Other than that night, one could say Burton didn't have a memorable career.

3. SKIP TO MY LUE

The 76ers won only one game in the 2001 Finals against the Lakers, but it was a doozy, as Allen Iverson scored 48 points in a 107–101 overtime win at the Forum, breaking the Lakers' 19-game winning streak. Iverson scored 38 points before the third quarter was over, as the 76ers took a 15-point lead, and then hit some memorable shots in overtime, including a key baseline jumper over Tyronn Lue, whom he would then step over for emphasis. The 76ers were the clear underdogs in the Finals, and they didn't win another game against Shaq and Kobe, but it was fun while it lasted.

2. NOT THIS TIME, CELTICS

The 1981–82 season wouldn't end with the 76ers winning the championship, but in just getting to the Finals, the 76ers overcame adversity and the rival Celtics. Boston was the number one Eastern Conference seed, having won five more games than the 76ers. A year before in the East Finals, the Celtics trailed 3–1 against the 76ers and came back to take the series and get to the Finals. In 1982 the 76ers came close to letting it happen again, but didn't. The 76ers went up 3–1 again, Boston convincingly took Games 5 and 6, and the series went back to

Beantown for the expected Celtics win. This time the 76ers won 120–106, and Boston fans chanted "Beat L.A., Beat L.A." in the waning seconds, rooting the 76ers on. Unfortunately, the 76ers didn't beat L.A. in the Finals until the following season.

1. A SWEET SWEEP

With Moses aboard, the 1982–83 76ers couldn't be stopped, and while the final game of any series sweep might be a bit anticlimactic, watching a joyous Maurice Cheeks dunk in the closing seconds certainly wasn't. That is probably the lasting image of the win, of a little point guard jumping high enough to dunk, then showing emotion we didn't often get from him. The 76ers won the first three games of the Finals against the Lakers, and in Game 4 fell behind by double digits early and still trailed by 16 in the second half. The Lakers held a 106–104 lead late, but then Julius Erving took over, announcing during a timeout he'd shine. He got a steal and dunk, then a key three-point play, and another bucket on a finger-roll made it seven points in the final minute-plus. Cheeks's dunk finished off the jubilant 115–108 win.

WERE THE 1966–67 76ERS THE BEST TEAM EVER?

Well, Wilt Chamberlain said at the time that the 1966–67 76ers were the best team ever, but since he was the starting center, he might have been a bit biased. The 76ers went 68–13, the best record in history at the time, though soon to be topped by a Wilt-led Lakers team in 1971–72 and two decades later by Michael Jordan's 72-win Bulls. What would Wilt say today?

The 76ers were deep, so deep that they were able to bring Hall of Famer Billy Cunningham off the bench as sixth man. Chamberlain's talents were undeniable, but he was hardly alone. Four players averaged at least 18 points per game, led by Chamberlain, with Hal Greer, Chet Walker, and Cunningham not far behind. Walker could do it all at small forward, averaging 19.3 points and 8.1 rebounds, and leading the team in free throws made per game. Luke Jackson was a rough, 250-pounder who played power forward, and he averaged nearly nine rebounds per game. Greer and his pin-point jumper averaged 22.1 points per game, while Wali Jones started at point guard and had a solid campaign. Cunningham came off the bench with guard Larry Costello, while veteran forward

Dave Gambee earned 12 minutes per game. The 76ers averaged 125.2 points per game, most in history for a season.

Chamberlain, still capable of scoring at will despite turning 30, was asked by new coach Alex Hannum to play a more team-oriented role and show his passing skills, which he did. Chamberlain had won league MVP awards, averaged 50.4 points per game for a season, and led teams to the playoffs, but he hadn't been able to top nemesis Bill Russell. Five times in seven years Wilt's teams were beaten in the playoffs by Russell's Celtics. Wilt focused more on defense this time, leading the league in rebounding at 24.2 per game and blocking who knows how many shots per game. The stat wasn't officially kept by the league until, ironically, the year after Chamberlain retired. Wilt also led the league in field goal percentage with a staggering .683 mark, and was third in assists. There was nothing Wilt couldn't do.

The 76ers stopped the Celtics' record streak of consecutive championships at eight, finally exorcising the demons of the past by beating Boston in five games to earn a trip to the Finals, where they beat the San Francisco Warriors.

Okay, so Philly finally won the big prize, with an unmatched array of offensive firepower, depth, and defense. But what about other contenders for best NBA team ever?

The Celtics won so many championships in the Russell era it's hard to spotlight only one squad, but the 1964–65 team broke its own league record for wins in a season with 62 and won its seventh straight title. The Eastern Finals series against the 76ers will always be remembered for John Havlicek stealing the ball in the final seconds of Game 7, leading to Johnny Most's legendary radio call. The Celtics were led by Sam Jones scoring 25 points per game, and five others averaged in double figures, including Havlicek, Russell, and Tom Heinsohn. It's a great team, maybe Boston's best, including the Larry Bird era. The Philly 1966–67 squad was stronger.

The Lakers team that won 69 games five seasons later is probably better known for its record 33-game winning streak. That team, which didn't lose for more than two months, also featured Chamberlain, but not in his prime, and three others on the team scored significantly more. Guards Gail Goodrich and Jerry West each scored nearly 26 points per game, with West leading the league in assists per game. Chamberlain led the league with 19.2 rebounds per game and was a defensive mainstay. This team won the most games in league history to that point and breezed through the playoffs, winning the title over the Knicks. While this team had it all, the 1966–67 76ers had a younger, stronger Chamberlain and more depth, and didn't rely so much on guard play. We'll take that 76ers team in six games.

The 1995–96 Bulls won 72 games, featuring an in-his-prime Michael Jordan and rebounder extraordinaire

Dennis Rodman. Jordan won his eighth scoring crown, Rodman his fifth rebounding title, and Scottie Pippen's stats took a small hit in scoring and rebounding but he still averaged 19.2 points per game and played a terrific defense. The Bulls had no problem winning the title, losing only one playoff game. But it also didn't have a center remotely like Wilt, as the Bulls didn't get much offense or defense from the position. Bill Wennington? Luc Longley? Are you kidding? Wilt would have eaten them alive. Sixth man Toni Kukoc was the third and final Bulls player to average double-digit points, but this team didn't have the depth the 76ers had. Sure, Jordan might have averaged 40 points a game if he faced the 1966–67 76ers in a series, but ultimately Wilt would have trumped the much-smaller Rodman, and the 76ers had plenty of scoring options. This one also goes to the 76ers.

By the way, what about the 1982–83 76ers? They were pretty good, eh? In sum, the 1966–67 76ers went 79–17, while Doc and Moses went 77–18. But that first 76ers team was better, scored more, and could have defended if it wanted to, no contest.

There you have it. Matched up against the greatest teams of all time, the Philadelphia 76ers would have certainly held their own, and beaten any of them.

WHAT WERE THE 76ERS' FIVE BEST TRADES?

55 Wilt Chamberlain was arguably the greatest player in the history of the NBA, and one might wonder: how can such a player ever be involved in a trade? If Chamberlain, who put up some absurd numbers in his career, was that good, then why would any team send him packing, and what could possibly be worth it in return?

Chamberlain was traded twice in his career, and in each case he would go to a team he'd help win a championship. The Philadelphia Warriors drafted Chamberlain in 1959, and three years later they were on the way to San Francisco. A year later the City of Brotherly Love got the fine Syracuse Nationals franchise. Midway through the 1964–65 season, Chamberlain was headed back to Philly, though with a different franchise. Got all that? A few years later, the Big Dipper was dipping back on the West coast, when the Lakers acquired him.

One could certainly make the argument that the best trade the 76ers franchise ever made was getting Chamberlain...and the worst was dealing him away. So, is that true?

5. JOHN KERR TO BALTIMORE FOR WALI JONES—SEPTEMBER 22, 1965

Jones was a star at Overbrook High and at Villanova, and the 76ers certainly had a chance to draft him in 1964, but instead went with the legendary Ira Harge from New Mexico. Detroit selected Jones, but he never played for the Pistons, instead being shipped to the Baltimore Bullets. Jones didn't get much chance to play as a rookie, but still made the league's all-rookie team. Then his hometown 76ers swooped in and dealt Kerr to get him. Kerr was 33 when traded, a fine rebounder in his day but on the way out, and he'd play just one more season in the league. Jones would become a starter on the 76ers team that lays claim to being the best ever, and the point guard averaged in double digits for points in all but one of his six seasons, while also being a capable assist man.

4. GEORGE MCGINNIS AND 1978 FIRST-ROUND PICK TO DENVER FOR BOBBY JONES, RALPH SIMPSON, AND 1984 FIRST-ROUND PICK—AUGUST 16, 1978

The 1976–77 76ers had plenty of offense, scoring 110.2 points per game and featuring six players who scored in double digits, led by Julius Erving and McGinnis, both athletic forwards who rebounded but weren't exactly standout defenders. The 76ers had role players to do the defending, led by long-time center Caldwell Jones. But being a high-flying, scoring team didn't lead to a championship. Up 2–0 in the Finals against Bill Walton and Portland, the 76ers didn't win again.

Meanwhile, the Nuggets were a 50-win team, but concerned about Jones's health as he dealt with asthma, occasional epileptic seizures, and a chronic heart disorder. McGinnis was a fine player, an annual 20-point scorer, and he would play only a year and a half in Denver. Jones was the premier defensive player of his era, maybe the best big-man defender other than Bill Russell, and played in Philly eight seasons. As for the draft picks, the one Philly dealt became journeyman Mike Evans, who averaged 7.7 points per game in nine seasons. Meanwhile, the 76ers used their pick on Leon Wood, who averaged 6.4 points and later became a league referee.

3. FRED CARTER TO MILWAUKEE FOR 1977 AND 1978 SECOND-ROUND PICKS. DECEMBER 8, 1976
LLOYD FREE TO SAN DIEGO FOR 1984 FIRST-ROUND PICK, OCTOBER 2, 1978

Okay, these deals seemed like robberies at the time, but in favor of the teams dealing with the 76ers. Carter was finishing up his career, and after this December trade he would play only 47 games for Milwaukee before retiring. The Bucks thought they were getting the guy who averaged

18.9 points in 1975–76, but Carter no longer wanted to play. Free was still a darn good scorer. The Clippers had hired former Philly coach Gene Shue, and he was willing to take on the selfish Free, who just wanted to score and didn't care if anyone else was on the court with him. Later he would change his name to World B. Free. In his two years in San Diego he'd finish in the top 4 of scoring both times, and lead the league in free throws made, and eventually score nearly 18,000 points. Anyway, 76ers fans didn't know the inside scoop, so they didn't get the deal. These were productive scorers sent away.

Hmmm, what ever happened to the draft picks in those deals? Glad you asked. The 1977 draft pick was used on Wilson Washington, who played 14 games his rookie season and then got dealt to the New Jersey Nets for future considerations. Washington played 100 career games. One of the future considerations was a 1979 draft pick that became Clint Richardson, a key reserve on the 1982–83 title team. The second-round pick in 1978 was used on a quiet point guard from West Texas A&M University named Maurice Cheeks. That turned out okay, right? Cheeks ended up the team's all-time leader in assists and steals, and the sight of him dunking near the end of the 76ers championship becoming secured still resonates today.

Meanwhile, the Clippers still stunk in 1984, but in Los Angeles, when the Free draft pick became relevant, the 76ers used it on…Charles Barkley. He turned out okay, too.

171

2. PAUL NEUMANN, CONNIE DIERKING, LEE SHAFFER, AND CASH TO SAN FRANCISCO FOR WILT CHAMBERLAIN—JANUARY 15, 1965

See, there are reasons why teams deal Hall of Famers for players who aren't quite at that level, and in this case it was because the cash-strapped Warriors couldn't afford Chamberlain. So, the 76ers lucked out. Neumann was averaging 14.4 points at the time of the deal, Dierking 7.8 points and 6.3 rebounds, and Shaffer hadn't played in a year and would never play again. The 76ers threw in $150,000, well worth it for the price of a championship. Philly fans had seen Wilt start his career with the Philadelphia Warriors, and then watched that franchise moved to San Francisco. This deal brought him back.

Chamberlain averaged 30.1 points per game in the 35 games he played in that season for the 76ers, though he couldn't guide the team to the playoffs. He would the next year, and soon he would help bring home a title.

1. CALDWELL JONES AND FIRST-ROUND PICK TO HOUSTON FOR MOSES MALONE— SEPTEMBER 15, 1982

Okay, so the trade was consummated a bit after the fact, but still, the Houston Rockets got something out of this. Malone was an unrestricted free agent after the 1981–82 season, which ended with his Rockets getting swept in the first round of the playoffs against the Seattle SuperSonics.

172

Malone signed an offer sheet with the 76ers and wanted to go there, but the Rockets matched the offer and decided to recoup something at the same time, so the 76ers and Rockets worked out the trade.

It was obvious early in the 1982–83 season that Malone was the difference-maker, a scoring/rebounding monster who would take the team to heights it had never reached. Jones gave his new team two solid seasons before moving on to Chicago and Portland. The Rockets sank without Malone, going from 46–36 to 14–58, and chose Ralph Sampson with the first overall draft pick the next season. The pick acquired from the 76ers became the third overall pick, since it was picked up from Cleveland in 1977, and it was Rodney McCray, a fine swingman who averaged 11.7 points per game in 10 seasons. By the way, with the number 2 overall pick the Indiana Pacers chose Steve Stipanovich, who played only five seasons. Draft picks are always a risk.

But none of that mattered. The 76ers had Moses Malone, and he would lead them to the promised land.

WHAT WERE THE 76ERS' FIVE WORST TRADES?

56 Okay, so we've established that one of these worst trades has to involve Wilt Chamberlain, and we also know that dark day of June 16, 1986, saw a pair of terrible deals get made. Like the Phillies, it seems the 76ers just don't know how to send revered veterans packing and get something good in return.

5. KENNY THOMAS, BRIAN SKINNER, AND CORLISS WILLIAMSON TO SACRAMENTO FOR CHRIS WEBBER, MATT BARNES, AND MICHAEL BRADLEY—FEBRUARY 25, 2005

No, the 76ers didn't really trade anything of importance, but that's the entire reason the Sacramento Kings were willing to make this deal. It was addition by subtraction, though the 76ers didn't know it. On the surface, it was a bold move by 76ers general manager Billy King to take on Webber's hefty contract, paying him more than $18 million per season and trying to make a run at a championship. But Webber couldn't play at the level people were used to seeing him at. He wasn't even close. Immediate reaction was that the Kings got hosed, as the players they got back wouldn't help them much, and they had bad contracts.

Webber, however, wasn't as productive as expected and was not a very good teammate or role model. The 76ers would make the playoffs a few months after C-Webb was acquired, but got bounced in five games by the Pistons, winning once. Webber played one full season in Philly, and did average 20.2 points per game with 9.9 rebounds during the year, but he and Allen Iverson didn't get to the postseason. So, King took on tons of contract for one playoff win, and on January 11, 2007, Webber's contract was bought out. The 76ers had to pay Webber $36 million so he would leave and sign with the Pistons.

4. WILT CHAMBERLAIN TO THE LAKERS FOR JERRY CHAMBERS, ARCHIE CLARK, AND DARRALL IMHOFF—JULY 9, 1968

As average as the characters were that the 76ers dealt to San Francisco to get Chamberlain, this group doesn't appear so great in return three and a half years later, but that's just because people don't know the names. Chamberlain didn't want to play in Philadelphia any longer, and forced management's hand. He could have retired at age 32, leaving the 76ers with nothing. Chamberlain's Lakers famously won 69 games in 1971–72, a new record, and the big center led the league in field goal percentage and rebounds. As for the new 76ers, the team didn't disintegrate at all—not right away at least. They rode Billy Cunningham to three more playoff berths, but then things fell apart four years later. Clark and Imhoff were actually very productive, but in the shadow of Wilt weren't given much credit. Imhoff averaged more than nine points and nine rebounds his first season in Philly, and 13.6 points and 9.5 boards the next season. Clark averaged 19.7 points his second season, 21.3 points in 1970–71, which was more than Chamberlain did with the Lakers. Sure, dealing Chamberlain wasn't fun, and not one of the best, but the 76ers actually did okay in the deal, all things considered.

3. CHARLES BARKLEY TO PHOENIX FOR JEFF HORNACEK, ANDREW LANG, AND TIM PERRY—JUNE 17, 1992

Six years and one day after the Moses-Ruland-Hinson debacles you will see next, the 76ers sent their best player to the Valley of the Sun for role players. At least in the case of Moses Malone, one could say he was past his prime, no longer a fan favorite, and one of the brittle players received in return was an All-Star. Barkley was drafted by the 76ers, made one of their own, and played eight interesting seasons with the club, unlike Malone who was clearly rented for a title run. Barkley made headlines off the court, and that certainly played a role in his dismissal. On the day of the trade, Barkley was acquitted on assault charges stemming from an incident in Milwaukee. He found out he was dealt while at an airport, and called the deal out of

Philly one of the best days of his life. So, yeah, he wanted to leave, too. Seems like it's a theme. Anyway, Barkley would soon lead the Suns to the NBA Finals against Michael Jordan's Bulls, while the 76ers freefell to 26 wins, then 25, 24, and 18 in 1995–96, which would welcome the Allen Iverson era. Hornacek was paroled to the Utah Jazz within two seasons. Lang played one underwhelming season in town. Perry, a Temple University product, played three-plus seasons before being dealt to the New Jersey Nets. This would be the worst trade in 76ers history, except for...

2. FIRST OVERALL 1986 DRAFT PICK TO CLEVELAND FOR ROY HINSON

1. MOSES MALONE, TERRY CATLEDGE, AND TWO FIRST-ROUND DRAFT PICKS TO WASHINGTON FOR JEFF RULAND AND CLIFF ROBINSON—JUNE 16, 1986

Yeah, it was that bad, and these bad boys come in a package deal, because that's how owner Harold Katz treated them. There's very little to justify these trades, and they deserve their own chapter, which they got (see next). Which deal was worse, you might ask? Well, Ruland played in five games his first season! At least Hinson, while no first overall pick Brad Daugherty, had some game.

WHAT WAS HAROLD KATZ THINKING ON JUNE 16, 1986?

 57 Even with the aid of hindsight, there seems little justification, if any, for what 76ers owner Harold Katz did in a pair of controversial trades that fateful June day. The 76ers were still very good at the time. Since winning the championship four seasons earlier, the team had won 52, 58, and 54 games, finishing second in the Atlantic Division each time and heading to the playoffs, though encountering no luck once they got there. The goal on this day, just before the draft, was not to rebuild, but get stronger. It sure didn't seem like it at the time, or later, but luck didn't help.

First of all, how did the 76ers even get that first overall draft pick for 1986 if they were so good? Well, 76ers fans might not like Kobe Bryant, but his father was responsible for getting the 76ers the pick. The then-San Diego Clippers wanted Joe Jellybean Bryant so badly in 1979 that they parted with a first-round draft pick seven years off. Maybe the Clippers figured they wouldn't even be around in seven years. Turns out they weren't in San Diego anymore, but Los Angeles; and they were still bad, bad enough to be in the lottery and win it, giving that 1986 first overall pick to Philly.

Anyway, Bryant did a decent job in Philly, and sired a Hall of Famer for Philly fans to boo, but this trade gave the 76ers the first pick and the rights to any player. North Carolina center Brad Daugherty seemed like the wise choice. He was a senior, which at the time wasn't necessarily a positive, as people would wonder if he was so good, why hadn't he left school early? In retrospect Daugherty was the smart pick in what became a dreadful draft. The Celtics had the second overall pick and used it on Maryland's Len Bias, who tragically died of a drug overdose less than 48 hours after the draft. Many of the other early first-rounders also turned into bad picks, like Chris Washburn and William Bedford.

But Katz apparently didn't want the pick, maybe because he didn't want to pay so much money for an unproven player. Didn't matter that Daugherty would become one of the league's premier centers and prove he wasn't as soft a player as people believed. Katz sent the rights to the number 1 pick to the Cleveland Cavaliers for Roy Hinson. Hinson wasn't a bad player by any means; he just wasn't a star. An athletic leaper who at 6'9" was more power forward than center, Hinson was coming off the best of his three seasons in the NBA, averaging 19.6 points and 7.8 rebounds, and he could defend other big men. The 76ers, who had supposedly drafted Andrew Toney to combat Boston, needed someone to stop Kevin McHale. Hinson could do this. Did he make any statistical leaderboards during that 1985–86 season? Um, sure, he was second in the league in personal fouls.

Katz wasn't done yet. Moses Malone had been the final piece to getting the championship puzzle a few years earlier, but now he was getting old, and looking old. He still remained a very productive player in 1986, averaging a team-leading 23.8 points per game, and he could rebound, but the 76ers couldn't run with him on the floor. At the time, dealing Malone didn't seem so silly. Fans just wanted more in return. Maybe it wasn't even rational: did Katz and Malone simply have a falling out, and the best way for Katz to win was to trade his starting center? Possibly. Whatever the case, Malone, Terry Catledge, and two first-round picks were sent to the Washington Bullets for Jeff Ruland and Cliff Robinson.

Where do we begin on this one? Malone wasn't done. He was only 30 and he still had six more seasons as a productive starting center, going to three more All-Star games. Catledge, who played one season in Philly after being a first-round pick, would be a helpful forward for Washington and Orlando, never a star.

And what about Ruland? A strong jump shooter, a capable, rugged rebounder, and a solid passer, Ruland had missed more than half the Bullets' games with foot problems the two previous seasons before the trade. To be exact, he played in 67 games in 1984–85 and 1985–86 total. Maybe Katz didn't think this was a long-term problem, or maybe he thought his billion-dollar NutriSystem franchise could heal the center. In 1986–87, Ruland played five games for the 76ers and was essentially done. He made a comeback five years later, but played in only 13 games. What did he hurt this time? Ruland claimed he hurt his Achilles when a Boston Celtics employee slammed a luggage cart into it. Ruland missed the rest of the season. He played 18 total games with the 76ers.

Likewise, Robinson wasn't a bad player before coming to the 76ers. In his three seasons in Philly the journeyman scored some points, including 19 per game in 1987–88, but he too was not durable. Robinson missed nearly half the team's games, including a 14-game season in 1988–89.

What ever happened to the draft picks? Ah, nothing big, really. They became Anthony Jones and Harvey Grant. But had Katz just stuck with what he had, it would have been a terrific front line of Charles Barkley, Brad Daugherty, and Moses Malone. Wow.

In retrospect, everything Katz tried to do with those trades blew up in his face. Should Katz have planned for this? Maybe, but nevertheless June 16, 1986, was a dark day for Philly hoops.

WHO'S BETTER: IVERSON OR DOC?

58 One guy flew through the air with the greatest of ease, redefining the game of basketball through the dunk. The other zoomed past defenders with the greatest of ease, wowing fans with his speed. Both brought excitement to the game. But who was better?

Julius Erving came to the 76ers from the ABA when the cash-strapped New York Nets basically couldn't afford him. Erving had shown his stuff in the soon-to-be defunct league, winning titles, awards, and fame, but needed a larger stage, and got that with the 76ers. He didn't just bring the dunk to the NBA; he was the most famous player of the time, an ambassador of the game, a pitchman, an idol to many.

Allen Iverson was the first overall draft pick in 1996 out of Georgetown, and instantly he became someone fans paid to see. In his Philly days, and now with the Denver Nuggets, Iverson brings excitement by being a prodigious, relentless scorer; a flash of light moving faster through defenses than the camera can follow.

TOOLS

Both Erving and Iverson are tremendous athletes. Erving was a playground legend in New York City, with remarkable jumping ability and large hands, an elegant player. Watch the old highlights from dunk contests, or various moves in Finals appearances against the Lakers, and it seemed he could fly. Iverson can't fly, but he has proven his speed and toughness since before joining the NBA. Iverson was a high school quarterback. In the NBA he has dealt with numerous injuries, but is renowned for playing through them. It's difficult to compare players from different eras both statistically and for ability, but Erving gets the nod for being one of the first players of his era to show these skills at such a high level, and in a way he reinvented the way the game was played.

LIKEABILITY

Both men have been idolized for who they are and what they bring to the game, but Erving developed a style that everyone wanted to emulate. Who wouldn't want to fly over defenders and slam the ball through the hoop? Few can. More Iverson posters have probably hung in the bedrooms of young boys, but back in the 1970s the ratio would have tilted toward Erving. It wasn't until after his career ended that skeletons in Erving's closet became public knowledge, like having fathered tennis player Alexandra Stevenson. Iverson has an entirely different hip-hop reputation in and out of the game, is seen by some some as a thug, and was in trouble with the law as early as high school. Erving is the choice again.

SCORING

Only three players have scored more points in the NBA and ABA combined than Erving. In an era of scoring, Erving annually led his teams in points with an array of moves and shots, not only the dunk. He improved his jump shot throughout his career, had a sick finger-roll, and got to the line at a strong rate and shot a decent percentage. However, Iverson has the third-best scoring average of all time, at 28 points per game, trailing only some guys named Wilt and Jordan. He's won scoring titles and averaged better than 30 points per game multiple times. Nobody his size ever won a scoring title. Iverson is the better scorer.

OTHER BASKETBALL SKILLS

At 6'0", if that, Iverson isn't a rebounder or shot blocker, but he's been named to the league's all-defense team numerous times and led the league in steals. Iverson isn't a master of the three-point shot, but he does have more range than Erving ever did. Iverson has also been one of the better passers in the game, an important part of playing point guard, and he never feared driving into the lane to draw fouls even though the men hacking at him were often a foot taller and had 100 pounds on him. Erving was a decent rebounder for the small forward position, and a very good one early in his career. He was also one of the better passers and shot blockers for the position. Erving didn't have to draw the opponent's best player, with the presence of stalwart Bobby Jones, but he could defend. He just couldn't defend like Iverson, who has exceptional quickness and has been among the league leaders in assists most years. Iverson gets the nod.

AWARDS

Erving is the only player to win MVP awards and team championships in the NBA and ABA, and he was an All-Star in each of his 16 professional seasons. Iverson is also a regular attendee of the All-Star festivities and in 2000–01 became the shortest player to win the league's MVP award. He was also Rookie of the Year. While Iverson has his share of hardware on his shelf, Erving accumulated more in his career.

AND THE WINNER IS...

Erving led the 76ers to the NBA Finals four times, winning once. He also won titles in the ABA. Iverson, though he hasn't had nearly the talent around him, led the 76ers to one Finals appearance, but it was a series loss to the Lakers. Erving gets the nod for winning, and ultimately the nod head-to-head.

WHO WAS THE TOP ALLEN IVERSON SIDEKICK?

59 Allen Iverson played 10-plus seasons in Philadelphia after being the first pick in the 1996 draft, and nobody can say the little guy wasn't productive. The Answer won four scoring titles and one MVP award. Of course, the 76ers went far in the playoffs exactly one time, in 2000–01. Is that really Iverson's fault?

The common theory behind why Iverson's teams didn't win a championship and generally underachieved come playoff time was that he didn't have enough help. Michael Jordan had Scottie Pippen; Magic Johnson had Kareem Abdul-Jabbar; Larry Bird had no shortage of solid players around him; but whom did Iverson have to pick up the slack on the nights he struggled, or to take that last shot if he was double-teamed? When the 76ers traded their superstar to Denver, there was a ready-made sidekick in place in Carmelo Anthony. Then again, the Nuggets didn't make it out of the first round of the playoffs.

Iverson did have help in the Philly years; it just wasn't the right help, or the team still wasn't good enough. In his rookie season, Jerry Stackhouse, the number 3 pick from the year before, averaged more than 20 points per game. Stack's numbers were a bit down the next season and he got sent to Detroit for Theo Ratliff and Aaron McKie. The 76ers felt Iverson needed a big man to guard the paint. Ratliff did fine, but he was no scorer. Derrick Coleman was his main wingman in 1997–98. The next year the team's second-leading scorer was Matt Geiger.

The big prize in February 2000 was supposed to be sweet-shooting Toni Kukoc, picked up in a three-way deal with the Warriors and Bulls to unload Larry Hughes, another top pick who didn't pan out. Kukoc wasn't special either, and a year and a week later he was moved to Atlanta in the Dikembe Mutombo trade. Mutombo was in the prime of his career, a monster defender who made life easier for everyone on that end of the court, but he and McKie combined didn't approach Iverson's points-per-game average.

Is it possible Iverson's style of play just didn't lend itself to developing another high-profile scorer? Iverson handled the ball, took most of the shots, and it's possible nobody could coexist with him. Stackhouse, Coleman, Hughes, and Kukoc failed, followed by Keith Van Horn. In the summer of 2003, the 76ers thought they had figured it all out when they concocted a four-team deal with the Knicks, Timberwolves, and Hawks that landed them Glenn Robinson. The Big Dog, as he was called, had averaged 20 points per game eight out of nine seasons in his career. With the 76ers, in 42 games he averaged 16.6 points per game. Robinson didn't quite work out with the 76ers. He was rarely healthy, and when he was dumped on the New Orleans Hornets for the Jamal Mashburn expiring contract and Rodney Rogers in February 2005, he hadn't played for the 76ers that entire season. Robinson would never play for the Hornets; Mashburn never suited up again.

The day before the Robinson deal, Chris Webber was picked up from the Sacramento Kings. Webber didn't score any more than Robinson when he was acquired, but in 2005–06 he averaged 20.2 points per game. But the 76ers went 38–44. That experiment failed as well.

Really, you could make an All-Star team of players who were acquired to work with Iverson. They weren't all nice guys, mind you; but these were productive players. And still the 76ers didn't win a title, getting to the NBA Finals only one time.

When it comes down to it, the best sidekick Iverson had was Mutombo, a critical defensive piece to the puzzle and one of the few players who didn't demand shots and didn't try to break up the clubhouse with petty complaints. Mutombo played only one full season with the 76ers, but also got to the Finals. It's ironic, really, that seemingly every season in the Iverson era the 76ers were looking for a big scorer to accompany their best player. However, the season Iverson took the team furthest in the playoffs, his sidekick wasn't really a scorer at all. If only the 76ers had learned their lesson.

WOULD DR. J HAVE WON THE TITLE WITHOUT MOSES?

60 The short answer is, "Probably not." The 76ers went to the Finals three times before Moses arrived via the Houston Rockets, and each time Julius Erving and pals lost. In 1977 the 76ers won the first two games of the Finals against Bill Walton's Trail Blazers, and lost the next four. Three seasons later, a rookie named Magic Johnson lined up at center to help eliminate the 76ers in six games, and then in 1981–82 another accomplished 76ers squad managed to skip by the Celtics in seven games to get to the Finals, where the Lakers were waiting to deliver a four-games-to-two series win. The 76ers were one of the best teams in the league and, as the team's motto went, they owed their fans one (or more), but whether they faced Bird's Celtics or Magic's Lakers, they couldn't get over the hump. Three Finals losses in Erving's first six seasons in Philly were not cutting it.

Erving wasn't to blame, but he needed more help, mainly in the middle. Nothing against Caldwell Jones and Darryl Dawkins—the first a veteran, skilled shotblocker and rebounder who didn't demand shots; the latter a mammoth of a man known more for naming his dunks and committing fouls—but the 76ers hadn't had a dominant center since the days of Wilt Chamberlain. Erving was among the league leaders in scoring every season, and 1981–82 had five others averaging in double digits (Andrew Toney, Bobby Jones, Maurice Cheeks, Lionel Hollins, and Dawkins), but no big-time center.

Malone was a big-time center. The league's rebounding champ and number 2 in scoring to George Gervin in 1981–82, Malone, Kareem Abdul-Jabbar, and Robert Parish were the top centers in the game. Philly's center was Caldwell Jones. Malone had won two MVP awards. Malone was a restricted free agent, and on September 2, 1982, the 76ers signed him to a mammoth $2.2 million offer sheet. The Rockets decided to match the deal and recoup something for their efforts, dealing Malone to Philly for Jones and a first-round pick. 76ers owner Harold Katz badly wanted a title and was willing to pay for it. Now he had one of the best forward-center combos in league history.

With Malone on board, the 76ers were unstoppable. The team won 65 regular season games, as Malone led the team in scoring and was fifth in the league, and his 15.3 rebounds per game easily dwarfed the number 2 boardman, New Jersey's Buck Williams at 12.5 rebounds.

Entering the playoffs, the 76ers were the favorites, destined to meet the rival Lakers, who had won 58 games. When prompted for his playoff predictions, Malone famously said "fo', fo', fo'," meaning that all three playoff series would be sweeps. He came close. The 76ers swept the New York Knicks and took the first three games of their series with the Milwaukee Bucks, only to lose Game 4 on May 15, 1983, 100–94. Three days later the series was over, and the 76ers romped over the Lakers, winning the title in Los Angeles.

Even Malone admitted along the way it was still Erving's team, and Erving played magnificently, but he couldn't have done it without a near prophet named Moses.

WHAT IS WILT'S GREATEST ACHIEVEMENT?

61 You can't look at the NBA record book without seeing the name *Chamberlain, Wilt*, littered throughout. From the time he came into the league to his final years, Chamberlain did it all. But among the myriad things Wilt did that nobody else could, which is his greatest accomplishment?

SCORING POINTS

Nobody could amass points the way Chamberlain did. The year before he entered the NBA, Bob Pettit of the St. Louis Hawks won the scoring title at 29.2 points per game, and that was the new league record, surpassing the top scoring season of George Mikan's career. Wilt joined the Philadelphia Warriors and trumped that mark, scoring 37.6 points per game. He won the scoring title his first seven seasons in the league, and when he left the game, nobody had scored more points. Only Kareem Abdul-Jabbar, who played longer, has more career points.

THE 100-POINT GAME

What Wilt did that memorable day in Hershey,

Pennsylvania, in 1962 is just incredible. Consider other one-game records across sports, and how close the new record is to the old. In baseball, for example, three pitchers have struck out 20 hitters in a game. In hockey someone named Joe Malone once scored seven goals in a game, back in 1920, but seven others have tallied six. Chamberlain scored 100 points in one game; the next-best total is 81 by Kobe Bryant in 2006. The most points scored in a game by someone before Chamberlain was Elgin Baylor with 71, and after was David Thompson with 73, until Bryant's 81. Those numbers aren't all that close to 100, are they? What else is amazing from this game? While Wilt excelled at just about every area of basketball, he was not a good free throw shooter at all. But on this night, he made 28 of 32 freebies.

AVERAGING 50.4 POINTS IN A SEASON

When someone scores 50 points in a game now—be it Kobe Bryant or LeBron James—it leads ESPN *SportsCenter*. It's a big deal. Even the great Michael Jordan managed to score 50 points in a game only 30 times in his wondrous career. Chamberlain *averaged* that in the 1961–62 season. The next best scoring average in a season for someone with a different name is Jordan, when he averaged 37.1 points in 1986–87.

REBOUNDING

Of course, Chamberlain wasn't a sieve on the defensive

THE BEST PHILADELPHIA SPORTS ARGUMENTS

end, either. He won 11 rebounding titles, on two different occasions leading the league in four consecutive seasons; he holds the record for career rebounds, highest average per game, and the top three marks for rebounds in a season. He twice averaged better than 27 rebounds in a season, and once had 55 in a game. If only blocked shots had been kept as a category back in Wilt's day, we'd probably find nobody had more in league history.

ASSISTS TITLE

Later in Chamberlain's career, when the 76ers had plenty of talent, coach Alex Hannum asked the big man to be more of a passer. Chamberlain didn't need to be told twice. He wanted to prove his versatility, and he wanted to win, and in the great 1966–67 season he finished third in the league with 7.8 assists per game. Of course, that wasn't enough. The next season while aiming to defend the championship, Chamberlain became the only center in history to win the assist title, averaging 8.6 per game. No big man could do this today.

DURABILITY

One of the reasons Chamberlain was able to attain the statistics he did was because he was always on the floor. He never fouled out in more than 1,000 career games, and in 1962–63 he averaged 48.5 minutes per game. Um, aren't there only 48 minutes in a regulation NBA game? Yes, but when you count overtime, you get past 48. Chamberlain played in 3,882 of a possible 3,890 minutes that season, and even later in his career rarely missed games due to injury.

WINNING

While rival Bill Russell won more championships, and it's not even close, Chamberlain was a force on the 1966–67 team, arguably the greatest NBA team assembled. Later in his career Chamberlain won another title with the Lakers, when that team won 69 games, best ever at the time.

WOMEN

Well, while it might not be the most politically correct thing to point out, Chamberlain made headlines by claiming in his second autobiography, *A View From Above* (published in 1991), that he had had sex with 20,000 women. Almost immediately people started doing the math to see if this was even possible. Could Chamberlain have had sex 1.14 times per day every day from the age of 15 until his death? The reaction to this proclamation was intense, and drew the ire of many who didn't believe it and felt it to be irresponsible. We'll never know if it's true, and to some that's a good thing. For the purposes of this argument, let's focus more on what Wilt did on the court.

So which one of these accomplishments is Wilt's greatest in a storied career? While the name of the game is

THE BEST PHILADELPHIA SPORTS ARGUMENTS

winning, Chamberlain is not known for this. He took part in only two title-winning teams. What does everyone remember? The scoring—on the court, of course. Chamberlain's scoring marks still boggle the mind, so whether it's career or single-season, we'll go with those for top achievement.

STARTING A FRANCHISE: WILT OR BILL RUSSELL?

62 It's often said that in order for a rivalry to be a good one, both teams or players have to have success. For years the New York Yankees, for example, owned the Boston Red Sox. It was a rivalry, but a one-sided one. Then a certain team blew a 3–0 AL Championship Series lead, the ghost of the Babe was dead, and the rivalry blossoms.

Wilt Chamberlain and Bill Russell certainly had a rivalry, with one man earning the personal accolades and the other winning the championships, so what kind of rivalry was this? Wasn't it one-sided? Let's figure out who really was better.

TOOLS

The NBA hadn't really seen anyone like Russell when he came into the league in 1956. He dominated on the defensive end and scored enough, but it was instantly clear he was a winner. Russell could have scored more if he wanted to, but the great Boston Celtics teams weren't interested in that. They were winning championships. Chamberlain, on the other hand, was three inches taller and the larger man to boot. He entered the league in 1959 and averaged 37 points and 27 rebounds. He scored at will, abusing smaller players but also featuring a good shooting touch, and, while he wasn't as defensive-minded as Russell, he toyed with opposing shooters who dared enter into the lane. In their 142 meetings, Chamberlain averaged 28.7 points and 28.7 rebounds, far better than Russell's 14.5 points and 23.7 rebounds. Both these Hall of Fame centers had tremendous ability, but Chamberlain had more.

INTANGIBLES

Chamberlain played on some fantastic teams in his career, and while he was traded a few times, don't let that fool you into thinking he was a bad teammate. Chamberlain was motivated to score, rebound, and win, and one can argue nobody has ever done the first two of those things better. But Russell won the championships because he was a better team player, willing to do whatever it took to get a victory, and he eventually became a coach. Could Chamberlain have done that? In fact, the presence of Chamberlain four years into his career probably lifted Russell to even greater heights. Being faced with a foe who could match him only made Russell better.

ONE GAME

Unless someone like Russell was covering, Chamberlain couldn't have been stopped if he didn't want to be. He didn't commit fouls. He didn't come out of games. He scored whenever he wanted to. He even won an assist title. Chamberlain could have adapted to any situation. But when faced with Russell in a few Game 7s (or other elimination games) Chamberlain rarely came out on top. Russell might have better teammates, other than the spring of 1967; on the other hand, Russell wasn't capable of scoring 50 points a night, yet alone 100. But for one game, especially if you had to have the win, he's the choice. These guys went head-to-head 142 times and Russell was the winner in 85 of them, or six out of 10 times. But statistics tell only part of the story, which brings us to...

ONE SERIES

These guys played for the Eastern Conference title six times in a nine-year span, and twice they met for the NBA championship. While each was in their prime with both in the league, Russell took home nine championships; Chamberlain just one. Sorry, Philly, (and San Francisco and Los Angeles), but Wilt takes home the stats and the awards, and thus if you're starting a fantasy team he's the choice. In real life, though, we'd give the nod to Bill Russell. Russell might not have had the stats, but the goal is to win, and in this case the Big Dipper has to be second best.

DOES THE 76ERS-CELTICS RIVALRY EVEN MATTER ANYMORE?

63 Once upon a time the Boston Celtics and Philadelphia 76ers were two of the signature teams in the NBA, staging meaningful games almost every season. In fact, even while the Bill Russell Celtics were winning the championship just about every season, the 76ers would represent a sizable speed bump. Russell and Wilt Chamberlain had the greatest individual rivalry; thus their teams weren't exactly pals.

In fact, Larry Bird and Julius Erving continued the rivalry into the 1980s, with their teams often representing the Eastern Conference in the championship series, and they even famously threw punches on a Friday night, November 9, 1984. It was early in the season, the 76ers were defending champs, and both teams were undefeated. Emotions were high, and late in the third quarter a fight ensued, leading to each star being ejected and later fined. The Celtics won the game, and later that year, the championship.

Ah, such fond memories. So what happened?

Well, to be blunt, when Bird and Erving retired and the teams stopped being good, the rivalry died down. What good is a rivalry if neither team has anything to play for?

From 1993 to 2001, the Celtics failed to win more than 36 games in a season. In that same time period the 76ers finished in last place twice and didn't start to win more than they'd lose until Allen Iverson's third season, 1998–99.

Plus, look at the players themselves. Russell vs. Chamberlain. Bird vs. Erving. Great stuff. What about Allen Iverson vs. Paul Pierce or Tyrone Hill vs. Antoine Walker? These guys weren't covering each other, and there were no epic playoff matchups. The Celtics and 76ers were no longer owning the Atlantic Division, either. Since the 76ers won the title in 1983 they have won two division championships, and in only one of those years were the Celtics any good.

The 2007–08 Celtics found a way to acquire Kevin Garnett and Ray Allen, and won the NBA championship, and with the 76ers getting Elton Brand and obviously improving, it could spark the rivalry again.

Rivalries still exist in sports, but nowadays Boston fans aren't too worried when the 76ers come to town, and when Philly is the host, the prime visiting team to boo is from Los Angeles, thanks to Kobe Bryant. The rivalry is gone...for now.

WHO DESERVES THE MOST BLAME FOR THE 9–73 SEASON?

64 Ever since that forgettable season, every time an NBA team is horrible, it gets compared to this sad-sack group that couldn't win double digits.

The dreadful 1972–73 76ers ended up with the worst record in NBA history, going 9–73. Since 1950, no team in the league has failed to finish a season with fewer than nine wins, or a winning percentage of .110. Awful, truly awful. The 76ers lost their first 15 games of the season and, after the calendar turned to 1973, would lose 20 straight and 34 of 35. Other than a magical February stretch with five wins in seven games, they actually lost 71 of 75 games!

So whose fault was it? The affable Fred Carter, who to this day professes to be the best player on the worst team ever, led the team in scoring, so he can't be the fall guy. But someone has to take the blame because, only six years earlier, the 76ers were arguably the greatest NBA team assembled.

BILLY CUNNINGHAM

The beloved Kangaroo Kid was a fan favorite as a part of the 1966–67 title team, being the number 4 overall pick in the 1965 draft, going to four All-Star games and later adding to his legend by coaching the 1982–83 team to the championship. But Cunningham also bolted for riches with the Carolina Cougars in the American Basketball Association before the wretched season. Was it worth it? Sure, Cunningham had no regrets, and no reason to feel guilty. He got paid, went back to the place near where he went to college at North Carolina, and was the ABA MVP in his first season. Only after being slowed by injuries the next year when the ABA's future was in jeopardy did Cunningham opt to come back to Philly for his final two seasons. Philly fans were happy to have him back and, surprisingly, showed no bitterness. Billy C had a Hall of Fame career, but if he had been on the 76ers in 1972–73 the team would have done a lot better than nine wins.

WILT CHAMBERLAIN

Wait, how could another of the greatest players in franchise history—maybe the best in league history—be blamed for this mess? Wilt got out of town only a year after winning the championship. It was a complicated scenario that resulted in one of the worst trades the team ever made. New general manager Dr. Jack Ramsay, a Philly native and really nice guy who led St. Joseph's University to a Final Four and who would eventually take the Portland Trail Blazers to the 1977 title against the 76ers, was forced to move Chamberlain to the Los Angeles Lakers for Darrall

Imhoff, Archie Clark, and Jerry Chambers. As the rumor goes, Chamberlain was once promised part ownership in the 76ers, but when one of the team's owners, Ike Richman, passed away, the other owner, Irv Kosloff, refused to honor the deal. Chamberlain threatened retirement, and with his contract having been restructured to a one-year deal, the 76ers took what they could get—which in this case wasn't much. While Clark and Imhoff were productive players, both were gone by 1972. Things went downhill from there. Ramsay would later dump more of the title team stars for little in return and become the team's coach, but the talent was seriously waning. And it all started when Wilt forced his way outta town.

ROY RUBIN

A fine college coach for 11 years at Long Island University, Rubin also authored a book about defense and taught clinics on the game. He couldn't turn down a three-year contract to coach in the NBA, starting with that miserable 1972–73 campaign. However, it was clear early on—from the introductory press conference when he admitted to not knowing who Hal Greer was, to when the players walked over the rookie coach when games began—that he was in over his head. It took 16 games for Rubin to get a win. For 105 days Rubin was the coach, and he went 4–47 in that time, beating only Buffalo, Houston, Kansas City, and Seattle, hardly strong teams, and all of which would be changing coaches soon as well. Rubin's problem was that he tried to lead the way he did in college, and rarely, if ever, ripped into his team, which sorely needed it. Being a large man, some good did come from this disastrous situation, as the added stress helped him lose 45 pounds along the way—though he still lost more games. He was mercifully replaced by Kevin Loughery, who at the time was one of the players. Loughery acted as a player-coach and fared a bit better than Rubin, actually directing five wins, though they all came in two weeks from Valentine's Day, 1973, through the end of February. Still, three of them were against good teams, including the eventual champion Knicks and division-winning Bucks. Go figure.

DON DEJARDIN

One could make the case that Rubin wasn't at fault at all, since he didn't have the horses and didn't make the mistake of hiring himself for the job, only of being the one entrusted with leading this collection. Rubin would never coach again, though he still fields interview requests when a current NBA team threatens the record. DeJardin, the general manager in 1972–73, actually kept his job a bit longer. Why is a mystery.

While numerous folks were at fault, he gets the ultimate blame for putting this crew together. He was responsible for Rubin as coach. And while DeJardin had taken over as GM from Ramsay in 1970 and had to deal with what was left behind, he is the one responsible for the drafting of Fred Boyd, Dana Lewis, and Al Henry with first-round selections. Only Boyd even played for the team in the disastrous season. DeJardin would go on to become a player agent for the likes of Gary Payton and Derrick Coleman and replaced as team GM by Pat Williams, who built the franchise back up. When people look back at the mess that was the league's last single-digit-win season, chances are they won't know who the GM was, but DeJardin is the main culprit.

WHY DOES PHILLY HATE KOBE BRYANT SO MUCH?

65 Kobe Bryant entered the 2007–08 season as one of the most prolific scorers in league history, averaging nearly 25 points per game.

By then he had won three scoring titles and was a part of three consecutive championship-winning teams with the Lakers. Philadelphia basketball fans applaud fine play and are smart enough to appreciate great players, and Bryant's father played with the 76ers in the 1970s. Kobe grew up in the area.

So why does Bryant get booed out of the building when he comes back to town?

The question doesn't have an easy answer, but here are some theories.

First of all, he's the enemy. He's not on the 76ers, nor has ever expressed interest in being on the 76ers. He's on a rival team, and not just another team Philly fans could care less about like Memphis or Sacramento, but a long-standing rival that won the 2001 NBA title against the 76ers with him on the court (and that's not to mention all the battles of the early 1980s). It's one thing for Philly fans to welcome back a native son for a somewhat meaningless regular season affair, but this was the Finals. Then again...

Bryant wasn't exactly aiming to be loved by the Philly fans for those 2001 Finals. In his words, he was "coming to Philly to cut their hearts out." Philly fans didn't take kindly to hearing that—can you blame them?

Another matter is that he's not really from Philly, and he doesn't take pride in the fact he grew up in the area. Maybe this is getting a bit too technical, but not everyone who says they are from Philly really is. There are many suburban areas surrounding the city, and some hard-core city folk take exception when a young lad who never had to take public transportation tries to act like he's from the town. Nothing about Bryant screams Philly. He doesn't have the attitude, the passion, doesn't live by Philadelphia code. Bryant went to Lower Merion high school in the ritzy Main Line section of the nearby suburbs, and probably played hoops in his back-yard. (In contrast, Wilt Chamberlain went to Overbrook High School in Philly and played street ball.) While Bryant was born in Philadelphia, his family moved to Italy when he was six, as Joe Jellybean Bryant joined a professional team there. The Bryants moved back to the Philadelphia area in 1991. When it was time for Bryant to look at colleges, it didn't seem like he gave the local Big 5 schools a second thought, even though his father attended LaSalle University. It's said Bryant would have attended Duke, had he not confidently jumped right from high school to the NBA.

Bryant isn't the only athlete from the Philly suburbs to make it big, but Phillies fans didn't boo Norristown's Mike Piazza with the same ferocity. Phillies fans didn't get the chance to boo Reggie Jackson, from Wyncote, but it's doubtful he would have been hated either. (Okay, the New York Rangers' Mike Richter was from Flourtown, and he was on a rival team, but how many fans even knew he was a local?) Bryant stands out as being from the Philly region and not welcomed back to town at all.

Nobody can dispute the success Bryant has had on the court or how talented he is, but unless he's on your team, do you *want* to like him? Bryant engineered the draft-day trade out of Charlotte in 1996, ostensibly to go to a big-market team not only for a better chance at winning, but for endorsement possibilities. He and Shaquille O'Neal had a much-publicized falling out while they were winning championships, eventually resulting in the likable O'Neal being traded to the Miami Heat. The theory was Bryant wanted to win a title on his own, thus getting the credit not as a sidekick, but a star. As of early 2008, it hasn't happened yet. Meanwhile, 76ers fans just longed to win. Some of the fans Bryant did have moved on after the star was accused of sexual assault. The case was later settled, with no guilt admitted. Did he do it? Who really knows? What can't be denied is that Bryant fits the mold of today's rich, pampered athlete, and for that even non-76ers fans dislike him. This might not be a Philly thing at all.

So why don't Philly fans like Kobe Bryant? All the above reasons have merit, but ultimately, he's not truly a Philadelphian, and plays for a rival.

WHO MAKES—AND MISSES—THE ALL-TIME 76ERS DREAM TEAM?

Young Philadelphia 76ers fans probably think the team has been around forever, but that's not officially true. The franchise, yes, has been around the longest of any NBA entrant, but not always in Philly. There was actually one season in which no NBA team played in the City of Brotherly Love. It was 1962–63: the Philadelphia Warriors were sold by Eddie Gottlieb to a San Francisco group before the season. There went Wilt Chamberlain out west, and a rich hoops town had to look elsewhere to follow the NBA. That didn't last long, though, as Irv Kosloff and Ike Richman bought the Syracuse Nationals early in 1963, and after the season moved the franchise to Philly.

The Nationals had entered the league when the league was born in 1949, and were very successful, becoming an annual playoff entrant and winning the championship in 1955. Dolph Schayes became a Hall of Famer in Syracuse, and like most Nationals he moved with the team to Philly, though he'd play only one more season. Since this is a book about Philadelphia arguments, you won't find much mention about the Nationals; and since the Warriors are no longer Philly's team, they aren't mentioned much either.

Even without piggybacking off the Nationals and Warriors, there is no shortage of terrific players who have worn the colors of the Philadelphia 76ers. If we were building one perfect team, here is how it would look. And boy, this team would win a whole lotta games.

66 CENTER: WILT CHAMBERLAIN (1959–1962 WITH THE WARRIORS, 1964–1968 WITH THE 76ERS)

What about: Moses Malone? There's been only one championship NBA team in Philly for 40 years, and Moses was the catalyst behind it. He played in Philly for only four seasons, and things went downhill for the team after his first campaign, but Malone was a statistical monster, averaging nearly 24 points per game and more than 13 rebounds. He won the league MVP in his first season as a 76er, as well as Finals MVP—and let's just say his confident "fo', fo', fo'" statement, while ultimately off by just one game, was very popular with Philly's atty-tude.

What about: Darryl Dawkins? If breaking backboards was a stat, Dawkins would have most everyone beat. Dawkins was drafted right out of high school, a year after Moses Malone helped blaze the trail, and while it took him a while to become a productive regular in the NBA, it eventually happened. Dawkins became more than a dunker by his third season in the league, and in his best season in Philly averaged 14.7 points and 8.7 rebounds in 1979–80.

Okay, so Dawkins was a little odd, naming his ferocious dunks all kinds of crazy names, and he once claimed to be from the planet Lovetron, where he spent the off-season practicing interplanetary funkmanship with his girlfriend Juicy Lucy. Ah, they don't make 'em like Darryl Dawkins anymore.

Yeah, but: That Chamberlain guy, the one with all the records, he was pretty good. What, you were expecting maybe Caldwell Jones here? Nobody has ever put up the statistics Sir Wilt did, and it's not even close. If only he were around today to tell us about them.

67 POWER FORWARD: CHARLES BARKLEY (1984–1992)

What about: Dolph Schayes? One of the greatest 50 players in NBA history, but he played a grand total of 24 games in Philly as a member of the home team. Everything else came with the Syracuse Nationals. Sure, it's the same franchise, but it's not Philly.

What about: Clarence Weatherspoon? He never got enough credit for how well he played in Philly, mainly because he had to replace Barkley, and 'Spoon wasn't his equal on or off the court. Similarly undersized and forced to guard taller, bigger players, Weatherspoon was also a top-10 overall pick who had to carry his teams. Problem was, his 76ers weren't very good, and he never appeared in a playoff game with the team in his tenure, which was

1992 through 1997. Weatherspoon's best statistical season in Philly was his second year, with 18.4 points and 10.1 rebounds, and after five-plus seasons of playing both forward spots he was dealt with Jimmy Jackson to Golden State for Joe Smith and Brian Shaw.

What about: Luke Jackson? The underrated Jackson was the fourth overall pick in the 1964 draft, a bruising 6'9" rebounder who did exactly what the 76ers needed. Jackson twice averaged a double-double over the course of an entire season, with his best numbers coming as a rookie with 14.8 points and 12.9 rebounds. When Wilt Chamberlain came back to town Jackson did less of both, but remained a key part of the 1966–67 title-winning team. He played his entire career with the 76ers, averaging 9.9 points and 8.8 rebounds per game.

Yeah, but: Barkley owned Philly while he was in town, for better or worse. Statistically, Barkley is one of the best power forwards in NBA history, one of four players ever to amass 20,000 points, 10,000 rebounds, and 4,000 assists. The Round Mound of Rebound managed to get his sizable butt near tons of missed shots, enough to average 8.6 boards per game as a rookie, then double digits every year after. In his third year in the league he was a man on a mission, garnering 14.6 rebounds per game. Oh, and he could score, too, finishing in the top 5 in scoring twice in his 76ers tenure. Only four men have scored more points in franchise history, and three of them are in the Hall of Fame

213

and Allen Iverson is on his way. Barkley was no angel, of course, but he managed to bridge the gap after the Dr. J era pretty well. And by the way; he wasn't 6'6". Try 6'4", maybe. Philly loves its overachievers.

68 SMALL FORWARD: JULIUS ERVING (1976–1987)

What about: Do you really think anyone else deserves serious consideration against Dr. J? We'll point out the other choices as well, just to be thorough. Chet Walker started at the three-spot for the 1966–67 team, and averaged more than 19 points and 8 rebounds per game. Walker was a consistent scorer for six years in Philadelphia, seven with the franchise. Also, Billy Cunningham was a small forward and a future Hall of Famer, but we're going to place him in the sixth-man category so he doesn't get dwarfed here.

Yeah, but: Um, Doctor J was pretty good. He dunked, he scored, he won a title. And he fought Larry Bird. Could Philly have asked for more?

Erving was exactly what the 76ers needed when they bought his contract from the New York Nets before the 1976–77 season. The American Basketball Association, where Erving made his bones as a magical dunker, was about to fold, and it was time to join the NBA. While in the ABA, Erving won two championships after being dealt by the Virginia Squires to New York. He had the look, the style, even the Afro, and Philly knew it was getting a superstar to lead them to a championship.

That didn't happen overnight, of course, but it eventually did. Erving once starred in a movie called *The Fish That Saved Pittsburgh.* Well, it can be argued that when the 76ers found a way to acquire Erving, he became The Doctor That Saved Philly's NBA team.

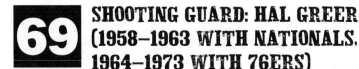

69 SHOOTING GUARD: HAL GREER (1958–1963 WITH NATIONALS, 1964–1973 WITH 76ERS)

What about: Hersey Hawkins? He played the first five seasons of his career with the 76ers, though he was actually drafted by the Los Angeles Clippers with the sixth overall pick in 1988. The 76ers acquired Hawkins for the draft rights to Charles Smith. Hawkins was a pure shooter and solid defender, one of the league's top rookies, and generally the number 2 scorer in the Charles Barkley years. Hawkins averaged better than 20 points per game twice in his Philly tenure, and was one of the league's best in three-point shooting and free throw percentage. He never scored like he did in Philly, though, after being dealt to Charlotte in the Dana Barros trade in 1993.

What about: Doug Collins? He was the first overall draft pick in 1973, and spurned other offers in the ABA to play with the 76ers. He didn't play much as a rookie, foreshadowing what would be an injury-plagued career, but he was

215

a pretty good scorer when healthy. Collins played parts of eight seasons with the 76ers, three of them near-full seasons, and averaged 17.9 points over his career while shooting 50 percent from the field. His best season came in 1975–76, when he averaged 20.8 points per game; and in 32 career playoff games he averaged 21.5 points per game. He also played in three All-Star games.

What about: Andrew Toney? He gets the final nomination over World B. Free and Fred Mad Dog Carter, but the truth is none of them get serious consideration. Toney was a master marksman who averaged 15.9 points per game in his career, though he's known more for the nickname the Boston Strangler, as some of his best games came against the team's biggest rival. Much of Toney's career, however, was marked by injury. Free, who changed his name from Lloyd to World B., was a scorer-for-hire who played the first three seasons of his career with the 76ers, arguably the worst of his career until he was just about through. Free averaged 16.3 points in his second year, but struggled in the playoffs. In 1980 with the San Diego Clippers he averaged more than 30 points per game. And Carter is best known for being the best player on the worst team in history, but other than averaging 20 points per game a few times for bad teams, his career in Philly wasn't noteworthy.

Yeah, but: Greer is the 76ers all-time leading scorer, with more than 21,000 points, and he was a consistent, durable player for 15 seasons in Syracuse and Philly from

1958–59 through the 1972–73 season. Sure, not all of his 21,000 points came in the City of Brotherly Love, but he won a title. Even just in his time in Philly, Greer was a terrific, underrated player, and he appeared in 10 straight All-Star games and was elected to the Basketball Hall of Fame in 1982. Greer was the consummate shooting guard who hit jump shots, was able to drive to the hoop, and could shut down opposing guards. He's also second in franchise history in assists and third in free throws attempted and made. While Wilt Chamberlain always made headlines in Philly, Greer was the soft-spoken star of the team, a well-respected gentleman who did his job and wasn't flashy about it. When Greer retired he was the NBA's all-time leader in games played. Philly's had some solid shooting guards, but Greer tops them all.

70 POINT GUARD: ALLEN IVERSON (1996–2006)

What about: Drafted in the second round of the 1978 draft, Maurice Cheeks wasn't supposed to end up one of the more underrated point guards in history, but when he retired in 1993 nobody had more steals and only four players had more assists. Cheeks was the consummate professional, a leader who let his game do the talking. About the only time he showed emotion was late in the championship-clinching game against the Lakers when he dunked and began to jump around in celebration.

Cheeks played 11 seasons in Philadelphia and was named to the league's all-defensive first team four consecutive seasons from 1983–86.

What about: Larry Costello and Wali Jones? They manned the point during the 1966–67 season, and while neither were big-time scorers or assist men, each played a key role for the team. Costello played for the Philadelphia Warriors and Syracuse Nationals, then was traded to the 76ers and actually had retired from the game in 1965. When 76ers coach Alex Hannum asked the six-time All-Star to play in 1966, Costello agreed, but missed half the season with a torn Achilles tendon. That opened the door for Jones to start, and the younger, more explosive player did a fine job, finishing second on the team to Wilt Chamberlain in assists per game. Jones was a Philly kid who went to Overbrook, and later Villanova University, and he played six seasons in Philadelphia.

Yeah, but: Iverson has been one of the most prolific scorers in NBA history, ranking third all-time in scoring average and winning MVP awards, and he led the 76ers to their only Finals appearance since 1983. While Cheeks did win a title, he had some help. Iverson went through numerous number 2 scorers in his Philly tenure and was often the only player the fans wanted to see. The Answer was the first overall pick of the 1996 draft, an obvious choice out of Georgetown, and he became the Rookie of the Year. Iverson was a polarizing figure with the 76ers, putting up great statistics but often disagreeing with management on, well, you name it. Iverson and coach Larry Brown had noted battles in their love-hate relationship, including the one about the star player missing practice. "We're talking about practice," Iverson said over and over again. It's a legendary monologue that made the rounds on *SportsCenter*, that's for sure.

71 SIXTH MAN: BOBBY JONES (1978–1986)

What about: Billy Cunningham? Younger 76ers fans, and by that we mean in their 40s, probably remember him for coaching the team that finally won it all in 1982–83, but The Kangaroo Kid was also a Hall of Fame player and one of the 50 greatest players in NBA history. So why isn't he the top sixth man or small forward in 76ers history? Cunningham wasn't always a sixth man. His best statistical seasons came as a starter, but as popular as he was, he's not going to beat out Julius Erving for those honors. Cunningham averaged more than 20 points and 10 rebounds per game in his NBA career, all spent in two terms with the 76ers, and was a key member of the title-winning 1966–67 team. He's the number 2 small forward and sixth man in 76ers history, but he gets the nod as best coach.

Yeah, but: Mere statistics don't do Bobby Jones justice— unless the number you're talking about is eight, for the number of times he was named to the NBA's All-Defense first team. Sure, Billy C scored and rebounded more, and won as many championships (one), but Jones was one of the quintessential sixth men of his era, along with Boston's Kevin McHale, and a crucial member of the 1982–83 team that zipped through the playoffs nearly unscathed. The 76ers always had scorers in the late 70s, guys like George McGinnis and World B. Free, but they didn't have a defensive stopper. Jones was that guy. The 76ers acquired him from the Denver Nuggets for McGinnis, a sure sign the 76ers "got it" and knew what they were missing. Jones averaged more than 10 points and five rebounds in his 76ers career, which lasted eight seasons, and he was one of the most accurate field goal shooters ever, currently ranked number 10 at .558. Jones was always a Philly favorite because he'd hustle and dive, do all the little things that didn't show up in box scores, and he was unselfish. He overcame a lot in his career, including asthma, occasional epileptic seizures, and a chronic heart disorder, and was one of the most respected players in the league.

FLYIN' HIGH AGAIN

WHAT WERE THE FIVE MOST MEMORABLE WINS IN FLYERS HISTORY?

72 Sure, it's been quite some time since the Flyers played a memorable game, at least according to the arguments listed below. The Flyers have actually been one of the most successful regular season teams in the NHL since their inception for the 1967–68 season, being one of the expansion teams to join the league. The Flyers won the Western Division that season, and seven years later would become champions of the league. It's not surprising the top games in team history would be in the years around 1974–1976, when the team was at its best.

5. STANLEY CUP FINALS, GAME 6 VS. OILERS—MAY 28, 1987

The Flyers and Edmonton Oilers met two seasons earlier for hockey's prize, and the Oilers won that series in five games. In the finale against beleaguered goalie Bob Froese, the Oilers scored early and often in an 8–3 win. The Oilers again had a 3–1 lead in the 1987 Finals. This time the Flyers didn't fold in Game 5, getting the final three goals of the game from Doug Crossman, Pelle Eklund, and

Rick Tocchet to send the series back to Philadelphia. Again the Flyers fell behind in a potential clinching loss, this time 2–0. The Flyers were getting waxed in their own building, getting outshot 15–5 in the opening period. Lindsay Carson scored a second-period goal to halve the lead, and in the final period Brian Propp and J. J. Daigneault scored 84 seconds apart to send the Spectrum crowd home happy. The Flyers lost Game 7 in Edmonton, but played valiantly, and Ron Hextall walked away with playoff MVP honors.

4. STANLEY CUP FINALS, GAME 6 AT SABRES—MAY 27, 1975

The Flyers won their second—and still last—Stanley Cup in Western New York. Up 3–2 in the series after taking Game 5 by a resounding 5–1 score, the Flyers went back to Buffalo to finish things off. The series was notable not only for the Flyers win, but because of an odd Game 3 in which fog encompassed the ice in Buffalo's Memorial Auditorium. It was warm that spring day in Buffalo, and the building didn't have air conditioning. The Sabres won the game in overtime, 5–4. Maybe the Flyers would have won Game 7 at home anyway, but armed with the chance to end the series in six games, they got a Bob Kelly goal just 11 seconds into the third period, and Bill Clement scored late in the 2–0 win.

3. STANLEY CUP FINALS. GAME 2 AT BRUINS—MAY 9, 1974

The big, bad Bruins had won Stanley Cups in 1970 and 1972, while the young Flyers were an expansion team in their seventh season of existence. The Bruins had Bobby Orr, Phil Esposito, and quite an aura about them. The Flyers were in their first Finals. The Bruins took Game 1 3–2, getting an Orr goal with only 22 seconds remaining. The Flyers weren't demoralized, but when they fell behind 2–0 in Game 2, certainly things weren't looking good. Then Bobby Clarke tipped home a Bill Flett shot in the second period, and the 2–1 score stuck into the final minute of regulation. With Bernie Parent pulled for an extra skater, the Flyers dumped the puck into the Boston zone, Rick MacLeish fed a wide-open Moose Dupont, and his slapshot tied the game in the final minute. Into overtime the game went, and 12 minutes in Clarke tipped home his own rebound over Bruins goalie Gilles Gilbert and celebrated. It was finally a series.

2. BEATING SOVIET RED ARMY—JANUARY 11, 1976

One has to remember that, back in 1976, relations were different between the USA and Russia than they are today. The U.S. Olympic hockey team wouldn't topple the Russians for four more years. And this Soviet Red Army team was really good, seemingly invincible. The Flyers, off to a splendid start and hoping for a third straight Stanley

Cup, wanted this game badly, as they were representing the NHL (even though the NHL didn't approve of the Flyers' roughhousing tactics). This Soviet team had already beaten the New York Rangers and Boston Bruins and tied the eventual Cup champion Montreal Canadiens, while another Soviet team had won three of four games against NHL teams. Bobby Clarke, guilty of slashing a star Russian player in the 1972 series against NHL All-Stars, was quoted as saying, "I hate the sons of bitches." Coach Fred Shero said he'd been looking forward to the game for months, and would later say it was the biggest game in the history of the franchise, a must-win game. Of course, these Flyers and the Soviets played very different styles. The Flyers were tough, took penalties, and hit hard. When Flyers defenseman Ed Van Impe elbowed a Russian player in the first period, it prompted the Russians to leave the ice in protest. After a 17-minute delay and a two-minute penalty assessed for delay of game, the Flyers quickly scored on a Reggie Leach tip-in. Rick MacLeish, Joe Watson, and Larry Goodenough also scored in the 4–1 win as the Flyers outshot the enemy 49–13. Flyers defenseman Joe Watson said the win compared to winning the Stanley Cup.

1. STANLEY CUP FINALS, GAME 6 VS. BRUINS—MAY 19, 1974

After the big win in Boston in Game 2, the Flyers took the next two games at home to build a 3–1 series lead. In

Game 5 at Boston, the Bruins pushed the Flyers all over the ice, scoring an early goal en route to a 5–1 rout. The Flyers felt they had to win Game 6 on home ice, knowing that the seventh game was in Boston. Kate Smith was brought out to sing another stirring rendition of "God Bless America," and the crowd was in a frenzy before the game even began. MacLeish and Dupont again hooked up for a critical goal, this time early in the first period. MacLeish won the faceoff back to Dupont, who took an ordinary shot from the right point on net. MacLeish, while battling for position with Bruins defensemen Dallas Smith and Carol Vadnais, felt the puck hit his leg, then his stick, and watched it soar past Gilles Gilbert for a 1–0 lead. Bernie Parent had a lead he'd never relinquish, playing brilliantly. When Orr took a hooking penalty against Clarke with 2:22 to go, the Flyers knew they were about to win their first Stanley Cup. Joe Watson held the puck behind Parent's net as the clock ran out, and just after 5:00 p.m. ET on May 19, 1974, the Flyers had won it all.

WHAT WERE THE FIVE BEST INDIVIDUAL PLAYOFF YEAR PERFORMANCES IN FLYERS HISTORY?

73 It's been a long time since the Flyers won a Stanley Cup, but they do have a pair of wins to their credit, and have been back to the Finals five times since. Overall in their 40 years of existence, Philly has made the playoffs 32 times and won 38 series, losing 30. In total games, the Flyers have won 189 times, lost 174. While only two of those playoff runs ended up with the Flyers hoisting the Cup, there have been memorable playoff performances since. Bobby Clarke had four assists in a playoff game against Boston, one of five Flyers to hold that mark. Tim Kerr scored four goals in one period against the Rangers, three of them on the power play. And our favorite Hammer, Dave Schultz, once had 42 penalty minutes in a game against the Maple Leafs. And we're not even counting the terrific goaltending play yet.

The NHL playoffs are like their own season, really. Some would say they last nearly as long as the regular season in the first place, and that the regular season is meaningless because it guarantees nothing in terms of postseason success. This is true. The Flyers have made numerous long playoff runs, and have seen some extraordinary second-season performances, so many that Bobby Clarke, the franchise's leader in playoff games, points, and assists, doesn't make this list statistically with a noteworthy enough performance. Let's count down the top five.

5. BRIAN PROPP, 1987

4. PELLE EKLUND, 1987

The Flyers' 1987 run to the Finals against Edmonton is generally credited to Ron Hextall, who carried the team and won the league's playoff MVP award, but Propp and Eklund played a major role with their offensive playmaking. Someone had to score the goals, and it wasn't going to be leading scorer Tim Kerr, who was out the final two series with one of his many injuries, this time a dislocated shoulder. Propp, who would finish his underrated Flyers career second in playoff points, with 112 in only 116 games, set a club mark with 28 points in the four rounds against the Rangers, Islanders, Canadiens, and Oilers. In Game 5 of the Finals at Edmonton, with the Flyers needing a win to keep the series alive, Propp assisted on all four Flyers goals in a 4–3 win. While Propp was a veteran in the playoffs for the eighth time, Eklund was a young, playmaking center from Sweden in his second playoffs, finally playing a major role on the club. Eklund, a gifted skater and passer, registered 20 assists in 26 playoff games that year, plus seven goals. Only Wayne Gretzky tallied more assists that playoff year. Eklund's 20 assists remain a team record.

3. REGGIE LEACH, 1976

Leach scored 19 goals in the 1976 playoffs, and to put this in perspective, nobody has broken the record since. That's right, Leach scored 19 goals in 16 playoff games, and while the season ended with a Montreal Canadiens sweep in the Finals, ending Philly's two-year run as Stanley Cup champs, Leach was awarded the Conn Smythe Trophy as playoff MVP, the first time a player on a losing team had won it. Leach scored five goals in the May 6 Game 5 clincher against the Bruins, despite getting drunk the night before. In fact, coach Fred Shero didn't want to play Leach, but was convinced by Clarke. Leach would also play well in the 1980 playoff run but he never had a goal-scoring postseason to top this one. Nobody ever has.

2. RON HEXTALL, 1987

A year after the Flyers lost Pelle Lindbergh to a tragic car accident, the team found a worthy on-ice replacement in Hextall. It didn't know it right away, however, as Hextall was no lock to even make the team. The rookie made it, played with poise and passion, and led the club to a terrific playoff season, one that ultimately ended with a Game 7 loss to the powerful Edmonton Oilers. Nobody was blaming Hextall for the loss. Without him, the Flyers would have gone nowhere. Hextall won 15 games that postseason, with a 2.77 goals against average. He shut out the rival Rangers twice in the first round, endured some rough moments in the Islanders series, which went seven games, then really shined against the defending champion Canadiens, as a number of key Flyers were injured. Hextall played poorly in the Game 2 loss and was pulled for Chico Resch. How would he play in Game 3 at Montreal? The Flyers fell behind 2–0 in the first period, but Hextall had made 19 saves to keep the club in the game. The Flyers came back and won, and took the series in six games, with Hextall carrying the club, especially in the three wins at the Forum. The powerful Oilers awaited, and took three of the first four games, but Hextall got the Flyers back to Edmonton for Game 7. He lost, but won the Conn Smythe Trophy anyway, pretty significant considering it was only the second time that had been done (Leach was first), and the Oilers had Wayne Gretzky, Jari Kurri, and a dynamic offense.

1. BERNIE PARENT, 1974

It's tough to imagine the Flyers winning either of their Stanley Cups without Parent, who won the Conn Smythe Trophy as playoff MVP in both 1974 and 1975. Each Cup was won in a shutout with Parent at the top of his game. However, the 1973–74 season stands out more. Parent had been reacquired before the season, after a year-plus in

Toronto. The Flyers had won only one playoff series before the 1973 season; Doug Favell played capably but didn't carry the team. Parent carried the team. In the opening round against the Atlanta Flames he allowed one goal in each of the first three games, then started the New York Rangers series with a shutout. In the Finals against Boston, Parent held strong in the Game 2 overtime win, then stifled the team with Phil Esposito and Bobby Orr back in Philadelphia the next two games, allowing three goals total. In the wondrous Game 6, Parent allowed nothing, for a 1–0 win. In the playoffs he permitted 35 goals in 17 games, barely two per game, for a 2.02 goals against average, and had a .933 save percentage. Most importantly, though, he registered the 12 wins needed to take the Cup.

WHAT WERE THE FLYERS' FIVE BEST TRADES?

74 Most of the top Flyers on the Stanley Cup winning teams came from the draft. Bobby Clarke was a second-rounder in 1969, and later in that draft came Dave Schultz and Don Saleski. Bill Clement and Bob Kelly came with the team's first two picks the next year, and the fine 1972 draft featured Bill Barber with the seventh overall pick, plus Tom Bladon and Jimmy Watson.

When it came to trades, the Flyers have generally been just as astute in mining for talent. Most of the team's top trades came early in franchise history, when building for the Stanley Cup wins: Barry Ashbee, Bernie Parent, and Reggie Leach came via trades, as did Rick MacLeish, Moose Dupont, and Ross Lonsberry. The Flyers haven't made many memorable trades since then, because for a deal to not be forgotten there had to be major impact. People on the streets of Philly don't talk about the big Sami Kapanen trade of 2003, because while Kapanen has been a nice player, he hasn't been a great one. The players in the top trades either won Cups or had long, distinguished Flyers careers. So let's see what those best deals were.

5. DARRYL EDESTRAND AND LARRY MCKILLOP TO HERSHEY (AHL) FOR BARRY ASHBEE—MAY 22, 1970

Nobody knew at the time how significant this deal would be, as Ashbee had logged many miles in the minor leagues with the American Hockey League's Hershey Bears. This was one of the first trades new general manager and former coach Keith Allen made—but why acquire Ashbee, then 31? Edestrand would go on to play 455 NHL games, McKillop none, but what did Allen see? Ashbee gave the young Flyers grit and leadership from the back line, something they desperately needed. Ashbee would soon become a beloved player and was named to the league's All-Star second team in 1973–74. His playing career sadly ended in the playoffs that season, when Rangers defenseman Dale Rolfe's shot inadvertently hit Ashbee in the right eye, causing severe damage. Ashbee was taken from the Madison Square Garden ice on a stretcher and never played again. He became an assistant coach the next year. In April 1977 he was diagnosed with leukemia and died a month later, one of the revered heroes in team history. The team's best defenseman award is named for him, and the annual Flyers Wives Fight for Lives campaign, which raises money for leukemia research, was also dedicated in his honor.

4. LARRY WRIGHT, AL MACADAM, AND 1974 FIRST-ROUND PICK TO CALIFORNIA FOR REGGIE LEACH—MAY 24, 1974

The Flyers' first Stanley Cup team wasn't particularly longing for more offense, but when Bobby Clarke's old friend and linemate from Flin Flon, Manitoba, became available in trade, the Flyers pounced. Leach was acquired a week after the team won the 1974 Cup. MacAdam played only five games with the Flyers as a rookie, and would go on to play in two All-Star games and win a Masterson Trophy with the Golden Seals, Cleveland Barons, Minnesota North Stars, and Vancouver Canucks, but Leach was the key to the deal. With the California Golden Seals and Boston Bruins, his first three full seasons he scored 58 goals. His first year in Philly he used his blistering slap shot to score 45 goals, and the next year he set what remains a franchise record with 61 goals. In the playoffs that year Leach was the best player in hockey, scoring 19 times in 16 games—even though the season ended with a sweep at the hands of the Montreal Canadiens—and winning the Conn Smythe Trophy for playoff MVP. Even later in his career, when properly motivated and sober, Leach remained a terrific goal scorer.

3. FRED SHERO TO THE RANGERS FOR 1978 FIRST-ROUND PICK—JUNE 2, 1978

Coach Shero had kind of worn out his welcome in Philly, with the 1977–78 season being the end for him. The Bruins swept the Flyers from the playoffs in 1977 and followed it up with a series win in five games in the semifinals. No coach has a better winning percentage in Flyers history, and certainly no other coach has won a Stanley Cup, but at the time Shero even said the Flyers needed a change, whether they realized it or not. So, on May 18, 1978, Shero submitted a letter of resignation to Flyers officials. The team refused it. To make a long story short, the Flyers got wind of Shero, who had a year left on his contract, wanting to go to the Rangers to be coach and GM. The Flyers didn't like it. This was a major rival. A few weeks later, realizing Shero couldn't come back to Philly, and with the Rangers worrying about tampering charges being filed, the teams worked out a deal, and Philly got the Rangers' first-round pick, number 7 overall, and cash to pay for him. The player became Ken Linseman. The Rat, as he was affectionately called, had three-plus good seasons in Philly and became a fan favorite with his scrappy play, resembling Bobby Clarke. In 1981–82, Linseman tallied 68 assists and registered 275 penalty minutes, an odd combination, but Linseman was a pain in the butt for opponents. The Flyers moved him after that season to Hartford in the Mark Howe trade, which is also one of the best deals in club history. Why is this deal better? Shero was leaving anyway, and for the rival Rangers. The Flyers got Linseman, and eventually Howe, for him. Bon voyage.

2. MARK RECCHI AND 1995 THIRD-ROUND PICK TO MONTREAL FOR JOHN LECLAIR, ERIC DESJARDINS, AND GILBERT DIONNE— FEBRUARY 9, 1995

Recchi was a terrific scorer for the Flyers, netting back-to-back 100-point seasons after the Flyers got him from Pittsburgh, and he would remain productive in Montreal, but the Flyers got two building blocks in return. LeClair played left wing in Philly for 10 seasons, scoring 50 or more goals three times and moving into the number 5 spot in team history for goals. Desjardins played the rest of his fine career in the orange and black, ending up the number 2 scorer among defensemen in team history, behind only Mark Howe. Seven times Desjardins was honored with the team's Barry Ashbee Trophy for top defenseman. Dionne never scored a goal in 22 Flyers games, but it doesn't matter, considering the other parts. Another best part of this trade: Recchi returned to the Flyers in March 1999 in a deal for Dainius Zubrus and had five more 20-goal campaigns for the Flyers.

1. 1973 FIRST-ROUND PICK AND FUTURE CONSIDERATIONS TO TORONTO FOR BERNIE PARENT AND 1973 SECOND-ROUND PICK— MAY 15, 1973

Parent was one of the original Flyers, getting plucked out of the 1967 expansion draft from Boston along with fellow goalie Doug Favell. Both were Bruins, and they'd share the Flyers goaltending job for a few years, though Parent was clearly the number 1 choice. Midway through the 1971 season, desperate for offense, the Flyers dealt fan favorite Parent to the Maple Leafs with a draft pick for Mike Walton, Bruce Gamble, and a first-round pick. Fans weren't pleased. Teammates weren't pleased. However, Walton was dealt to Boston that day for Rick MacLeish, and that turned out all right. Two years later, after tiring of Favell as the goaltender, Parent was reacquired from Toronto. Favell was the future consideration, and the draft pick sent to the Maple Leafs became Bob Neely, who played 283 career games. But who cares? Parent led the immediate charge to a pair of Stanley Cup wins, winning playoff MVP in each season, and ended up in the Hall of Fame.

IS THE LINDROS TRADE THE WORST IN FLYERS HISTORY?

 The Flyers have actually been a pretty smart franchise when it comes to making trades. While there is no shortage of very good or great trades since the team came into being, how many truly bad trades can you find?

Certainly dealing Bernie Parent in 1971 was not a popular thing to do, but Rick MacLeish came back in the deal and Parent returned to lead the club to a few Stanley Cup wins. The 1978 deal that send Tom Bladon, Orest Kindrachuck, and Ross Lonsberry to Pittsburgh for a first-round draft pick who became Behn Wilson seemed one-sided. But the Flyers moved former Stanley Cup pieces who were on the decline, and Wilson, while mostly an underachiever, did end up second only to Bladon in scoring by a defenseman in Flyers history, before Mark Howe and Eric Desjardins came along and pushed him to fourth. In recent years, the Adam Oates trade deadline deal to Washington, which sent numerous high draft picks, didn't quite work out, but it didn't set the franchise back much. See, these trades really aren't that bad.

Now, that Eric Lindros trade: how did that work out?

The Quebec Nordiques made Lindros the first overall draft pick in 1991, and wisely so, even though he didn't want to play there. Lindros was a big kid, physically larger than most, and with terrific playmaking abilities. His talent couldn't be denied, and really, even with the Flyers, it never was. The guy was going to be a star. But Lindros was also trouble from the beginning, becoming embroiled in controversy in junior hockey, refusing to play for a team in Sault Saint Marie, then balking at playing in Quebec when he was drafted. The team worked out trades with the Flyers and the Rangers, and eventually an arbitrator ruled in favor of the Flyers. Looking back, was that such a good thing for the Flyers?

The Flyers sent six players to Quebec, plus two first-round draft picks and a cool $15 mil in cash, all for this special player. The Quebec franchise moved to the U.S. and became the Colorado Avalanche, and one of the six, Peter Forsberg, would actually end up being a more special player than Lindros! Also ironically, Forsberg played for the Flyers in his later years, well after Lindros had left. In Colorado, Forsberg helped lead the Avalanche to eight division titles and two Stanley Cups. Each time the Avalanche won a Cup, fans in Philly squirmed in their seats. Ron Hextall was in the deal. So were Chris Simon, Mike Ricci, Kerry Huffman, and Steve Duchesne, and all played in the NHL, to various levels of success.

The Lindros deal might have seemed like a good idea at the time, because nobody knew just how good Forsberg would be, and it was believed Hextall was on the downside of his career. Forsberg is ticketed for the Hall of Fame, and Hextall actually came back to Philly a few years later and was very good. Had Lindros been on the ice more, maybe Philly fans wouldn't be able to look back with such negativity at the deal.

If Stanley Cups are the ultimate measure of a trade's effectiveness, then the Lindros trade was a big bust. The Flyers never did win a Cup with him, though the Flyers did make it to the Finals in 1997 to face the Red Wings, but never won a game. So, the Lindros era, while it did feature an MVP award and a lot more points than games played, never did result in the success the Flyers expected. And considering who was in that deal, that was the only reasonable goal.

In the end, the Flyers can't be faulted for wanting Lindros's talent, but they certainly paid too steep a price to get the entire package. Had Lindros led the Flyers to the pinnacle of hockey and drunk from the Cup one more time, it would have all been worth it. For a franchise that has not made horrible trades, the Lindros trade stands out.

WHAT IS LINDROS'S LEGACY IN PHILLY?

76 We've established that expectations were so sky-high for Lindros, it would have been hard for him to reach them, but all the good that came from his numbers on the ice got over-shadowed by the bad. And there was plenty of bad. So how will Philly fans remember Lindros?

THE DEALS

Since Peter Forsberg, the Hall of Fame prize draft pick of the Lindros deal, eventually came to Philly and had no more success in the playoffs than the Big E, it's likely the trade will forever be remembered—but not as Lindros's legacy. If a team has a chance to get a player of his stature, it's normally worth going for it. Of course, Flyers fans also remember the trade that sent Lindros packing. Years after the Flyers fought so hard to get Lindros away from the Rangers, who also had worked out a deal with the Quebec Nordiques, now the Flyers were desperate for the Rangers to take him on.

THE INFIGHTING

Lindros seemed to always be hurt, so naturally he came to question the training staff on more than one occasion for misdiagnosing his injuries. While there might be something to a claim or two, it's still not the proper thing for a franchise player—and team captain—to do. When Lindros's contract ran out and he became a restricted free agent, he turned down what seemed like a reasonable deal from Flyers icon/general manager Bobby Clarke, with the contentious negotiations becoming public knowledge. Clarke made the offer more for appearance's sake and to let the fans know he was trying to build a winner. However, it was clear Clarke just wanted Lindros out of town, whatever the cost, and the franchise player demanded a trade as well. (Lindros's teammates didn't seem too sad to see him go, either.) Lindros ended up on the Rangers in a trade for Kim Johnsson, Pavel Brendl, Jan Hlavac, and a draft pick, but let's just say that wasn't worth it either. Really, the Lindros era also took a toll on Clarke, whose playing career was the stuff of dreams. As an administrator, he took grief for Lindros and was viewed as a failure.

FAMILY INVOLVEMENT

When the Lindros era ended, Clarke was quoted as saying he should have never let Lindros's family become as involved as they did with his professional life, but it was too late. Lindros was labeled as difficult even before he turned pro, spurning two teams that had drafted him, and while with the Flyers Clarke became tired of reading quotes in the media from Lindros's parents, defending their son. Rumor has it his parents were involved with everything involving their son and the team, even which lines he should play on and which players the team should acquire to play with their son. Said Clarke, "We don't want his mom and dad. We've had enough of them."

INJURIES

Ah, what was it first: the knee problem in his rookie season that cost him 21 games? In year two he missed nearly as many, though he was more productive. Still, no playoffs. In 1996–97 a groin injury was the cause of missed games. Lindros's first concussion came the following season, and there would be more. Later in 1999 in Nashville, Lindros nearly died when he suffered a collapsed lung, and wouldn't play again that season. By the time he left Philly, he had suffered at least three concussions.

THE SCOTT STEVENS HIT

The last time Lindros suited up as a Flyer came in Game 7 of the conference finals against the New Jersey Devils, in the 2000 playoffs. The Flyers had beaten the Sabres and the Penguins without Lindros, but now he was finally healthy and ready to go by Game 6. The Flyers, who had a 3–1 series lead without Lindros, fell in Game 5 and welcomed the star back for Game 6, which was a 2–1 loss. It was on to Game 7, but early on Lindros would exit. Devils enforcer Scott Stevens drilled Lindros with a legal shoulder hit to the head, and Lindros hit the ice with a thud and was taken off the ice. The Flyers lost the game and the series, the hit became legendary, and Lindros never played for the Flyers again.

PLAYOFF FAILURE

Lindros played eight seasons in Philadelphia, and led the team to the postseason five times. Is that enough? The haul to acquire Lindros rivals any deal in hockey history, including the Wayne Gretzky trade, and the players dealt for him won Stanley Cups. Lindros did not. While we can all focus on the injuries, his attitude, questionable behavior, and the damage done to the organization and Clarke, the bottom line is he was supposed to deliver Stanley Cups to Philly, and never did.

That's his unfortunate legacy.

IS BOBBY CLARKE ULTIMATELY LOVED OR HATED IN PHILLY?

77 As a player, Bobby Clarke was one of the best Philly had ever seen. He overcame diabetes to get drafted by the Flyers in the second round in 1969 and became an instant hit in Philly. He was tough, gritty, determined, his work ethic was second to none, and he had one thing on his mind: winning.

As a player, Bobby Clarke did win. The Flyers won a pair of Stanley Cups in 1974 and 1975, and Clarke was the captain and unquestioned leader of those teams. Clarke owns the franchise record for career points, by a wide margin, and is tops in points for postseason as well. He's a Hall of Fame player and arguably one of the top 20 players in league history.

While a generation of Flyers fans remember Bobby Clarke for all the good in the 1970s and early in the 1980s, there's another generation that never got to see the feisty player on the ice. All it knows about Bob Clarke—the retired adult who chopped off the y in his name to sound older—is that he was in the team's front office for nearly 20 years, and in that time never delivered a Stanley Cup. The first few seasons as GM went okay, with two trips to the Finals that ended with losses to the Edmonton Oilers. Things generally went downhill after that, however, with the Eric Lindros era placing a cloud over Clarke's tenure off the ice, even though he wasn't in charge when the trade was made. Clearly the Clarke-as-GM era was not as successful as the one when he played; though in fairness, Flyers teams were still making the playoffs every season. It's not like the Flyers had become the Washington Capitals. Still, Clarke did deserve blame for how the Lindros situation played out, and he didn't make things better.

In fact, by the time Clarke resigned from his role as GM early in a disastrous 2006–07 season, arguably the worst and most embarrassing in club history, it looked like the game had passed Clarke by. He wasn't an astute talent evaluator anymore and admitted he didn't know much about the draft or making trades. Assistant Paul Holmgren, also a tough former Flyers player, was the one behind the scenes making the key moves like trades and evaluating talent. How could nobody higher up in the Flyers front office see that Bob the administrator wasn't even close to the same as Bobby the player?

So is Clarke loved or hated in Philly these days? By the time the Lindros era wound down in 2000, Clarke wouldn't even present the team's yearly MVP trophy at center ice of games anymore, because of negative reaction from fans.

Ultimately, though, Clarke will be remembered fondly, and fans will forgive and forget his title-less reign as GM.

All it takes is for the Flyers to get really good again and give fans something to cheer about. New villains will always be found in Philadelphia, the city where fans demand excellence and let you hear it if it doesn't come, and time should heal this wound.

DID LEON STICKLE COST THE FLYERS A STANLEY CUP?

78 The short answer is no: contrary to popular opinion, he did not. Veteran linesman Stickle clearly missed an obvious offside call in the first period of the sixth and final game of the 1980 Stanley Cup Finals, and New York's Duane Sutter scored a big goal, but folks, it was only the first period, and there was plenty of hockey to be played!

While Flyers fans still whine to this day about the worst official's call in Philly history—and it is—the truth of the matter is, the Flyers tied the game at 2–2 later in the first period. Sure, both Islanders goals in that period were dubious, this first one coming on what appeared to be a high stick, but this game was far from over. In fact, it went to overtime. The infamous offside goal was not the one that decided the game, the series, or the season. It was just an unfortunate play that became historic.

Flyers officials were mad after the game, from owner Ed Snider saying the officials had it in for his team to coach Pat Quinn noting officials shouldn't have such a strong influence in such a key game. They had reason to be angry, as the Flyers felt they were the better team and would have gotten to play Game 7 on home ice had Game 6 turned out differently. But Stickle wasn't the one who took penalties, missed open nets, didn't convert on 2-on-1s, and let in goals.

Here's what happened on the play in question: the Islanders' Clark Gillies was the one who skated into the Flyers zone in a 1–1 game, dropping the puck behind him for Butch Goring. The problem was, the puck clearly went past the blue line, maybe as much as two feet. It was clear to Flyers players this was an offside, and to the announcers on the rare CBS broadcast (it was a Sunday afternoon). Flyers players began to let up on the play, assuming Stickle, who was in perfect position to make the call, would actually make it. He didn't. Goring found Sutter on the side of the net and he beat goalie Pete Peeters top shelf. There was no call, but Brian Propp scored soon after to tie the game anyway. Sure, it could have given the Flyers the lead, but it's impossible to predict what would have happened had the offside goal been disallowed.

The Islanders scored twice in the second period to take a 4–2 lead, but by the middle of the third period Bob Dailey and John Paddock had scored goals to tie the game at 4–4. The resilient Flyers certainly weren't playing as if they held a grudge over the events of the opening period.

The overtime goal that won the first of four Stanley Cups for the Islanders was a clean play, with winger Bob Nystrom taking a John Tonelli pass and deflecting it past Peeters for the winner seven minutes into overtime. The

Flyers had plenty of chances earlier in overtime to win the game against Islanders goalie Billy Smith, but failed to beat him.

The bottom line is, Stickle made a big mistake in not blowing the whistle on the offside, and later he'd even admit he'd blown the call, but he's not the reason the Flyers lost.

DID KATE SMITH REALLY HELP THE FLYERS WIN?

79 It seemed an odd pairing, to say the least. Kate Smith was one of America's most beloved entertainers for 50 years, on radio and TV, and with a recording career that began in 1926. What did she know about hockey?

Probably nothing, and after watching the Broad Street Bullies, she probably didn't want to know. Professional hockey had been around for decades by the 1960s, but it's hard to believe Smith was much of a fan. Unbeknownst to her, the Flyers and Smith would begin a unique relationship on December 11, 1969, when Flyers vice president Lou Scheinfeld decided to shake things up and play something other than "The Star Spangled Banner" before a home game with Toronto. Looking for a patriotic song to wake the fans up, he chose Smith's rendition of Irving Berlin's "God Bless America." The Flyers were struggling in their third season, Bobby Clarke's rookie year, and whether or not the new song worked can never be measured, but the Flyers beat the Maple Leafs 6–3.

A few games later, with the team stuck on five wins, Scheinfeld opted to bring Smith's song out again, and the

Flyers won. A good luck charm was born, and every so often, without planning and warning, the home crowd would hear Smith's taped voice from years earlier and, far more often than not, the end result was a win. Smith, then 66 years old, even showed up in person at the Spectrum for the 1973 season opener against Toronto, a 2–0 Flyers win.

When the Flyers brought Smith out for Game 6 of the 1974 Finals, needing only a win over the Boston Bruins to win the Stanley Cup, the team's record with her singing either live or on tape was an astounding 35-3-1. Smith wasn't just a good luck charm; she was money in the bank, and the Flyers were champions. For whatever emotional reason, when Smith sang, the Flyers won.

Then again, the Flyers had a great team in 1974, and again the following playoff season when Smith sang live before Game 7 of the semifinals against the New York Islanders, a series in which the Flyers won the first three games, then lost three straight before really needing Smith's help. It worked, of course! After the Stanley Cup years, however, Smith's beautiful voice wasn't such a sure thing. Her final record was 69–13–3, but it's almost irrelevant in the big picture. Smith died in 1986, and a statue in her honor was dedicated outside the Spectrum in 1987. Her voice is still heard every so often before home games, even after her passing. One of the most memorable times since then came before the 2001 opener, not long after the September 11 attacks on America, when

Smith and Lauren Hart were joined together for a special mixed duet.

Kate Smith didn't score any goals for the Flyers, nor did she prevent any, but whenever her powerful, inspirational voice played before a game, you knew something special was happening. Three of the four times she appeared in person at the Spectrum, the home team was victorious. If her dulcet tones helped get the players motivated and excited as the fans got, then yes, Smith did help the Flyers win.

WHO WERE THE FIVE TOUGHEST FLYERS?

80 Look, they were named the Broad Street Bullies, so there had to be some pretty tough members of the team. There were. The Flyers' brand of hockey might not have been what the NHL wanted in the early 1970s, but it worked, leading to a pair of Stanley Cup championships. Being tough wasn't solely about fighting, but it didn't hurt. If fighting was the only criteria, the Flyers would have way too many players good at this part of the game to narrow this list.

Some great fighters have come through town, from the early days when Dave Schultz, Moose Dupont, Bob Kelly, Gary Dornhoefer, and Don Saleski were the big names, to the 1980s when Dave Brown, Glen Cochrane, and Ed Hospodar roamed the ice. Even in the 1990s, as the NHL tried to distance itself from the old days of brawling, Dan Kordic, Ryan McGill, Shawn Antoski, and Craig Berube picked up the slack.

What about the best Flyer ever: could he have been the toughest? Consider what Bobby Clarke had to overcome just to make the NHL and earn respect, dealing with diabetes growing up and having it affect when he was drafted. Not only did Clarke hate to lose, but he refused to be outworked or outplayed. Clarke played with venom inside. Surely he played through injuries, as most hockey players have to, but he never used health as an excuse. He wasn't liked by all opponents, and he had his moments of questionable play, such as when he dropped Soviet goal scorer Valeri Kharlamov with an ankle slash in the 1972 Canada-Soviet series, but Clarke was always able to back it up. Even while the Flyers always had enforcers around to protect Clarke, he didn't shy away from violence, even late in his career when the penalty minutes began to pile up again. So why isn't Clarke on this list? Well, he wasn't much of a fighter. Clarke was tough, but the players below didn't have his ability, and really had to fight for everything they earned.

To be on this list, you had to have stood up for teammates, been able to deliver bone-crushing hits and, of course, drop the gloves and mix it up from time to time and win.

5. BOB KELLY

The Hound wasn't blessed with great scoring ability, but that wasn't his role on the Flyers. His job was to be a thorn in the side of opponents, defend teammates, let his aggressive style do the talking and, of course, brawl often. Kelly played in Philadelphia for 10 seasons, averaging nearly 13 goals per season, and accumulating more than 1,100 penalty minutes. Kelly would throw his body around with abandon and be known as one of the key sparkplugs on the ice, a true leader.

4. DAVE BROWN

At 6'5", 220 pounds, Brown never backed down from a fight and, as the legend goes, he never lost one either. Brown played most of his career with the Flyers, with his career bests in penalty minutes coming in 1985–86 and the following year with 277 and 274 PIMs, respectively. Brown certainly wasn't shy in the playoffs, knowing that in the biggest games he could get the crowd and teammates going with a well-placed dropping of the gloves. How can one measure the intimidation Brown inflicted on other teams? How many Flyers playmakers were safe on the ice because Brown was out there? Brown's career high in points for a season was 17, but he still managed to play in 10 seasons with the Flyers, and that speaks volumes.

3. BEHN WILSON

A big, strong defenseman who was ready for the NHL from day one, Wilson totaled 49 points and 197 penalty minutes as a rookie and earned a reputation as someone opponents didn't want to mess with. Wilson had an erratic personality at times, even with teammates, and was a terrific fighter. He made waves around the league in his first year, as he seemed to score a point or win a fight just about every night early on. Flyers fans gave him grief later in his career, but they couldn't deny Wilson was tough.

2. RICK TOCCHET

In the 1970s the Flyers were led offensively by guys named Clarke, Barber, MacLeish, and Leach. When the team drafted Tocchet in the sixth round in 1983, they thought they were getting a tough winger who might score an occasional goal. Tocchet approached 300 penalty minutes in his second, third, and fourth NHL seasons, then turned into one of the league's premier two-way forwards, while not forgetting his fighting roots. Tocchet was only 6'0", but regularly challenged taller enforcers, and held his own.

1. DAVE SCHULTZ

Schultz was drafted to be the team's enforcer, its tough guy, and boy did he deliver. The expansion Flyers got pushed around in their first few years, then decided to make over the team by selecting fighters like Schultz. Never before had the NHL seen a guy pile on the penalty minutes the way Schultz did. The league didn't like it, but Flyers teammates and fans loved him for his style. Schultz would regularly tangle with the other big-name tough guys of the day like Terry O'Reilly, Keith Magnuson, Steve Durbano, and Tiger Williams. He loved the notoriety, since he knew he would never be known for scoring goals, though he did have a 20-goal season in 1973–74. The Hammer totaled 259 penalty minutes as a rookie, then 348 when the Flyers won their first Cup; and a staggering league record of 472 PIMs in 1974–75. Think about that number, averaging more than 6 penalty minutes every game of the long season. Even today, Schultz remains a hero in Philadelphia for an era of yesteryear, a symbol of who the Broad Street Bullies were.

WHO MAKES—AND MISSES—THE ALL-TIME FLYERS DREAM TEAM?

Considering how good the Flyers have been over the years, with the second-best winning percentage in the league since 1967 (trailing only the Montreal Canadiens), there are plenty of players to choose from for honors. At least 13 people who were members of the Flyers organization have found their way into the Hockey Hall of Fame. Three are players who played large roles on the Stanley Cup winning teams: Bobby Clarke, Bernie Parent, and Bill Barber. Keith Allen, the Flyers' first head coach and later GM and Executive VP, is in; as well as longtime owner Ed Snider, original GM Bud Poile and even announcer Gene Hart.

So, while the top players in team history tend to have a bent toward the Stanley Cup years, let the argument begin as to whether some of the statistics put up by those in the organization years later can match up.

81 CENTER: BOBBY CLARKE (1969–84)

What about: Eric Lindros? The cost to get this franchise player was great, and while it continues to leave a bad taste in people's mouths, the guy did have a very productive career when he was on the ice.

Clarke remains the only pure center, not counting Rick MacLeish, to score more points in team history. Lindros was a hitter and a playmaker, and he scored more points than games played in each of his eight controversial seasons in Philly. But it never ended with a Stanley Cup, and ultimately he will be remembered for the trade, the concussions, and the sour relationship with the team's signature player and executive.

What about: Rick MacLeish? That nasty wrist shot played a major role in scoring 328 goals as a Flyer. Fans weren't so pleased initially when MacLeish was acquired from Toronto because fan favorite Bernie Parent was in the deal, but the Flyers didn't have much to bargain with and needed offense. It took MacLeish two seasons in the minors to become a regular in Philly, but in his first full season he scored 50 goals and was a star on the power play. MacLeish scored the lone goal in the Flyers' Game 6 win over the Bruins to win the first Stanley Cup, and could always be counted on for a clutch goal. While Bobby Clarke, Bill Barber, and Reggie Leach often drew the opposing team's top line, MacLeish was the smooth-skating sniper on the second line.

What about: Dave Poulin? The Flyers captain for much of his tenure in Philly, succeeding Clarke's second run as the official team leader, Poulin was a terrific defensive forward, joining Clarke as the only Flyers to win the Frank J. Selke Trophy for defensive skill, and his 27 shorthanded goals rank third in club history. Poulin was known for defense and work ethic, but wasn't a bad scorer either. A product of Notre Dame who went undrafted by the NHL and played a year in Sweden, he set the Flyers record for points by a rookie in 1983–84 and played in a pair of All-Star games. While the Poulin-led Flyers did reach the Stanley Cup Finals, it was still odd to see Poulin, unceremoniously stripped of his captaincy for Ron Sutter and dealt to Boston, in the 1990 Finals for another team. Unfortunately for Poulin, he never did win a Cup, but Philly fans remember the good times.

What about: Rod Brind'Amour? When you've got *amour* in your name, chances are you'll be a big hit with the ladies. Brind'Amour was a very popular Flyer, but also productive on the ice. He came to Philly from the Blues for Murray Baron and Ron Sutter for the 1991–92 season, and would be a point-per-game scorer in the orange and black until the 1999–2000 season. Brind'Amour was very popular in Philly, mainly because he wasn't Eric Lindros and was one of the league's most durable players, holding the club record appearing in 484 consecutive games. Unlike Poulin, Brind'Amour won a Stanley Cup after leaving Philly, with the Carolina Hurricanes.

Yeah, but: Are you kidding? Clarke is the best player in Flyers history, the best draft pick, the one name most recognizable with the franchise, even close to 40 years after the team selected him in the second round of the

1969 draft. Clarke was a bit of a controversial pick, because teams feared his diabetes would hold him back. Flyers scout Jerry Melnyk persuaded Flyers brass to draft the 19-year-old from Flin Flon, Manitoba, however, and it turned out to be the most important act of his Flyers career. In the first round, the team chose a center named Bob Currier, who would never play in the NHL. Ten teams passed on drafting Clarke, including the Flyers, but as soon as Clarke was picked a number of teams started offering players to acquire him. Clarke was an All-Star as a rookie, the team's leading scorer as a sophomore, and would go on to win MVP awards and Stanley Cups. No Flyer has registered more points or assists, regular season or playoffs, or had a better gap-toothed smile.

82 LEFT WING: BILL BARBER (1972–84)

What about: Gary Dornhoefer? He didn't pile on big stats, but he was one of the first Flyers, having been chosen in the 1967 expansion draft from Boston, and would remain a Flyer the rest of his playing career, and beyond as an announcer. Dornhoefer scored 202 of his 214 career goals with the Flyers, where he made his reputation more as a grinder, hard hitter, and leader who would often crowd the opposing net and wreak havoc wherever possible. Injuries were a big part of Dorny's career, but he played through the pain and earned fans that way. In the

1973 playoffs, with the Flyers battling the Minnesota North Stars and looking for the franchise's first-ever series win, Dornhoefer scored the overtime goal in Game 5 to give the Flyers a crucial win and 3–2 series lead. The goal was immortalized forever as a statue outside the Spectrum.

What about: Brian Propp? The 14th overall pick in the 1979 draft, and one of the most prolific junior hockey scorers ever, Propp ended up the number 2 goal scorer and assist man in club history. One year in the minors Propp had 94 goals and 194 points in only 71 games. Basically, the Flyers knew when they drafted Propp they were getting a productive player, and he certainly was, scoring at least 90 points four times in a consistent career. Like a number of Flyers who joined the team after the winning Cup years, Propp played with the Flyers teams that lost to the Oilers in two Finals, then moved on to another stop and had success, but couldn't win it all. Propp went to the Cup Finals five times, and never won. Often overshadowed by flashier players, Propp was the consummate team player and remains with the Flyers family doing radio work.

What about: John LeClair? He came to the Flyers in the Mark Recchi deal with Montreal; this after LeClair had won a Stanley Cup in 1993 and scored overtime goals to win two of those Finals games. LeClair was merely okay in a few regular seasons with the Canadiens but blossomed in Philly, reaching the 50-goal plateau three straight seasons, becoming the first American-born NHL player to do so. He scored 382 goals as a Flyer, fifth on the team's all-time list.

Yeah, but: Barber is the all-time leading goal scorer in franchise history, with 420 goals, and only Clarke scored more points. While others grabbed the headlines, Barber just went on the ice and didn't stop scoring goals. He was the seventh overall pick in the 1972 draft and needed only 11 games in the minors with the AHL's Richmond Robins before he was ready for full-time NHL duty. Barber scored 30 goals his rookie season, registered 50 in 1975–76, and also ended up tied for the team mark in career playoff goals.

83 RIGHT WING: TIM KERR (1980–91)

What about: Rick Tocchet? This rough guy came to the Flyers in the 1984 draft and was an instant fan favorite, and that's before he learned how to be a good offensive player. Eventually the big hits and fights came with goals, and Tocchet became one of the premier power forwards in hockey when he scored 45 goals during the 1988–89 season. Tocchet played seven-plus seasons in Philly the first time, before having his best statistical season in Pittsburgh and winning a Stanley Cup. He would then become a well-traveled player and finish his playing career in Philly. In 2006, Tocchet was accused of financing a nationwide sports gambling ring based in New Jersey, likely from his playing days with the Flyers, and in 2007 he pled guilty to conspiracy and promoting gambling and was sentenced to two years probation.

What about: Mark Recchi? His 395 assists rank fourth all-time for the Flyers. Originally acquired from Pittsburgh in a deal for Tocchet and Kjell Samuelsson, Recchi had two tours of duty in Philly. The first was far more productive, as Recchi played in two All-Star games and twice topped 100 points. After playing four years in Montreal as part of the trade that brought John LeClair and Eric Desjardins to Philly, Recchi had five more productive seasons. Recchi still holds the Flyers record for most points in a season, with 123 in 1992–93.

What about: Reggie Leach? He was an incredible goal scorer, especially in the 1975–76 regular season when he lit the lamp 61 times and in the playoffs added another 19 goals in 16 games. The Flyers lost the Cup to the Montreal Canadiens in a sweep that season, but Leach was named the Conn Smythe Trophy winner for MVP of the playoffs, despite not playing for the winning team. Leach had played with Bobby Clarke in Flin Flon, Manitoba, where they became a dynamic goal-scoring team. When Clarke became established in Philly, Leach would eventually be acquired for Larry Wright, Al MacAdam, and a first-round pick. Leach possessed a blistering slap shot, and while the years after the Cup seasons weren't as productive for him, he dialed things up one last time in 1979–80 with 50 goals.

Yeah, but: Kerr gets the nod here for his incredible streak of goal-scoring in the 1980s and what he made of a career that wasn't expected to be much. Four straight seasons he scored 54 or more goals, and after missing most of 1987–88, he came back with 48 goals in 1988–89, further dominating with 14 goals and 25 points in the play-offs. Like Leach, Kerr was talented, but went about his work in a totally different way. He wasn't given anything and wasn't drafted by an NHL team. Kerr was big and wide, with soft hands and excellent hand/eye coordination, and parked himself in front of opposing nets, often scoring garbage goals. Well, they all count the same, don't they? Kerr came up big in playoff games, notching four in one period in a 1985 game against the hated New York Rangers. The Flyers trailed 3–2 in the second period, and Kerr would score four times in a little more than eight minutes, three of them on the power play. Not everything was a positive with Kerr. He underwent many shoulder operations, and in 1990 had to deal with the death of his wife Kathy, who passed away from complications due to childbirth. Kerr kept on playing, able to overcome the adversity and not wasting a day of his talents.

84 DEFENSE: MARK HOWE (1982–92) AND ERIC DESJARDINS (1994–2006)

What about: Tom Bladon? He was Philly's first true offensive defenseman, and he's the owner of one of the hallowed records for a D-man, scoring eight points in one game. It came on December 11, 1977, when the opposing Cleveland Barons watched Bladon tally four goals and four assists. The Flyers didn't have anyone like Bladon for a long time, mainly going with stay-at-home types on the blue line like Ed Van Impe and Barry Ashbee; so when Bladon had his big game, it was actually the first time a Flyers defenseman had ever scored as many as three goals in a game. Bladon was also a plus-10 in the game, an 11–1 Flyers win. Bladon was the 23rd overall pick in the 1972 draft by the Flyers, and in his six years with Philly he averaged 11 goals per season. That was a lot back then. Howe and Desjardins are the only Flyers defensemen to top Bladon in career goals or assists.

What about: Behn Wilson? An offensive defenseman from the beginning, the Flyers traded three members of the Stanley Cup teams, including Bladon, to the Penguins for the rights to the number 6 overall pick in 1978. Even as a rookie, Wilson had no problem fitting in, scoring 18 goals and registering 197 penalty minutes. His career in Philly would be remembered for good and bad. He could score and deliver bodychecks and was never afraid to start or finish a fight, but as a defenseman he also made poor choices at times, making mistakes in the Flyers zone and taking penalties. One of the toughest Flyers, but also much maligned (pre-Lindros, of course).

What about: Joe Watson? Remember back in the old days defensemen weren't supposed to score goals and pile up the points? The older Watson was an original member of the franchise, who played for 11 seasons in Philly, always a vocal leader in the clubhouse and solid stay-at-home defender. He scored only 36 goals in those years, but was a dependable rock on the blue line, for some of those years with younger brother Jimmy with him as a pairing.

Yeah, but: Howe was easily the best offensive defenseman in Flyers history. But that's not to imply he couldn't defend: Howe was a three-time runner up for the Norris Trophy as the league's top defenseman, and his 1985–86 season was remarkable, with 82 points, seven shorthanded goals, and a plus-minus of 85. Howe wasn't a physical presence on the blue line, but he saw the ice better than most and would often lead the rush up the ice from end to end, showing off his skating and passing skills. To put his Flyers statistics in some perspective, if you remove Desjardins from consideration, no other Flyers defenseman in team history has even half the goals, assists, or points that Howe does.

Yeah, but: Desjardins ranks second to Howe in Flyers history for defenseman in goals, assists, and points, and he won the Barry Ashbee Trophy for top Flyers defenseman seven times in 10 years. In 17 NHL seasons, Desjardins's teams never missed the playoffs. Acquired from the Canadiens in the John LeClair-Mark Recchi deal, Desjardins ranks eighth in club history in games played.

85 GOALIE: BERNIE PARENT (1967–71, 1973–79)

What about: Ron Hextall? This guy sure had an interesting career with the Flyers; but then again, he was a pretty interesting guy. He was an intense, aggressive competitor who protected the goalie crease like someone from the 30 years prior, but also had no problem leaving the crease to help the offense. A third-generation player, Hextall was ready for the NHL the minute the Flyers brought him up from AHL affiliate Hershey. Hextall had a memorable rookie campaign, culminating in being named the Conn Smythe Trophy winner as playoff MVP, even though the Flyers lost to Edmonton. Hextall carried the club like Parent had a decade earlier. Hexy had a number of memorable events as a Flyer before being involved in the infamous Eric Lindros trade. Twice he scored goals. No other goaltender had ever scored a goal by shooting the puck until Hextall did it, once in a playoff game against Washington. He also holds the league record for penalty minutes in a season, with 113. Twice Hextall committed angry sins in the playoffs that resulted in suspensions at the start of the following season: one a slash to the legs of Edmonton's Kent Nilsson; the other a blocker to the head of Montreal's Chris Chelios. All this did was endear him to Philly fans even more.

What about: Pelle Lindbergh? What a shame. He didn't accrue the career stats other top Flyers goalies did, but the

Swedish import was seemingly on his way before tragedy struck on November 10, 1985. Leaving a party on a Saturday night—or technically a Sunday morning— Lindbergh crashed his Porsche 930 Turbo into a wall at a New Jersey school. He and two others died. Lindbergh, 26, was voted an All-Star that season, despite playing in only eight games. Lindbergh was the first European goaltender to win the Vezina Trophy, as he won 40 games in 1984–85. Lindbergh ranks seventh in victories for a Flyers goalie, and who knows how much higher he'd rank if he hadn't left that party drunk.

What about: Pete Peeters? He doesn't seem to get much credit for his role on the amazing 1979–80 team that went months without losing a game, but Peeters registered 22 wins and 5 ties that year before losing a game in February. He shared the nets that season with veteran Phil Myre. Most people who remember Peeters recall the highlight of Bob Nystrom scoring over his diving body in overtime of Game 6 of the Finals against the Islanders, but Peeters does rank fourth in games for a goalie in club history and seventh in wins.

Yeah, but: The Flyers have won two Stanley Cups, and Parent was in the nets for both. In fact, he was so durable those seasons, backup goaltender Bobby Taylor barely played. Parent started 73 of a possible 78 games in 1973–74, an amazing feat, and held the NHL record for wins with 47 in a season until 2006–07 when Martin

Brodeur topped him. Parent got passed in games and wins by Hextall, but his 2.42 goals against average is much better, and his 50 shutouts dwarf Hextall's 18. Hextall was, no doubt, a great goalie for the Flyers, but Parent is one of the best of all time.

PHILLY THINGS

WHO ARE THE FIVE BEST PRO COACHES IN PHILLY HISTORY?

86 A great coach needs players, of course, or he's not going to look like a great coach. Or will he? What's the bottom line on coaching—to get the best out of the players, or to win a championship? Is winning everything? For college coaches, there's a lot more at stake than championships; there's the molding of young men and women for future ambitions and goals. At the professional level, however, improvement is seldom enough. Today's salaries for coaches are so exorbitant, and the patience level of most owners is so thin, that a coach has to win it all or be deemed a failure.

We'll get to the worst coaches in Philly history, but there's a common theme among the best, and that's a championship. All five coaches or managers to make the list for top consideration won a title. Andy Reid has fallen short, despite having the most wins in Eagles history. Hey, the Reid era has been terrific, with four conference title games and a trip to the Super Bowl. In an era of free agency, what Reid has done is remarkable. He just hasn't won a title.

Not too many coaches in Philadelphia pro sports history have won a title. In fact, we can count the list of them on two hands, and we don't need all our fingers on that second hand to do it. Buck Shaw and Alex Hannum each won titles, with the 1960 Eagles and 1967 76ers, respectively, but neither spent much time coaching in Philly. Kudos to Andy Reid, Dick Vermeil, Mike Keenan, and Larry Brown, among others, for getting to the Finals. And to Danny Ozark we say: Greg Luzinski was not a good left fielder. Anyway, here are the greatest pro coaches in Philly sports history.

5. DALLAS GREEN

A controversial pick, to be sure, since his Phillies managerial record was only 169–130, and he quickly bolted town to Chicago to steal Ryne Sandberg and others, but did he or did he not win a World Series? Did anyone else do this in 125 years of Phillies baseball? One can say Green had lots of talent on that 1980 team, but really, Mike Schmidt and Steve Carlton sure seemed to have a better cast of talent around them for the Ozark years of the late 1970s. Green was the right manager at the right time, and he pushed the right buttons. The Phillies could have lost the division title in Montreal instead of prevailing and had numerous chances to blow the Houston playoff series; even in the World Series, when that 2–0 lead just about became a 3–2 deficit in Kansas City, Green guided the ship. Charlie Manuel, meanwhile, enters 2008 with as many Phillies postseason wins as Charlie Brown.

THE BEST PHILADELPHIA SPORTS ARGUMENTS

4. FRED SHERO

No Flyers coach has more wins, regular season or playoffs. No Flyers coach was in charge for more seasons. And most importantly, no other Flyers coach has won a Stanley Cup. Nicknamed The Fog, Shero was a brilliant motivator and tactician, and he brought out the best from those rough-and-tumble Flyers teams. While his famous blackboard quote, written before Game 6 of the 1974 Finals—"Win together today, we walk together forever"—stands forever, Shero also said something that defined his tenure as coach: "I'm like a duck: calm above the water, and paddling like hell underneath." It's best if we didn't know further details of that one.

3. CONNIE MACK

Cornelius Alexander McGillicuddy wasn't merely the manager of the old Philadelphia Athletics. He was the manager seemingly forever! Mack was not a terrific ballplayer in the 1800s, but in 1901 he became manager, general manager, and part owner of the fledgling A's franchise, a job not very much in demand at the time. Mack managed the team for the next 50 seasons, eventually becoming full owner in 1936. He won 3,582 games with the A's, as well as five World Series titles, finally retiring at age 87 after the 1950 season as a gentleman who managed with class, always dressed like a champ, and earned the respect of his players.

2. GREASY NEALE

Again, Eagles fans can debate Andy Reid vs. Alfred Earle Neale, but Neale's got him 2–0 where it counts most, in championships. Neale was a professional baseball player from 1916 to 1924, with all but 22 of his 768 career games as a Cincinnati Red. The others were with the Phillies. Neale was a speedy outfielder and one of the Reds' leading hitters for the 1919 World Series team that beat the Black Sox. He became Eagles coach in 1941 and stayed the rest of the decade, winning 66 games against 44 losses, with five ties, and leading the team to the 1948 and 1949 championships. Neale is credited with developing what later became the 4–3 defense as well.

1. BILLY CUNNINGHAM

So you think just anyone could win with Moses, Dr. J, Bobby Jones, and Mo Cheeks on their side? Well, maybe, but the 76ers had empty finishes to seasons before Cunningham led them to a remarkable 1982–83 campaign with a 65–17 regular season record and wins in 12 of 13 postseason games. Cunningham was the sixth man on the record-breaking 1966–67 76ers team that won it all, and he became coach of the team in 1977, not long after retiring as a player. He coached only one team in his career, and won 454 games against 196 losses, a staggering .698 winning percentage.

WHO ARE THE FIVE WORST PRO COACHES IN PHILLY HISTORY?

87 For as many good seasons as Philadelphia sports franchises have had, there are a lot more bad ones. No baseball franchise has lost more games than the Phillies. The Eagles were league laughingstocks for much of the time between 1960 and the Dick Vermeil era. The normally successful, playoff-bound Flyers entered 2007–08 coming off the worst record in the league, and no NBA team has had as dreadful a season as the 1972–73 76ers.

So where do we begin in discussing the worst coaches? If one of the criteria for being best coach is a championship, what goes into being the worst? Finishing in last place? Having the most losses for a period of years? If you're that bad, chances are you won't be keeping the job for very long. To be the worst coach, there had to have been some expectations that success was on the way, which pretty much disqualifies the Phillies managers for much of the 20th century. There weren't many wins for Kaiser Wilhelm, Art Fletcher, Burt Shotton, Jimmie Wilson, and quite a few other guys, but the Phillies weren't supposed to be any good those years. To be a really bad coach, you had to dupe the fans or management into thinking you were good. Also, mismanaging a potential title team, like Gene Mauch and Danny Ozark did, might mean these guys made mistakes, but they still did pretty well, at least in the regular season. Anyway, fair or not, here are the five worst coaches in Philly history.

5. TERRY FRANCONA

You've gotta hand it to Francona, who currently owns a pair of World Series rings for doing great work with the Boston Red Sox. As the Phillies manager, he wasn't a big winner, and didn't handle being in Philly very well. In Boston, the guy could run for mayor. What changed? Was he really so bad in Philly? Francona was a nice guy, but the media ate him alive. So did the players. After managing some former hoops player named Michael Jordan for the Double-A Birmingham Barons in 1994, the Phillies gave him a shot in 1996, and Francona finished fifth, third, third, and fifth. There were expectations for much better things. The Jim Fregosi Phillies went to a World Series prior to the Francona era and the Larry Bowa teams won 86 games three out of four years right after. Francona either figured things out after he left Philadelphia, or he just has really good players in Beantown. It's probably both.

4. RICH KOTITE

All the other guys on this list had losing records, but not Kotite. He went 37–29 in his four tumultuous seasons leading the Eagles, bridging the gap between the Buddy Ryan and Ray Rhodes eras. Rhodes lost six more games than he won. So what was so wrong with Kotite? He wasn't respected, the fans thought he was an incompetent joke, and his teams had loads of talent but consistently fell short. Kotite did guide the Eagles to a playoff win in New Orleans after the 1992 season, but what defines him most is how the 1994 campaign ended. The Eagles were 7–2, as the remnants of the Ryan-Bud Carson defense remained strong, but then the team lost its final seven games. New owner Jeff Lurie made the switch to Rhodes, and Kotite became the New York Jets' problem. There, without the horses he had in Philly, he went 4–28. Ouch!

3. DOUG MOE

Twenty years after Fred Carter's 1972–73 76ers set a mark for ineptitude that has never been matched, Carter was named to replace Doug Moe on the 1992–93 team. Moe went 19–37, not even finishing off his lone season as coach. The 76ers, pretty much unlike any other Philly pro team in the last 20 years, have seen some coaches accrue terrible records. Johnny Davis won 22 games in his only season. John Lucas averaged 21 wins in his two campaigns. Randy Ayers ended up coaching four fewer games than Moe. But Moe was an accomplished coach with the Spurs and Nuggets, and he bragged to 76ers fans how his run-and-gun style would work. It didn't. After a 56-point loss to

Seattle on March 6, 1993, when the 76ers allowed 149 points, Moe was relieved of his duties.

2. ROY RUBIN

As bad as the 1972–73 76ers were, and no team in NBA history was worse, it's really hard to win only four games— out of 51. It was Rubin's first and last NBA coaching opportunity. It should have been obvious at the introductory press conference that this wasn't going to go well when Rubin, asked about coaching future Hall of Famer Hal Greer, responded, "Who?" That's the question, Philadelphia fans, when trying to remember the coach of the 9–73 Philadelphia 76ers team.

1. JOE KUHARICH

No other coach in Philly team sports has been so disliked that the fans chanted his name in a derisive manner. The fans hated this guy. He was essentially wearing the Santa Claus outfit that dark day in 1968, a symbol of the fans' anger. Kuharich didn't have great players, in part because he made a few ridiculous trades to send good players packing, but it's not like the Eagles were going to win championships. The problem is, owner Jerry Wolman loved the guy. Before Kuharich's first season ended, Wolman bestowed upon him a remarkable 15-year contract for $50,000 per year. He would make it through five total years as Eagles coach. That contract is probably what set the fans off, knowing how poorly this guy did his job in relation to what he earned. Kuharich was the only coach with a losing record at Notre Dame, and he didn't win in Philly either. The Eagles lost the first 11 games in 1968, and there were "Joe Must Go" buttons, chants in the stadium, and actual banners flying from planes. Kuharich finally flew off after that 1968 season, going 28–41–1 in his ugly tenure.

WHO ARE THE FIVE GREATEST BIG 5 PLAYERS OF ALL TIME?

88 Philadelphians love their basketball, but with the 76ers having not won a title for 25 years, nor were they much of a threat for most of that time, the case can certainly be made that it's a college hoops town, not pro. In 1955 the Big 5 was formed to help showcase the city's basketball talent. It's not a conference, but an alliance of these schools: Pennsylvania, Temple, St. Joseph's, Villanova, and LaSalle. No, they don't officially have their own league together, though a few of the schools are in the same conference, and they haven't piled on the championships themselves, but for more than 50 years it's like a party when they meet in Big 5 city series games with pride and bragging rights on the line. How many 76ers games can you say that about?

Each Big 5 game used to be an even bigger event, with games played at the famed Palestra in doubleheaders and tripleheaders. For a city that doesn't have much to watch for college football, it celebrates hoops; and when one of the teams is really good and makes a run though the NCAA tournament, the entire city gets on the bandwagon, including the other Big 5 schools. These are all city schools, except Villanova, which is on the Main Line suburb and not far off. And the Palestra, still the site of most Big 5 games, remains one of the top places to watch the kids play. It's the college hoops equivalent of Yankee Stadium, rich in history and memories.

These schools have some pretty intense individual rivalries, like when Villanova and St. Joe's meet in the Holy War. Former Temple coach John Chaney, a pretty intense guy himself, created a special relationship with St. Joe's in his final years when he allegedly ordered a player to hurt someone from the other team. This isn't like Yankees-Red Sox, or any other professional rivalry, because the names change every year and there are five teams fighting for city supremacy. (Really, when you throw Drexel into the mix, even though the city school isn't officially part of the Big 5, there are six.) And the students make all the games worth watching. Standings are kept and the schools honor the round-robin format, even as they have league commitments to abide by. It's certainly a unique relationship.

Not every Big 5 star has gone on to make it big in the NBA, but some have. Cutting down the best in Philly college hoops history to five players isn't easy, but here are the best of the best. And by the way, we're well aware that a few of these guys played before the actual formation of the Big 5 in 1954, but we're throwing them in anyway. Pretend the question is Philly college basketball history, OK? C'mon, we couldn't leave these guys out.

5. KEN DURRETT AND LIONEL SIMMONS, LASALLE

Hard to leave either off the list, so we satisfy two generations by calling it a tie. Nobody in Philly scored more than the 3,217 points that Simmons did in college, and only Pete Maravich and Freeman Williams did in NCAA history. Simmons won the Naismith Award for top player as a senior in 1990, leading the Explorers to three NCAA tournaments. Durrett played at LaSalle from 1968–71 and scored 1,679 points in only 71 games, leading the Big 5 in scoring twice before suffering a serious knee injury his senior year. Neither Simmons nor Durrett had notable pro careers, but they certainly made their mark in the Big 5.

4. JAMEER NELSON, ST. JOSEPH'S

The top freshman in the country in 2000–01, Nelson was barely 6'0", but he made big play after big play and became a fan favorite as well as a top scorer. Nelson averaged 19.7 points, 5.1 rebounds, and 4.7 assists his junior season, and threatened to turn pro. Good thing he returned to school, leading the Hawks to a 27–0 regular season record and spot among the Elite Eight in the NCAA tournament. Oklahoma State ended the Nelson run, and the team finished 30–2, but it was a great ride that captivated the Philly sports scene. Nelson left St. Joe's as the school leader in points, assists, and steals, and remains a productive NBA player.

3. PAUL ARIZIN, VILLANOVA

Arizin apparently wasn't good enough to stick on the LaSalle College High school basketball team, but he made Villanova's team as a sophomore and was an instant hit. As a junior he averaged 22 points per game, and in a February 1949 win over Navy Air Material Center, he scored 85 points (though he always noted it was not an accomplishment he was proud of since it was an over-matched opponent). Pitchin' Paul was the college player of the year as a senior in 1950, averaging 25.3 points per game, and went on to play in 10 NBA All-Star games, twice leading the league in scoring.

2. GUY RODGERS, TEMPLE

When he graduated to the NBA he was the highest scorer in Temple history with 1,767 points, a two-time All-American from 1955–58, and the terrific playmaking guard who went on to success in the NBA. Rodgers played with Wilt Chamberlain for six seasons, registering 20 assists in the Stilt's 100-point game, and twice led the league in assists. At Temple he became one of the first black players to play a significant amount of time, and he led Hall of Fame coach Harry Litwack's teams to a pair of Final Fours.

1. TOM GOLA, LASALLE

The college basketball player of the year in 1954, Gola was voted the most outstanding player of the Final Four that season, leading the Explorers to the national champi-onship. In five tournament games he averaged 22.8 points and 20.4 rebounds. A Philly high school star who led LaSalle College High to a Catholic League title, Gola made All-American each of his four years and held the NCAA rebounding record of 2,201. Gola won an NCAA and NIT title in college and was on the 1956 Philadelphia Warriors championship team. He was enshrined into the Basketball Hall of Fame in 1976, and even though he technically played before the Big 5 was formed, he remains known as a Philly legend and top college hoops player.

WHO ARE THE FIVE GREATEST BIG 5 COACHES OF ALL TIME?

89 While the players come and go in college basketball, the coaches stay and often become more famous than the players.

Philadelphia has been blessed with some of the great coaches in NCAA history. Big 5 schools have made a total of nine Final Fours, with Villanova leading the way with three, followed by LaSalle and Temple with two each. Also, one of the biggest upsets in NCAA title game history came when a Big 5 team stunned a mighty conference counterpart.

One name you won't see on this list is Philadelphia University's Herb Magee, who is the all-time winningest Division II coach, breaking the record in February 2007 of 828 wins. Magee has been at the same school for 40 years, a testament to his loyalty, since he certainly could have bolted for a Division I job had he wanted to. Magee isn't on the list because he has never coached in the Big 5, though few doubt the success he could have had, had he jumped to Division I.

Let's check out the top Big 5 coaches.

5. ROLLIE MASSIMINO, VILLANOVA

Some might wonder why Rollie doesn't rank better on this list. The last championship won by any team in Philly was by his Villanova Wildcats in 1985, after all. Massimino's record has certainly been tarnished since the historic win over Georgetown, both at 'Nova and elsewhere, but hey, this was arguably the greatest upset in tournament lore. Villanova was a number 8 seed that March, but found its way through to the Final Four, then played a near-perfect game to knock off Patrick Ewing's Hoyas. Massimino coached 19 seasons at Villanova, winning 357 games, and was 20–10 in the NCAA tournament. He ranks only number 5 here because we don't want to overrate that one memorable win. The rest of the time at 'Nova, Massimino was a winning coach, but not legendary, and others on this list are more Philly.

4. FRAN DUNPHY, PENN/TEMPLE

Dunphy replaced John Chaney at Temple in 2006, becoming the first coach of two Big 5 schools. For 17 years at Penn, Dunphy was one of the top coaches in the Ivy League, leading the Quakers to 310 wins and 10 league titles. Dunphy graduated from LaSalle, acting as co-captain under coach Tom Gola and averaging 18.6 points per game as a senior, and later was an assistant coach there. He also earned a master's degree from Villanova, meaning Dunphy pretty much knows all the Big 5 schools well.

3. DR. JACK RAMSAY, ST. JOSEPH'S

A Philadelphia hoops institution, Ramsay attended Upper Darby High School and St. Joseph's College and later received doctorate degrees from Penn. Upon becoming coach of the Hawks in 1955, when the Big 5 was born, Ramsay guided teams to 10 postseason appearances and 234 wins, as well as seven outright or shared Big 5 titles. Ramsay went on to win an NBA title with the Portland Trail Blazers, knocking off his hometown Philadelphia 76ers, but he was hardly regarded as an enemy of the city. Ramsay was an innovative coach who helped put St. Joe's hoops on the map.

2. PHIL MARTELLI, ST. JOSEPH'S

Martelli played point guard at local Widener University, and served as an assistant coach at St. Joe's for 10 years before becoming coach in 1995. The Hawks made it to the NIT title game in Martelli's first year, and then the Atlantic 10 championships and NCAA tournament trips followed. The 2003–04 team, led by Jameer Nelson and Delonte West, went on to the Elite Eight. The colorful Martelli wrote a book about life lessons and should be at St. Joe's for a while longer, having signed a contract extension into the next decade. Entering the 2007 season he was second in school history in coaching wins, averaging 20 per season.

1. JOHN CHANEY, TEMPLE

A fiery Philadelphian who first coached at Cheyney State, Chaney moved on to Temple in 1982 and guided teams to a postseason tournament in 23 of 24 seasons, 17 times in the NCAA tournament. Chaney's teams were known for practicing hard and playing tough defense, and many of the noteworthy players under him excelled in hustle, energy, and defense. Chaney made some of the wrong headlines at times, like when he broke up a press conference to go after Massachusetts coach John Calipari, and when he sent one of his players to rough up a St. Joseph's player because he wasn't pleased with the officiating. However, Chaney is known to his players as a father figure who cared about not only winning, but learning. He won 741 games as a college coach, 516 at Temple.

WHICH IS THE GREATEST ROCKY MOVIE?

90 Let's be honest. This is a book about Philadelphia sports arguments, and we're going to skip the part about the best overall sports movies ever. *Rocky* wins. Or *Rocky II* wins. Or *Roc*...you get the point. Sylvester Stallone didn't know it when he created the character Rocky Balboa, but to this day, moviegoers think that was a real character from the streets of Philly running up and down the streets, jumping atop the steps of the Philadelphia Museum of Art, punching beef in a freezer, overcoming great odds for stardom. Balboa was Philly, true and true—even though Stallone was from New York.

As the story goes, Stallone watched journeyman fighter Chuck Wepner get battered around into the 15th round against Muhammad Ali on March 24, 1975. Wepner stayed on his feet, fought back, never stopped trying, knowing this was probably his only chance at the big time. In that fight, the role of Rocky was born. Stallone had appeared in some movies, in minor roles, but saw opportunity with Rocky. It might appear as some general rags-to-riches tale of an out-of-luck pug trying to live the American dream, but really, it was a story many in Philadelphia could identify with.

How could this story take place anywhere else? Not to rip on any other place, but it had to be Philly. The City of Brotherly Love always seems to be an underdog, nestled on the I-95 corridor between New York and Washington, D.C. Stallone was telling the Rocky story through a city that always seems to overcome as well. What a perfect fit.

So which Rocky movie is the best one? Let's not insult your intelligence by delving too deep and giving serious consideration to the final two versions. In 2006 *Rocky Balboa* was released. Rocky is supposed to be 59 years old, and he fights a guy half his age, which is the major problem. Actually, critics gave the movie solid reviews. The premise of the film, giving Stallone and moviegoers closure for the series, did work, and we knew going in its goal wasn't to compete with the other versions. So while it's not in consideration for being the best Rocky movie, it's not in consideration for the worst either. That honor would have to go to *Rocky V.* Rocky beating up Tommy Gunn, or Tommy Morrison to you and me, just didn't work. *Rocky V* was a colossal disaster; it's best to forget it happened.

The next entry we can eliminate from conversation is *Rocky IV*. Rocky's buddy Apollo Creed thinks he's still a bad dude, and that mean monster Russian Ivan Drago is no big deal. Then Creed dies. Or, as Drago famously says, "If he dies, he dies." Well, he does die. Rocky is crushed. He must avenge his friend's death, fighting Drago on Christmas Day in Mother Russia, against the toughest odds he's ever faced. And he trains with a beard. The premise is a bit hokey, contrived, and obvious. The movie is fun, and the music rocks, but it's still a distant fourth in the series.

You might assume that the next Rocky flick to get flicked out is *Rocky III*, since we're methodically going in order. Here's a shocker: that's not the case. We're skipping right to *Rocky II*. It finished up memorably with Balboa enacting revenge on Creed, but the first half of the movie puts you to sleep, as Rocky runs out of money and gets embarrassed by his wife and fellow fighters because he can't fight again. Then he does. One gets chills up the spine when Adrian, shockingly out of her coma, asks Rocky to win, and the training scenes are cool, but *Rocky III*, with the fascinating Mr. T, edges it out.

Clubber Lang doesn't just want the heavyweight title, he wants Rocky's heart. He wants to inflict pain. Balboa has to overcome the death of trainer Mickey, which paralyzed audiences at the time. Why does someone have to die in every Rocky movie? Who's the one getting punched the most? Everything works in *Rocky III*, as the villain Lang is believable—more so than the tired Americans-vs.-Russians routine—and the "Eye of the Tiger" is still played on radio stations today. I give it a thumbs-up.

Of course, nothing can beat the original. *Rocky I* is a classic, setting an industry standard and winning the 1976 Academy Award. The other movies in the saga might have had more action, better music, stronger lines, and more character plots, but *Rocky I* puts it all together in one complete package. You watch this movie, then afterward you start humming "Gonna Fly Now" and see if you can jog a mile. Then halfway through you crawl home to watch the movie again. Well, that's what I hear happens, anyway.

WHO ARE THE TOP FIVE FIGHTERS FROM PHILLY?

91 Don't let the name City of Brotherly Love fool you. Just like the name Sweet Science, which seems to paint the sport of boxing as friendly, Philly is a tough town and its fighters are even tougher. While Las Vegas is the home of many championship fights, Philly breeds fighters, and you can catch good fights there, too. If you've never seen a brawl between Philly fighters at the Blue Horizon on North Broad Street, one of the greatest, most energetic places to watch a fight, you've missed out.

Philly fighters don't back down; they intimidate and instill fear. They don't stop fighting until the final bell, they get up when knocked down, they are always throwing punches. Philly fighters are tough, and they have to be carried out of the ring. Rocky Balboa isn't a real figure, but there's a reason Sly Stallone chose Philly. It's a great fight town, with many memories.

Many Hall of Famers have called Philly home at one time or another, and narrowing down the list of the all-time greats forces us to leave a lot of names out. Heavyweight champ Sonny Liston, light heavies Philadelphia Jack O'Brien and Matthew Saad Muhammad, middleweights

George Benton and Bennie Briscoe, welterweight Gypsy Joe Harris, and all the way down to bantamweight Jeff Chandler—none make the cut. So who does?

5. JOEY GIARDELLO

A middleweight from South Philly, Giardello was always willing to get in a brawl, and most times he emerged victorious. Originally named Carmine Orlando Tilelli and born in Brooklyn, he lived most of his life in Philadelphia and turned pro in 1948, waiting more than 14 years for his first title shot. Giardello fought some of the top fighters of the era, beating Sugar Ray Robinson and Rubin Hurricane Carter and taking the title from Dick Tiger. Giardello finished with a record of 101–25–7, with 33 wins by way of knockout.

4. HAROLD JOHNSON

Less a brawler than a technician, Johnson turned pro in 1946 and fought at light heavyweight and heavyweight in his career. Like Giardello, it took a long time for Johnson, who had some epic fights with Archie Moore, to get his own title shot. In 1961 he finally took advantage, after Moore was stripped as champ, and beat Jesse Bowdry. He'd later beat Doug Jones for world recognition. Johnson went 76–11 in his career, with 32 knockouts, and entered the Hall of Fame in 1993.

3. TOMMY LOUGHRAN

The Ring magazine fighter of the year in 1929 and 1931, Loughran was an undersized light heavyweight champ who regularly fought larger men. As a light heavyweight he beat Max Baer and James J. Braddock, who would become heavyweight champs, and in a shot for Primo Carnera's heavyweight title he lost a close decision, though most at ringside thought he had won. (Carnera weighed 86 pounds more than Loughran.) The South Philly fan favorite went 109–30–11 in his career, with 17 knockouts, and fought many world champions.

2. BERNARD HOPKINS

The Executioner was born and raised in the Germantown section of North Philadelphia, and while in high school the self-described thug was sent to prison for strong-arm robbery, and served more than four years. Hopkins turned his life around while at Graterford State Penitentiary in the Philly suburbs, getting his high school diploma and committing to boxing. Hopkins became a solid middleweight and, even though he lost his first title shot against Roy Jones Jr., Hopkins toppled champ Segundo Mercado and would defend the middleweight title a record 20 times, beating some of the biggest names in the sport, including Felix Trinidad and Oscar De La Hoya. Some think Hopkins, who lost twice to Jermain Taylor, is sticking around too long, as he's 42 and has risen in weight from 160 pounds to the 175-pound neighborhood of light heavyweight, but Hopkins clearly still has goals to achieve. He's also been a defender of fighter's rights and testified before Congress in support of the Muhammad Ali Boxing Reform Act of 2000.

1. JOE FRAZIER

Born in South Carolina, Smokin' Joe became one of Philly's own as he was raised there and continued to make the town his home. Frazier won the gold medal at heavyweight in the 1964 Tokyo Olympics, turned pro, and became champion in 1970. Frazier and Muhammad Ali fought three times, with Frazier winning the first and defending the title in 1971 at Madison Square Garden. After Frazier lost his undefeated record and the title to George Foreman in Jamaica, Ali beat Foreman in New York in 1974. The third fight was the most memorable—the Thrilla in Manilla—and Ali won it with a 14th-round stoppage. Frazier didn't win another fight, and he opened up a gym and continues to represent Philly in a positive way.

WHAT WAS THE BEST DEFUNCT TEAM IN PHILLY HISTORY?

92 Who among us can't remember where they were the day the Frankford Yellow Jackets won the NFL championship in 1926? You were wearing your Two-Bits Homan powder blue and yellow jersey, weren't you?

Yes, the Frankford Yellow Jackets were the first NFL champions from Philadelphia, and Henry Homan—or, as he was called, Two-Bits, because of his diminutive stature at 5'5"—was real, too. So were Guy Chamberlin, Charley "Pie" Way, and Bull Behman. The Yellow Jackets called Frankford home, a section of northeast Philly known for the subway line that originates there. In 1926 this team went 14–1-1, a wins record that stood until the 1972 Dolphins tied it. There were no Philadelphia Eagles at that time. In fact, these franchises are not related. The Yellow Jackets folded during the 1931 season. Bert Bell and Lud Wray bought the rights to the franchise in 1933, calling the team the Philadelphia Eagles, and started a new team from scratch. This is why you won't find that 1926 title-winning team as a part of Eagles lore.

That said, the Yellow Jackets were one of the top teams of that NFL era, one of the finest defunct sports teams in

Philadelphia history. There are other teams that are no longer with us as well, notably in hockey: the Philadelphia Quakers were in the early NHL in 1930 (and weren't very good); and the Blazers were a World Hockey Association team in 1972–73, with Bernie Parent and Derek Sanderson the big names. A year later, Parent was back in Philly with the Flyers. Other hockey teams that called Philly home were the Arrows, the Firebirds, and the Ramblers, the latter playing in the Eastern Hockey League from 1955 to 1964.

In basketball, the Philadelphia Tapers were in the short-lived American Basketball League in 1961 and the Sphas competed in the Eastern Basketball League and American Basketball League. The name Sphas stood for South Philadelphia Hebrew Association, and most of its stars were Jewish. And in football, before Vince Papale became "Invincible" and tried out for the Eagles, he was in the World Football League with the Philadelphia Bell. The Bell played in JFK Stadium for a year-plus, and its cheerleaders were paraded around in the Bell Helmet Buggy. It's true!

And then there's the Steagles, but that 1943 crew isn't really a defunct team. For one year during World War II, the Philadelphia Eagles and Pittsburgh Steelers merged into one. That team went 5–4–1, actually the first winning season for Philadelphia's franchise.

Ah, such fond memories. But the greatest defunct team in Philly major sports history is actually the most recent one, those Philadelphia Stars of the United States Football

301

League. The USFL existed for three seasons, and the Stars were in Philly for two of them, winning 31 of 36 games, losing to the Michigan Panthers by two points in the 1983 title game, then beating the Arizona Wranglers the next season for the championship. Even when the Stars moved to Baltimore for the third season, forced out when the league moved its schedule to the fall, they remained good, winning the championship over the Oakland Invaders. That was the final game in USFL history.

The Stars were led by University of North Carolina running back Kelvin Bryant, who ran for more than 1,400 yards (in an 18-game season) both years in Philly, and the Penn State quarterback-wide receiver duo of Chuck Fusina and Scott Fitzkee was one of the league's best. Jim Mora Sr. coached the team, and Carl Peterson was its general manager. Mora would go on to coach in the NFL with the Saints and Colts, and Peterson has run the Chiefs since 1989.

The USFL didn't have a long run, and it was known more for being the starting grounds for Herschel Walker, who left Georgia a year early for the big bucks with the New Jersey Generals. Other college football stars would follow, including future Eagles great Reggie White and Pro Bowl quarterbacks Steve Young and Jim Kelly. The Eagles stunk for the two seasons the Stars were winning seemingly every week, and Philly fans had a team it could watch win. Well, for two seasons at least.

WHAT IS THE BEST ANNOUNCING DUO IN PHILLY SPORTS HISTORY?

93 Philadelphia sports fans have been blessed with some of the greatest announcers in history. While our teams have been losing, and for the few times they've won, it's been nice to enjoy the games with the home announcers. Before every household had multiple televisions with cable and young fans on the East coast could watch every Los Angeles Dodgers game, there was radio. Yes, today's youth might not believe it, but for generations prior, that was how we listened to our favorite teams playing ball.

By Saam was one of the broadcast pioneers of Philadelphia, calling more than 8,000 Philadelphia A's and Phillies games on radio or TV from the late 1930s through the mid-1970s. Saam began in Philly with Villanova and Temple football and, starting in 1939, for 12 years he called both Philly baseball teams, since the teams shared a stadium and radio announcers didn't travel. Saam teamed up with Claude Haring on A's games, then Bill Campbell and Richie Ashburn on Phillies telecasts. In 1970 Harry Kalas replaced Campbell. Saam never did call a pennant or division winner in Philadelphia, but did announce 13 no-hitters and the 100-point Wilt Chamberlain game in Hershey, Pennsylvania. Saam was awarded the Ford Frick award by the Baseball Hall of Fame for excellence in broadcasting in 1990. While some Philly announcers get too emotional for highs and lows, Saam was a true professional, even tempered and always under control. And he called more than 4,000 losses, so he needed to be.

Campbell is a Hall of Famer in his own right, as his career began in 1940 and he still does commentary on KYW-AM in Philadelphia. Campbell has been the play-by-play announcer for the Phillies, Eagles, and 76ers, with hockey the only major sport that he hasn't covered. Campbell worked with Kalas and Ashburn for Phillies games, was the voice of the Eagles from 1952–66, and handled the Warriors and 76ers as well. Campbell might have done his best work with Matt Guokas on 76ers telecasts. In 2005 Campbell was awarded the Curt Gowdy Award by the Basketball Hall of Fame.

There have been many other fine announcers in Philly sports history, with Merrill Reese going on 30 years as the voice of the Eagles and Gene Hart having a wonderful ride with the Flyers. Reese got a job with 610 WIP-AM in 1977 filling in for Charlie Swift, the Eagles' play-by-play man, and took over as the main voice after Swift committed suicide. Reese has had numerous radio partners over the years, including Swift, Herb Adderley, Bill Bergey, Stan Walters, and currently Mike Quick. How many Eagles fans repeatedly turn down the TV sound on Eagles games to listen to the WYSP broadcast with Reese? I've got my hand raised.

Hart was a local announcer in South Jersey when he found out Philadelphia was getting an expansion hockey team in 1966. He submitted tapes and got the job, thus beginning a 29-year relationship with the Flyers. Young fans used to listen to Flyers games in the 1970s on small transistor radios instead of going to sleep, and it was Hart's gentle voice informing everyone of what was going on. It took time for hockey to become big in Philly, and Hart was the one expertly describing and explaining the game. He worked with a number of broadcast partners over the years, including Stu Nahan, Larry Zeidel, Don Earle, and Bobby Taylor. Hart was elected to the Hockey Hall of Fame in 1997. His most memorable call was repeating over and over, "The Flyers win the Stanley Cup; the Flyers win the Stanley Cup!..."

When games ended, you'd listen to the post-game show and wait for the final words of the night, when Hart would deliver his signature phrase, "Good night and good hockey." With Hart, it always was.

But the greatest Philadelphia announcing duo came from baseball, where former Phillie Richie Ashburn and Harry Kalas formed a lasting friendship and shared it with viewers and listeners every night for six months of the season. Harry and Whitey began their unlikely partnership

305

when the Vet opened in 1971, and it didn't end until Ashburn's shocking passing after a game in New York in 1997. Philadelphia has dealt with deaths of sports heroes in the last 25 years, notably the Flyers' Pelle Lindbergh, Eagles' Jerome Brown, and Phillies' Tug McGraw; and when Ashburn moved on, generations of fans cried. Ashburn first played in Philadelphia in 1948, was an instant star as the leadoff hitter and center fielder, and ended up in the Hall of Fame, going in the same day as Mike Schmidt. Kalas himself was inducted in 2002.

Harry and Whitey were a wonderful, friendly duo, on and off the field, and Phillies fans were the big winners. Kalas has made some of the greatest calls in Phillies history, lucky enough—unlike By Saam—to announce for winning teams. Who can forget that ninth-inning home run Michael Jack Schmidt, as Kalas called him, whacked in Pittsburgh in 1987, number 500 for Schmitty's career? "Swing and a long drive! There it is! Number 500!"

Kalas and Ashburn, a generation of Phillies fans will never forget you.

WHAT WERE THE FIVE MOST MEMORABLE QUOTES IN PHILADELPHIA SPORTS HISTORY?

94 Professional sports athletes aren't always like you and me. They say things; sometimes really dumb things. They don't always think before they speak, and really, with all that money in the bank, who's to say they need to? The most memorable quotes in Philadelphia sports history weren't necessary the dumbest, but you be the judge. They are certainly memorable.

These aren't the *best* quotes in Philly sports history. To me, the best quote would have to be after a great win, or to motivate players before a big game; and in that case Flyers coach Fred Shero takes the cake with the words of wisdom he wrote on the blackboard prior to Game 6 of the 1973–74 Stanley Cup Finals against the Bruins: "Win together today, and we walk together forever." The Flyers did win, and have walked together ever since.

As for the 76ers, it was more of a motto than a quote, but certainly "We owe you one," was an annual mantra until Moses arrived and brought the city its last championship.

For those wondering about Tug McGraw quotes, the best ones appear to have been uttered while he was a member of the New York Mets. Here's my favorite: when asked what he would do with his share of the 1973 World Series money, Tug said, "I'm going to spend 90 percent of it on good times, women, and Irish whiskey. The other 10 percent I'm going to waste." Philly, and New York, will forever miss Frank Edwin McGraw. The Tugger was a beloved Philly favorite. Certainly some of those who did make our top five list were hardly viewed that way. Here are the best quotes.

5. MEDIUM RARE FOR OL' 5-FOR-1

Von Hayes wasn't the most popular Phillie, that's for sure. The trade to get him, five players for one with the Cleveland Indians, wasn't as one-sided as most people think. But that didn't mean Phillies fans, and teammates, shouldn't bust his chops every so often. Pete Rose dubbed him 541, as in 5-for-1. Hayes had a sweet swing, just not as sweet as expectations. He wasn't a bad player at all, but Phillies fans always wanted more, be it hustle or production. Anyway, he got booed a lot. Hayes's response: "They can do whatever they want. I'll still be eating steak every night." If only his best performances weren't so rare, but well done.

4. WATCH THOSE HANDS

Freddie Mitchell certainly didn't have a distinguished career with the Eagles, but he never lacked for confidence or bravado. Mitchell was a first-round flop who caught six touchdown passes in four years, including the playoffs, and made 107 receptions. None were bigger than the 28-yarder from Donovan McNabb on fourth-and-26 in the final minutes against the Green Bay Packers. Mitchell's heroics kept the drive alive; the Eagles tied the game and won it in overtime, advancing to the NFC Title game. After the game, the bombastic Mitchell put on a show for reporters, saying, "I'd like to thank my hands for being so great." You deserve a hand for that catch, Freddie, but not much else.

3. WHO, WHAT, WHERE?

Ricky Watters made no pretense about who he was and what he was all about. A significant free agent signing for the team who played for three seasons starting in 1995, Watters was productive. He was also selfish. In his first game with the Eagles, Watters short-armed a Randall Cunningham pass over the middle, letting it drop rather than catch it and get hammered by a Tampa Bay player. The fans booed. Teammates steamed. After the game when asked about the play, Watters said, "For who, for what?" as if to say it wasn't worth it. After retirement he'd write a book with that line in the title. Watters scored 32 touchdowns in three seasons, twice making All-Pro, but Philadelphians remember him for what he said.

2. LET TERRELL SPEAK!

The Terrell Owens era in Philly did have some good moments. He was clearly one of the most talented wide receivers in football, as his performance in coming back from multiple injuries for Super Bowl XXXIX showed. The Eagles lost, but Owens couldn't be blamed. However, Owens couldn't get along with coaches and teammates, with his main goal in the months after the Super Bowl being to renegotiate his contract. Owens played seven games during the 2005 season, but his off-field words continued to cause controversy. Finally, the team suspended Owens for a month on November 6. Two days later, in front of his New Jersey home, he and agent Drew Rosenhaus hosted a mockery of a press conference. Owens insincerely apologized, and Rosenhaus answered most queries from reporters with a terse, ridiculous, "Next question." The next time Owens would play in a game would be with the Dallas Cowboys.

1. WHAT ARE WE TALKIN' ABOUT?

Allen Iverson was one of the most productive and exciting players in 76ers history. But as you might have heard, he wasn't a big fan of practicing. He and coach Larry Brown did get the team to one NBA Finals appearance, but their love-hate relationship got just as much attention. In one memorable press conference on May 8, 2002, after Iverson felt he was attacked once again by Brown for missing practice, the talented guard responded:

If Coach tells you that I missed practice, then that's that. I may have missed one practice this year but if somebody says he missed one practice of all the practices this year, then that's enough to get a whole lot started. I told Coach Brown that you don't have to give the people of Philadelphia a reason to think about trading me or anything like that. If you trade somebody, you trade them to make the team better... simple as that. I'm cool with that. I'm all about that. The people in Philadelphia deserve to have a winner. It's simple as that. It goes further than that.... If I can't practice, I can't practice. It is as simple as that. It ain't about that at all. It's easy to sum it up if you're just talking about practice. We're sitting here, and I'm supposed to be the franchise player, and we're talking about practice. I mean listen, we're sitting here talking about practice, not a game, not a game, not a game, but we're talking about practice. Not the game that I go out there and die for and play every game like it's my last but we're talking about practice, man. How silly is that? .... Now I know that I'm supposed to lead by example and all that, but I'm not shoving that aside like it don't mean anything. I know it's important, I honestly do, but we're talking about practice. We're talking about practice, man. We're talking about practice. We're talking about practice. We're not

311

talking about the game. We're talking about practice. When you come to the arena, and you see me play, you've seen me play right, you've seen me give everything I've got, but we're talking about practice right now.... Hey I hear you, it's funny to me too, hey it's strange to me too, but we're talking about practice, man, we're not even talking about the game, when it actually matters, we're talking about practice.... How the hell can I make my teammates better by practicing?

In case you're trying to follow from home, this much-imitated monologue contained the word practice 20 times. Or seven more times than Rosenhaus said the words "next question." Now you try talking for that long in an animated voice and saying one word that often. What are we talkin' about? As Coach Brown said, Iverson said the word practice even more than he actually did practice.

SHOULD PENN STATE'S JOE PATERNO RETIRE?

95 Unlike college hoops, Philadelphia isn't much of a college football town. Ivy League entrant Penn has 11 perfect seasons to its credit in more than 130 years of football, and 13 league titles. But the Quakers don't win National Championships, and their last prime-time NFL player was Chuck Bednarik, 50 years ago. Temple's football program thrived when Pop Warner was coach and in the 1970s under Wayne Hardin (with a bowl game appearance!), but the last winning season came in 1990. Villanova, from the Main Line and outside the city, has done well for itself in Division I-AA since bringing the program back, but you won't see the Wildcats in the Cotton Bowl. It's really more of a basketball school.

Thus, each Saturday in the fall Philly college football fans tend to turn to State College, Pennsylvania, a good 200 miles west from Philadelphia in the middle of the state. Penn State is one of the largest public universities in the United States, and the football team is very successful, playing in the Big Ten conference and boasting two National Championships in the 1980s and seven undefeated, untied seasons in more than 120 years of college football. Basically, the Nittany Lions are expected to be contenders every season, and are held to among the highest of standards.

Joe Paterno has been there for all of it. Well, not all of it; but quite a bit of it. He's old, but not that old. And therein lies the point. When is enough enough?

Through the 2007 season, the 81-year-old Paterno has spent 58 years as an assistant or head coach at Penn State, the latter 42 as head coach. He's tied with Florida State's Bobby Bowden for most wins by a Division I football coach, and nobody has more bowl wins. What jumps out at you about Paterno? The wins? The championships? The fact he's contributed more than $4 million to the university? His teams' graduation rates, which recently have been very strong, especially for such a large program?

Hmm, how about the fact he's been eligible for Social Security benefits for 16 years?

It would be public relations suicide for Penn State to push Paterno out the door, even though there are plenty of school supporters who believe this would be good for the program. Hey, the guy is 81. Would you want to be recruiting at that age, knocking on doors trying to woo teenagers to play football for you? Dealing with the media scrutiny isn't fun at any age, but especially when there's a target on your back. Who wants to be working at age 81 in the first place? It's not like Paterno needs the money, or has anything left to prove. JoePa has carved his niche in college football history, and Penn State owes much gratitude to the man for all he's done.

In 2003 and the following season, when Paterno's teams went 7–16, he heard the cries that he was too old to handle the job, that the game had passed him by. It was hard to argue against that point. But since then, the Nittany Lions have gotten back on track. The 2005 team went 11–1, won the Big Ten and the Orange Bowl, and finished with a number 3 overall ranking. In 2006 and 2007, Penn State went 9–4 each year and won a bowl game. Kids still want to play for Paterno, the grand master, and they want to win, and there's little reason to think this is going to cease anytime soon.

Paterno should retire when he's good and ready, and only when it becomes obvious he can no longer properly lead the team. Sure, he was born before the constitutional amendment repealing prohibition was ratified, but so what? He owes Penn State fans nothing, except his best job leading young men on and off the field. Let's hope he can continue to effectively do this for years to come.

WHAT'S THE WORST DECISION IN PHILLY SPORTS HISTORY?

96

Baseball is the one sport in which coaching decisions seem to have the greatest impact. Or at least, the decisions we can all see. In football, a bad play call can lose a game, but the public isn't normally privy to such decisions. In hoops, so many points are scored and end-game plays ignored that coaches struggle for control. This is even more the case in hockey, where coaches are recycled just to spark a team. It has little to do with the decisions they make setting up lines.

Baseball managers are held accountable for much more in their line of work. Each day's lineup is scrutinized, every fat guy sitting on his couch thinks he knows when to make a pitching change, and there is much more strategy to consider than with the other major sports. As a result, one can argue that the three worst decisions in Philly sports history all came in different eras of Phillies baseball. Stunningly, all can be blamed on Mitch Williams! Why was he out there in Game 6 of the 1993 World Series? Why wasn't he out there down the stretch in 1964? Did he misplace his glove when he could have been a defensive replacement on Black Friday in the 1977 playoffs?

Okay, we joke because we care. Williams got over the fateful pitch he threw to Joe Carter seemingly moments after the game, and so should we. Williams is a pitcher, not a left fielder, so he can't be blamed for manager Danny Ozark's 1977 goof. And as the 1964 summer was coming to a close and manager Gene Mauch was blowing his best chance at a World Series, Williams was still in the womb. Can't blame him for 1964, either.

But we can blame Ozark and Mauch for the worst decisions in Philly sports history. Which is worse?

In Ozark's case, his 1977 Phillies had won 101 games during the regular season and led 5–3 in the ninth inning of Game 3 of the National League championship series against the Dodgers. The Phillies were three outs away from going up two games to one, and with ace Steve Carlton on the mound the next day, also at friendly Veterans Stadium. Earlier in Game 3 Phillies fans famously rattled Dodgers starting pitcher Burt Hooton so much that he couldn't stop walking hitters, and got booed/cheered off the field.

Anyway, the Phils had a 5–3 lead in the ninth. Gene Garber was on the mound. Greg Luzinski was in left. One of those guys was a problem. Luzinski was quite the hitter, but not a very good fielder. Jerry Martin, on the other hand, was the opposite, and he was The Bull's defensive caddy during the regular season. Why didn't Ozark make the defensive switch on this day? He claims he wanted Luzinski out there to celebrate the win, and maybe to bat

317

in the bottom of the ninth. Well, thanks in part to Luzinski, he needed to bat in the ninth, and the win never happened. How fitting that Luzinski got hit by a pitch in the ninth and Martin came in to pinch run. Celebration? There's no room for soft gestures like that in sports, not when a critical win isn't secured. Plus, this wasn't the series clincher. How much celebrating is there after going up 2–1 in games?

Well, it never happened. Garber registered two outs quite easily, then began a painful turn of events, a disastrous 10 minutes in Phillies history. Pinch-hitter Vic Davalillo beat out a bunt single. Then pinch-hitter Manny Mota hit a deep fly ball to left field, which Luzinski first misjudged, then let glance off his glove when he hit the wall. Was it an easy catch? Nope, but most Phillies said after the game Martin would have made it. Martin said it, too. Davalillo scored on the "double." Next up was Davey Lopes. This isn't Ozark's fault, but Lopes lined a ball off Mike Schmidt at third base, and it caromed to Larry Bowa at short. Bowa snared the ball with his bare hand and whipped it to first. Replays showed Lopes was out, but of course umpire Bruce Froemming called him safe. The game was tied. Lopes moved to second when a rattled Garber tried to pick him off and threw wildly, and Bill Russell knocked in the go-ahead run with a single up the middle. The Dodgers won 6–5, and the next day took the series in the Philly rain when Tommy John outpitched Carlton.

Ozark's lack of a decision on replacing Luzinski was ultimately blamed for the loss, forever known in Philly lore as Black Friday. The Dodgers lost in the Reggie Jackson World Series to the Yankees, but Phillies fans will always believe their team could have won it all.

The way history tells the story, what Ozark did—or didn't do—would pale in comparison to what Mauch did in 1964. There might never be another collapse like the 1964 Phillies. Sure, technically the Mets did blow a bigger lead just recently in 2007, and the Phillies caught them, but that will never have the same impact of '64. The problem is, did Mauch really make his four-man rotation into Jim Bunning and Chris Short, and that's it? Um, not really.

The Phillies, who hadn't won a thing since 1950, and even then got swept by the Yankees in the World Series, held a 6 ½ game lead with 12 games to play. They were in. Well, unless they were to drop the next 10 games; then they could still lose it if other teams played well—which is what happened. Losing streaks happen all the time, and managers can't always control them, but in this case, Mauch could.

The way history remembers it is, Mauch decided to abuse Bunning and Short, in an effort to clinch early so all Phillies could be rested. In reality, he used them more than others, but not solely. They did not pitch every other day. Let's investigate.

- On September 21, Cincinnati's Chico Ruiz stole home in the sixth inning of a scoreless game that Art Mahaffey started. That was the only run.
- On September 22, Short got lit in a 9–4 loss.
- On September 23, Dennis Bennett started and lost 6–4.
- On September 24, Bunning lost to the Braves 5–3.
- On September 25, Short started on two days rest, but John Boozer lost in 12 innings 7–5.
- On September 26, Mahaffey started and had a 4–3 lead in the ninth, when Bobby Shantz allowed three runs on a Rico Carty triple.
- On September 27, Bunning and future manager Dallas Green got pummeled in a 14–8 loss, despite Johnny Callison swatting three home runs for the Phillies.
- On September 28, the Phillies went to St. Louis and lost 5–1. Short started, Bob Gibson won.
- On September 29, Bennett started and didn't get out of the second inning in a 4–2 loss.
- On September 30, Bunning allowed six runs in 3 1/3 innings. Cards 8, Phils 5. That's 10 straight losses.

For the record, Mauch went not with a two-man rotation, but a three-man, involving four pitchers. In the 10 games, Bunning and Short each started three times, so four starting pitchers were used. Sure, Mauch relied more on his aces, and they didn't pitch so well, but Mahaffey pitched well in his starts. Bennett was a problem. I'd say Mauch panicked a bit, but he takes unfair criticism for what happened. The Phillies lost three games to the 92–70 Reds, four more to the 88–74 Braves, and three to the eventual World Series champion Cards, who won 93 games. It's a losing streak. I'd give the line that it happens from time to time, but never in history has it actually happened quite like this, except for this time. I don't blame Mauch for the losing streak, though he didn't do such a great job avoiding it.

Ozark, meanwhile, took a pair of 101-win teams to the playoffs, and his three division champs won two playoff games. Leaving Luzinski in left field is the worst decision in Philly sports history.

Don't blame The Bull, though. He wasn't a major leaguer for his glove.

WHAT ARE THE FIVE GREATEST NUMBERS WORN IN PHILLY SPORTS HISTORY?

97 Even now, many years after the last time Bobby Clarke laced up the skates in an NHL game, I still equate the number 16 with him. The greatest players always remind us of the number they wore. Nobody else on the Flyers wears 16, of course, but even when I see someone on the other team who has it, I think of Clarke. To Philly fans who grew up in the 1970s, any 16 in the game of hockey is Bobby Clarke.

The numbers our heroes wore and continue to wear are important to the fans. We bought their jerseys, read their baseball (and other sport) cards, and hung posters in our rooms growing up. Like narrowing down other lists in this book, some memorable numbers are going to get left out. Number 7, for example, was pretty big in 1980 when the quarterback (Ron Jaworski) and left wing sniper (Bill Barber) wore it to their respective championships. Number 10 was for the overachievers back then, the unselfish point guard (Maurice Cheeks) who would become coach and the vacuum-like shortstop who became manager (Larry Bowa).

Number 31 got the Eagles to their first Super Bowl (Wilbert Montgomery), covered center field for the Phillies like no other (Garry Maddox), and was on his way to becoming one of the best goalies in the NHL (Pelle Lindbergh), until tragedy struck. Number 2 was acquired to get the 76ers to the championship (Moses Malone), which he did in fo', five, and fo' games, while the best Flyers defenseman (Mark Howe) and Eagles kicker (David Akers) had the same number. Number 19 hit majestic home runs (Greg Luzinski) and scored 50 goals in a season (Rick MacLeish), including the Stanley Cup winner. Number 5 is still worn, and gets roundly booed, by the productive quarterback whom fans seem to want to be somewhere else this coming season (Donovan McNabb), and the productive left fielder whom fans seem to want to be somewhere else *every* season (Pat Burrell).

And none of those numbers is the greatest worn in Philadelphia sports history. Even Clarke's 16, unfortunately, misses the cut, since it isn't shared by other Philly greats; and it misses out when compared to the greatest hoops player ever. Another one that didn't quite make it is of the number that Philly fans never want to see on the ice again: the Eric Lindros 88.

So what are the greatest numbers?

5. WILT CHAMBERLAIN'S 13

Look, the guy set just about every record there is in the

game of basketball. Wilt wore this number with the Harlem Globetrotters, who retired it. He wore it with the Warriors and the 76ers, and nobody else has since. Even in other sports, can you remember a great player taking on this number, other than maybe Dan Marino? Maybe the best players didn't choose to wear the so-called unlucky 13, but it didn't seem to be a problem for Chamberlain.

4. JULIUS ERVING'S 6

Dr. J wore another number that shows up in Philly lore when he was with the ABA's New York Nets, but he took on this single digit with Philadelphia. That's how tons of young Erving wannabes honored him with photos of him on their walls. The Phillies have also had much luck with this number. A generation earlier, Phillies fans remember Johnny Callison professionally manning right field with the same number, and the 1950 World Series team saw third baseman Willie Puddin' Head Jones take that number. Currently, it's Ryan Howard, reaching 100 career home runs faster than anyone ever has. Ultimately, Bill Russell won more championships with Number 6, but Philly fans certainly recall the way Erving wore it more fondly.

3. MIKE SCHMIDT'S 20

All four pro franchises have had memorable players wear

this number, but Schmidt shines above all as the greatest third baseman of all time, and one of the greatest to ever wear Number 20 in sport. Even now, at Citizen's Bank Park, numbers of the current top players are recognized in youth jerseys in the stands, but many of the parents have a Schmidt throwback shirt or jersey. As for the other sports, Brian Dawkins still wears the number, Doug Collins wore it in college and with the 76ers, and among the Flyers to own the number are Jimmy Watson, Trent Klatt, and Dave Poulin.

2. STEVE CARLTON'S 32

Why Carlton over Schmidt? Well, that's not what we're saying here, but 76ers fans surely remember Billy Cunningham having the same one. Thirty-two is a famous number throughout sports history, with Jim Brown, O. J. Simpson, Magic Johnson, and Sandy Koufax among those who wore it. In Philadelphia it was two of Hall of Famers who were instrumental in championships: Carlton pitching the Phillies to the 1980 World Series; and Cunningham playing and coaching for NBA titles in Philly.

1. BERNIE PARENT'S 1

However, no number is more beloved in Philly history than the first number, assuming you don't count zero. Bernie Parent was the best goaltender in the world when he took the Flyers to a pair of Stanley Cup championships. His career might have ended too early, but while he was out there on the ice, Flyers fans could never complain about Bernie. If we had a chapter for greatest bumper sticker, "Only the Lord Saves More than Bernie" would clearly be the best, just beating out the Phillies one from the 1982 season about new manager Pat Corrales ("Corrales a pennant!"). Okay, it would beat that one by quite a bit. Parent could have been knighted by Philly fans, but so could a certain center fielder and broadcaster who spent more than half his life in our city. Richie Ashburn, like Parent, seemingly had no enemies, and he was Number 1 on the field and, later, in the booth.

WHICH ARE THE FIVE GREATEST PHILLY TEAMS TO NOT WIN A CHAMPIONSHIP?

98

It seems a rite of passage for young Philly fans to have their hearts broken by their favorite teams at the worst possible times: that is, before a championship is won. So few Philly entrants have won titles, one might wonder how many great teams there really have been. Well, the truth is, some of the Philadelphia teams that have won titles were not the best, and other teams that didn't win were just plain better. And winning a championship shouldn't be the lone criteria for a successful campaign.

To win a title in professional sports, it takes more than great players and coaching; it takes a bit of luck. Some of these teams could have used some of that to go with the players. For one reason or another, none of these teams won championships, but each could have done it.

5. 1986–87 FLYERS

The first full season after the death of Pelle Lindbergh was a very successful one, as rookie Ron Hextall carried the team to 100 points in the regular season, and playoff series wins over the solid New York teams (Rangers and Islanders) and the defending champion Montreal Canadiens. The only team with more regular season points than Philly was Wayne Gretzky's Edmonton Oilers, a buzzsaw of a franchise that was on its way to four Stanley Cup titles in five seasons. The Flyers were young, not just in goal, but offensively as Peter Zezel, Pelle Eklund, Rick Tocchet, Murray Craven, and Scott Mellanby were all 23 or younger, and joined forces with Tim Kerr, Dave Poulin, Brian Propp, and Mark Howe. Yes, 100 points is a season points total topped by numerous other Flyers teams who did not win it all, but considering this club's youth and the teams it faced in the postseason, it was one of the best.

4. 1979–80 FLYERS

The Islanders won the Stanley Cup in controversial fashion in overtime of Game 6, but the Flyers have nothing to be ashamed of. This team began with a win and then a 9–2 loss to a mediocre Atlanta Flames team. What happened from October 16, 1979 through January 6, 1980 was incredible. The Flyers didn't lose. Not once. The 35-game unbeaten streak was as unlikely as it was fascinating, and it set a North American pro sports record. Pete Peeters and Phil Myre played goal as well as they ever had. Seven players registered between 65 and 79 points during the regular season (Ken Linseman, Reggie Leach, Brian Propp, Bill Barber,

Bobby Clarke, Rick MacLeish, and Paul Holmgren). Among the team's surprising, unsung defenders were Norm Barnes, Mike Busniuk, and Frank Bathe. The Flyers finished the regular season with 116 points, second most in club history and 25 more than the second-place Islanders, who would, of course, win the title. The Flyers ripped through the first three rounds of the playoffs in Moses Malone-like fashion, winning 11 of 13 games. The Islanders, incidentally, won the first of four straight Stanley Cups.

3. 2004 EAGLES

The Eagles have had other fine teams that didn't win it all, that's for sure. Ron Jaworski, Wilbert Montgomery, and Dick Vermeil took the 1980 team to a 12–4 mark and the Super Bowl, until Rod Martin, Jim Plunkett, and the wild-card Oakland Raiders ended the run. Buddy Ryan's teams less than a decade later were also built for Super Bowl runs, generally on defense, but couldn't get over the hump. But the 2004 Eagles were the best team Andy Reid and Donovan McNabb had. That team finished number 2 in the league in points allowed, and McNabb had Brian Westbrook and Terrell Owens to help on offense. The Eagles began the season with wins in 13 of 14 games before clinching everything and sitting everyone for the final two weeks, which became losses. Big deal. The Eagles beat the Vikings and Falcons, finally exorcising the NFC Championship home game demons, and played the

New England Patriots toe to toe for much of the Super Bowl. In the end, it wasn't meant to be, but since 1960, no Eagles team has been better.

2. 1979–80 76ERS

The regular season, like others in that era, was a bit of a blur. The 76ers knew they were good, and so were the Boston Celtics and Los Angeles Lakers. Those other teams won a few more games than Philly did, but it didn't matter. All three were in the mix. We knew the Lakers would get to the Finals again. Kareem Abdul-Jabbar was still in his prime, and the rich got richer when a point guard named Magic Johnson fell into the team's lap. The Celtics won the most regular season games that year, with 61, thanks to their own superstar rookie Larry Bird. Who did the 76ers get in the draft for that season? Well, Jim Spanarkel, Clint Richardson, and Earl Cureton, of course! Regardless, the 76ers were led by what was arguably Julius Erving's best NBA statistical season, as he averaged 26.9 points, 7.4 rebounds, 4.6 assists, 2.2 steals, and 1.8 blocks. And he had plenty of help. Four others averaged double figures in the playoffs, including the emerging Darryl Dawkins. Maurice Cheeks and Lionel Hollins were a terrific back-court, while Bobby Jones and Caldwell Jones were terrific defenders. No, this was not the Moses Malone-led team that won it all, but it was deep and talented. The 76ers blew by rival Boston in the Eastern Finals in five quick games.

The 76ers and Lakers split the first four games. Kareem scored 40 points in Game 5 to give the Lakers a 3–2 edge, but badly sprained his ankle. The 76ers thought they had Game 6 locked up, and it was unlikely Abdul-Jabbar would be ready for Game 7 as well. What happened? What Magic Johnson did, a rookie playing center in Kareem's place getting 42 points, 15 rebounds, and seven assists, is arguably the greatest single-game performance against a Philly team, considering the importance. The 76ers didn't win it all, but would get revenge on Magic and Co. three seasons later.

1. 1977 PHILLIES

It might seem an odd choice, but this Phillies team won 101 games for the second consecutive year and appeared better than the year before. The 1980 Phillies wouldn't have stood a chance against this team, no matter what buttons Dallas Green could have pushed. The '77 Phillies not only won 10 more regular season games than the 1980 team, but slugged 69 more home runs, scored 119 more runs, had a better bullpen, and made fewer errors. Greg Luzinski, Bob Boone, Larry Bowa, and Garry Maddox were still in their prime. Bake McBride was acquired from the Cardinals and hit .339 for the Phillies, Davey Johnson slugged .545 off the bench, and Tim McCarver hit .320. Luzinski had team highs of 39 home runs and 130 RBIs and batted .309. Mike Schmidt and Steve Carlton were dominant in both seasons, as was Tug McGraw, but all three were on their own in 1980. In 1977, they each had more help. The 1977 team had four relief pitchers top 70 innings with an ERA of 2.75 or lower. Neither team had much rotation depth after Carlton and a big number 2 winner (Larry Christenson went 19–6 in 1977; Dick Ruthven 17–10 in 1980). The '77 Phillies had to hold off a 96-win Pirates team to win the NL East, and faced the 98–64 Dodgers in the playoffs. By now you must know what happened in that memorable series, but think about how close the Phillies came to winning this series. The Phillies had Game 3 won, a few times. Even if you forgive Luzinski for dropping the fly ball in the ninth inning, Bowa threw out Davey Lopes at first base on the next play, though Lopes was called safe. The Phillies lost, and had nothing left in the rain in Game 4. The Dodgers fell in the World Series to the Yankees. No Phillies team has ever won more than the 101 games this one did. It should have fared better.

WHERE DOES ONE GET THE BEST PHILLY CHEESESTEAK?

99 Of all the foods Philadelphia is known for—soft pretzels, hoagies, Tastykakes, water ice, and scrapple among them—there is nothing like the cheesesteak. Other cities copy them, but the cheesesteak is vintage Philly, having originated there in the 1930s.

When visitors come to Philadelphia, the Liberty Bell is an attraction, as is the Philadelphia Museum of Art, the zoo, and Independence Hall. Oddly enough, so is the corner of Ninth and Passyunk Streets in South Philadelphia, right near the Italian Market. This is where you'll find bitter competitors Pat's King of Steaks and Geno's Steaks. Pat's is older and always has longer lines. Geno's is right across the street on the other corner, with flashy neon signs. These establishments are well-known providers of cheesesteaks, and if you're headed to a sporting event in Philly, chances are you're either headed to this corner before the game or afterward. Or both before *and* after.

Of course, these aren't necessarily the best cheese-steaks in town. To acquire this city icon, you have to decide what's important to you: the cheesesteak itself, or the entire experience. Anyone can take thinly sliced pieces of steak, add some melted cheese, and dump it in a long roll, and it doesn't have to be done in Philly. All of these pieces are important. The top round needs to be griddled up and browned perfectly, the Amoroso's Italian bread sliced, and the cheese—whichever kind you choose—is best when melted. Throw in some onions, peppers, maybe some hot sauce if you so desire, and you've got a terrific sandwich.

This practice of devouring cheesesteaks is such a big deal in Philly, there's a right and wrong way to order one— a proper protocol if you will—so don't mess up. If you want cheese whiz and fried onions, then say "wiz, wit" and you're all set. Ask for "wiz, witout" and there's no onions. You can adjust the cheeses as well; or change the name of the sandwich. Try a "mushroom provolone witout." There will be a quiz later.

Naturally, if Philly fans can debate their favorite athletes, they can debate their favorite cheesesteaks. *Philadelphia Magazine* has a best-of issue every year, and for every year this decade a different restaurant has been honored with Best Cheesesteak. Some of these places are upscale; some not so much. Even five-star restaurants try their own variations of the cheesesteak. And of course, feel free to order this delicacy at the sporting event you're at.

Pat's and Geno's are fine places to get a cheesesteak. I recommend trying one from each in one sitting, or stand-ing if you will, and see if you can tell the difference. Jim's

Steaks on South Street is one of my favorites. Rick's Steaks, formerly in the Reading Terminal Market never fails to please, and Steve's Prince of Steaks in the great Northeast were the 2007 winners in *Philly Mag*. Personally, I've never had a bad steak—a misteak, if you will—at Tony Luke's on Oregon Avenue, not far from the stadiums or Interstate-95.

I certainly haven't eaten at every cheesesteak establishment in the Philadelphia region, though it is on my list of things to do before I pass on. Of course, knowing the nutritional value of the cheesesteak, a goal of eating a cheesesteak from every place would likely help me to pass on a lot earlier, so maybe I'll listen to my cardiologist and mix in a salad.

But if you ask me where to get the best cheesesteak, my answer is without question, in Philadelphia. You can't go wrong there. Hey, I'm not going to pick favorites. I've gotta live there.

WHICH PHILLY PRO TEAM WILL BREAK THE CHAMPIONSHIP DROUGHT?

100

It's going to end at some point. Really, Philly fans, it will. It might be when you least expect it, but a Philadelphia team is going to win a championship, the fans are going to go wild, and there will be a parade. And we will dance. Oh, how we will dance.

The main reason for Philly teams not winning a title since 1983 is just bad luck. These teams aren't poorly run. They haven't had horrid players. The Phillies went to a World Series, and if they had a bullpen, maybe they could have won it. The Flyers have been to the Finals a few times since 1983, the Eagles went to a Super Bowl and should have been to more, and even the 76ers went to the Finals. We've been close. So who's next to get over that proverbial hump?

As of this writing, the 76ers were in a bit of a rebuilding stage. The Allen Iverson era had been over more than a calendar year, Andre Iguodala was emerging into a stand-out player who might or might not be built around, and new team president and general manager Ed Stefanski had only been with the team a little while and certainly needs a year or two to fix the Billy King mess. The Western

Conference is the NBA's best, but in the East the 76ers aren't far from being annual playoff entrants. They're not close to a title, though. They're probably the furthest away of the Philadelphia teams, despite signing Elton Brand to a huge off-season contract and becoming relevant again.

The Flyers had a disheartening, franchise-worst campaign in 2006–07, and once Bob Clarke stepped aside, Paul Holmgren took over as general manager and started to rebuild things. He got a franchise goaltender, spent money on free agents like he was on a shopping spree, and was making the team relevant again. Stanley Cups can't be bought in the NHL, but just get into the playoffs and a run can be made. Plus, the Devils' Martin Brodeur can't play forever. The Flyers made a long and shocking playoff run in 2008, and can remain annual title contenders if Daniel Briere and Martin Biron carry the load.

Donovan McNabb isn't a kid anymore. Seems like only yesterday Eagles fans were booing his selection on draft day. Now on the wrong side of 30, McNabb still has life left in his arm and legs. The 2007 season was doomed from the start, as McNabb worked his way back from a torn ACL and into game shape during the actual games, but there should be no holding him back in 2008. The Eagles aren't a young team. Jon Runyan and Brian Dawkins are just about done. Brian Westbrook is running out of time. Andy Reid and McNabb think they have one more great season in them, and it could lead to playoff games in January 2009. Can it lead to the big game on February 1, 2009? It's possible, but not as likely as...

...Jimmy Rollins, Ryan Howard, Chase Utley, and Cole Hamels getting their chance on the big stage. The Phillies won the NL East in 2007 and have the kind of nucleus that should contend for years. And really, the Phillies have been contending for years. Philly fans tried not to notice, but Larry Bowa won exactly 86 games in three of his four seasons, and Charlie Manuel 85 or more in *each* of his first three. The Phillies are well-run, have on-field leadership, and seem hungry for a title. That's good. Don't be shocked if there's a championship run before the end of the decade.

And don't forget the parade. Nobody does a parade like Philly. If I were to rank them, I'd say the Phillies parade in 1980 was the best, then the first Flyers Stanley Cup title, then the 76ers in 1983. Man, we could sure use some more of those.

INDEX
by Subject

INDEX

by Name

ABOUT THE AUTHOR

Eric Karabell is a senior writer for ESPN.com, but began his passion for Philadelphia sports many years before joining the Worldwide Leader. Eric grew up in the Philadelphia suburbs and realized early on what it meant to be a Philly fan. While attending The American University in Washington, DC, Eric became a reporter for the *Washington Post*, and married his love of sports with journalism. Later he moved back to the Philadelphia area and became a reporter for the *Philadelphia Inquirer*, and a writer/editor at *The Ring Magazine*, before joining ESPN in 1997. Eric has coordinated ESPN.com's coverage of the NFL, NBA, and fantasy games. Since 2002 he has led ESPN's fantasy section, first as its deputy editor, now as a writer and presence across multiple media outlets. Eric frequently appears on *ESPNEWS* and *Baseball Tonight*, hosts a national ESPN radio show and a daily baseball podcast, and contributes to *ESPN the Magazine*. His online blog was recently honored by the Fantasy Sports Trade Association as best fantasy baseball series. He was twice named fantasy writer of the year.

Eric lives in the Philadelphia suburbs with his understanding wife, Emma, and children Zachary, Ryan, and Madeline. Household arguments are generally more about what to make for dinner than how to make the Eagles Super Bowl champs, but the kids are learning their priorities.